Consumer Marketing Strategies

CONSUMER MARKETING STRATEGIES

A Harvard Business Review Paperback

Harvard Business Review paperback No. 90087

ISBN 0-87584-283-6

The *Harvard Business Review* articles in this collection are available as individual reprints, with the exception of "Brandstanding: Long-Lived Product Promotion." Discounts apply to quantity purchases. For information and ordering contact Operations Department, Harvard Business School Publishing Division, Boston, MA 02163. Telephone: (617) 495-6192, 9 a.m. to 5 p.m. Eastern Standard Time, Monday through Friday. Fax: (617) 495-6985, 24 hours a day.

Editor's Note: Some articles in this book may have been written before authors and editors began to take into consideration the role of women in management. We hope the archaic usage representing all managers as male does not detract from the usefulness of the collection.

Printed in the United States of America by Harvard University, Office of the University Publisher.
93 92 91 5 4 3 2 1

Contents

Tactics for Retailers

The Changing Rules of the Game

Marketing Is Everything

by Regis McKenna

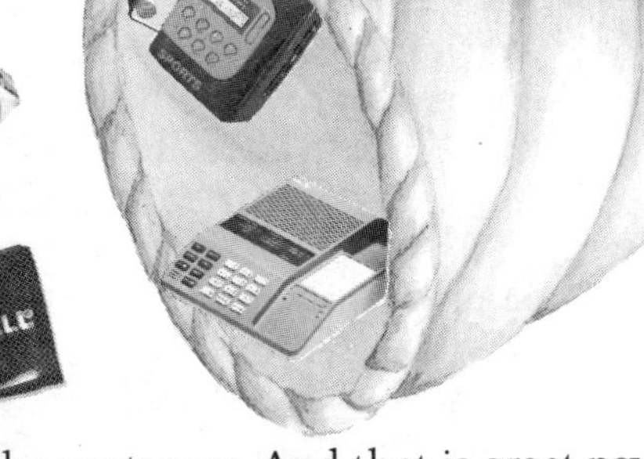

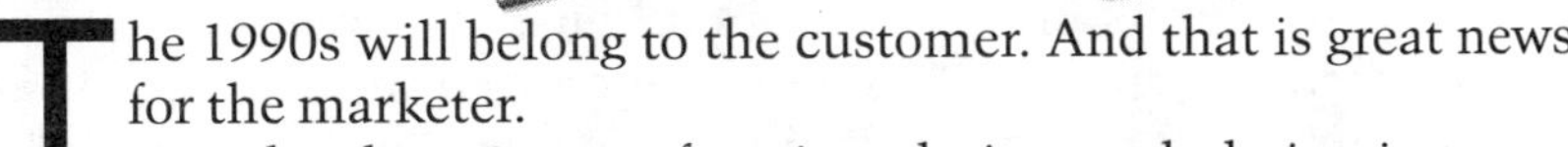

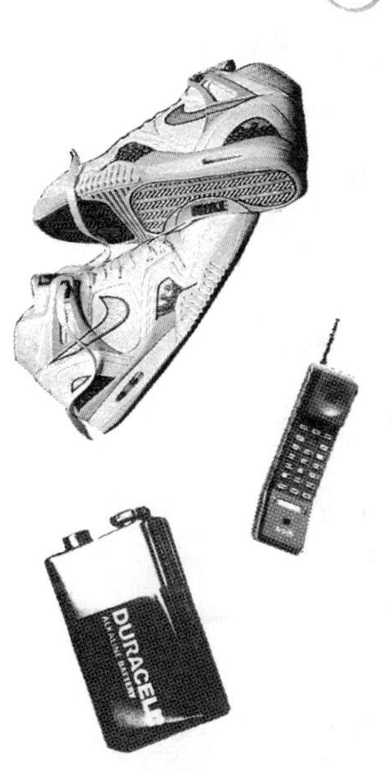

The 1990s will belong to the customer. And that is great news for the marketer.

Technology is transforming choice, and choice is transforming the marketplace. As a result, we are witnessing the emergence of a new marketing paradigm – not a "do more" marketing that simply turns up the volume on the sales spiels of the past but a knowledge- and experience-based marketing that represents the once-and-for-all death of the salesman.

Marketing's transformation is driven by the enormous power and ubiquitous spread of technology. So pervasive is technology today that it is virtually meaningless to make distinctions between technology and nontechnology businesses and industries: there are *only* technology companies. Technology has moved into products, the workplace, and the marketplace with astonishing speed and thoroughness. Seventy years after they were invented, fractional horsepower motors are in some 15 to 20 household products in the average American home today. In less than 20 years, the microprocessor has achieved a similar penetration. Twenty years ago, there

Regis McKenna is chairman of Regis McKenna Inc., a Palo Alto-headquartered marketing consulting firm that advises some of America's leading high-tech companies. He is also a general partner of Kleiner Perkins Caufield & Byers, a technology venture-capital company. He is the author of Who's Afraid of Big Blue? *(Addison-Wesley,* 1989) *and* The Regis Touch *(Addison-Wesley,* 1985).

DRAWING BY TIMOTHY BLECK

were fewer than 50,000 computers in use; today more than 50,000 computers are purchased every day.

The defining characteristic of this new technological push is programmability. In a computer chip, programmability means the capability to alter a command, so that one chip can perform a variety of prescribed functions and produce a variety of prescribed outcomes. On the factory floor, programmability transforms the production operation, enabling one machine to produce a wide variety of models and products. More broadly, programmability is the new corporate capability to produce more and more varieties and choices for customers – even to offer each individual customer the chance to design and implement the "program" that will yield the precise product, service, or variety that is right for him or her. The technological promise of programmability has exploded into the reality of almost unlimited choice.

Take the world of drugstores and supermarkets. According to *Gorman's New Product News*, which tracks new product introductions in these two consumer-products arenas, between 1985 and 1989 the number of new products grew by an astonishing 60% to an all-time annual high of 12,055. As venerable a brand as Tide illustrates this multiplication of brand variety. In 1946, Procter & Gamble introduced the laundry detergent, the first ever. For 38 years, one version of Tide served the entire market. Then, in the mid-1980s, Procter & Gamble began to bring out a succession of new Tides: Unscented Tide and Liquid Tide in 1984, Tide with Bleach in 1988, and the concentrated Ultra Tide in 1990.

To some marketers, the creation of almost unlimited customer choice represents a threat – particularly when choice is accompanied by new competitors. Twenty years ago, IBM had only 20 competitors; today it faces more than 5,000, when you count any company that is in the "computer" business. Twenty years ago, there were fewer than 90 semiconductor companies; today there are almost 300 in the United States alone. And not only are the competitors new, bringing with them new products and new strategies, but the customers also are new: 90% of the people who used a computer in 1990 were not using one in 1980. These new customers don't know about the old rules, the old understandings, or the old ways of doing business – and they don't care. What they do care about is a company that is willing to adapt its products or services to fit their strategies. This represents the evolution of marketing to the market-driven company.

Several decades ago, there were sales-driven companies. These organizations focused their energies on changing customers' minds to fit the product – practicing the "any color as long as it's black" school of marketing.

As technology developed and competition increased, some companies shifted their approach and became customer driven. These companies expressed a new willingness to change their product to fit customers' requests – practicing the "tell us what color you want" school of marketing.

In the 1990s, successful companies are becoming market driven, adapting their products to fit their customers' strategies. These companies will practice "let's figure out together whether and how color matters to your larger goal" marketing. It is marketing that is oriented toward creating rather than controlling a market; it is based on developmental education, incremental improvement, and ongoing process rather than on simple market-share tactics, raw sales, and one-time events. Most important, it draws on the base of knowledge and experience that exists in the organization.

These two fundamentals, knowledge-based and experience-based marketing, will increasingly define the capabilities of a successful marketing organization. They will supplant the old approach to marketing and new product development. The old approach – getting an idea, conducting traditional market research, developing a product, testing the market, and finally going to market – is slow, unresponsive, and turf-ridden. Moreover, given the fast-changing marketplace, there is less and less reason to believe that this traditional approach can keep up with real customer wishes and demands or with the rigors of competition.

Consider the much-publicized 1988 lawsuit that Beecham, the international consumer products group, filed against advertising giant Saatchi & Saatchi. The suit, which sought more than $24 million in damages, argued that Yankelovich Clancy Shulman, at that time Saatchi's U.S. market-research subsidiary, had "vastly overstated" the projected market share of a new detergent that Beecham launched. Yankelovich forecast that Beecham's product, Delicare, a cold-water detergent, would win between 45.4% and 52.3% of the U.S. market if Beecham backed it with $18 million of advertising. According to Beecham, however, Delicare's highest market share was 25%; the product generally achieved a market share of between 15% and 20%. The lawsuit was settled out of court, with no clear winner or loser. Regardless of the outcome, however, the issue it illustrates is widespread and fundamental: forecasts, by their very nature, must be unreliable, particularly with technology, competitors, customers, and markets all shifting ground so often, so rapidly, and so radically.

The alternative to this old approach is knowledge-based and experience-based marketing. Knowledge-based marketing requires a company to master a scale of knowledge: of the technology in which it competes; of its competition; of its customers; of new sources of technology that can alter its competitive environment; and of its own organization, capabilities, plans, and way of doing business. Armed with this mastery, companies can put knowledge-based marketing to work in three essential ways: integrating the customer into the design process to guarantee a product that is tailored not only to the customers' needs and desires but also to the customers' strategies; generating niche thinking to use the company's knowledge of channels and markets to identify segments of the market the company can own; and developing the infrastructure of suppliers, vendors, partners, and users whose relationships will help sustain and support the company's reputation and technological edge.

The other half of this new marketing paradigm is experience-based marketing, which emphasizes interactivity, connectivity, and creativity. With this approach, companies spend time with their customers, constantly monitor their competitors, and develop a feedback-analysis system that turns this information about the market and the competition into important new product intelligence. At the same time, these companies both evaluate their own technology to assess its currency and cooperate with other companies to create mutually advantageous systems and solutions. These close encounters – with customers, competitors, and internal and external technologies – give companies the firsthand experience they need to invest in market development and to take intelligent, calculated risks.

In a time of exploding choice and unpredictable change, marketing – the new marketing – is the answer. With so much choice for customers, companies face the end of loyalty. To combat that threat, they can add sales and marketing people, throwing costly resources at the market as a way to retain customers. But the real solution, of course, is not more marketing but better marketing. And that means marketing that finds a way to integrate the customer into the company, to create and sustain a relationship between the company and the customer.

The marketer must be the integrator, both internally – synthesizing technological capability with market needs – and externally – bringing the customer into the company as a participant in the development and adaptation of goods and services. It is a fundamental shift in the role and purpose of marketing: from manipulation of the customer to genuine customer involvement; from telling and selling to communicating and sharing knowledge; from last-in-line function to corporate-credibility champion.

Playing the integrator requires the marketer to command credibility. In a marketplace characterized by rapid change and potentially paralyzing choice, credibility becomes the company's sustaining value. The character of its management, the strength of its financials, the quality of its innovations, the congeniality of its customer references, the capabilities of its alliances – these are the measures of a company's credibility. They are measures that, in turn, directly affect its capacity to attract quality people, generate new ideas, and form quality relationships.

The relationships are the key, the basis of customer choice and company adaptation. After all, what is a successful brand but a special relationship? And who better than a company's marketing people to create, sustain, and interpret the relationship between the company, its suppliers, and its customers? That is why, as the demands on the company have shifted from controlling costs to competing on products to serving customers, the center of gravity in the company has shifted from finance to engineering – and now to marketing. In the 1990s, marketing will do more than sell. It will define the way a company does business.

Marketing Is Everything and Everything Is Marketing

The old notion of marketing was epitomized by the ritual phone call from the CEO to the corporate headhunter saying, "Find me a good marketing person to run my marketing operation!" What the CEO wanted, of course, was someone who could take on a discrete set of textbook functions that were generally associated with run-of-the-mill marketing. That person would immediately go to Madison Avenue to hire an advertising agency, change the ad campaign, redesign the company logo, redo the brochures, train the sales force, retain a high-powered public relations firm, and alter or otherwise reposition the company's image.

Behind the CEO's call for "a good marketing person" were a number of assumptions and attitudes about marketing: that it is a distinct function in the company, separate from and usually subordinate to the core functions; that its job is to identify groups of potential customers and find ways to convince them to buy the company's product or service; and that at the heart of it is image making – creating and projecting a false sense of the company and its offerings to lure the customer into the company's grasp. If those assumptions ever were warranted in the past, however, all three are totally unsupportable and obsolete today.

Marketing today is not a function; it is a way of doing business. Marketing is not a new ad campaign or this month's promotion. Marketing has to be all-pervasive, part of everyone's job description, from the receptionists to the board of directors. Its job is neither to fool the customer nor to falsify the company's image. It is to integrate the customer into the design of the product and to design a systematic process for interaction that will create substance in the relationship.

To understand the difference between the old and the new marketing, compare how two high-tech medical instrument companies recently handled similar customer telephone calls requesting the repair and replacement of their equipment. The first company – call it Gluco – delivered the replacement instrument to the customer within 24 hours of the request, no questions asked. The box in which it arrived contained instructions for sending back the broken instrument, a mailing label, and even tape to reseal the box. The phone call and the exchange of instruments were handled conveniently, professionally, and with maximum consideration for and minimum disruption to the customer.

The second company – call it Pumpco – handled things quite differently. The person who took the customer's telephone call had never been asked about repairing a piece of equipment; she thoughtlessly sent the customer into the limbo of hold. Finally, she came back on the line to say that the customer would have to pay for the equipment repair and that a temporary replacement would cost an additional $15.

Several days later, the customer received the replacement with no instructions, no information, no directions. Several weeks after the customer returned the broken equipment, it reappeared, repaired but with no instructions concerning the temporary replacement. Finally, the customer got a demand letter from Pumpco, indicating that someone at Pumpco had made the mistake of not sending the equipment C.O.D.

To Pumpco, marketing means selling things and collecting money; to Gluco, marketing means building relationships with its customers. The way the two companies handled two simple customer requests reflects the questions that customers increasingly ask in interactions with all kinds of businesses, from airlines to software makers: Which company is competent, responsive, and well organized? Which company do I trust to get it right? Which company would I rather do business with?

Successful companies realize that marketing is like quality – integral to the organization. Like quality, marketing is an intangible that the customer must experience to appreciate. And like quality – which in the United States has developed from early ideas like planned obsolescence and inspecting quality in to more ambitious concepts like the systemization of quality in every aspect of the organization – marketing has been evolutionary.

Marketing has shifted from tricking the customer to blaming the customer to satisfying the customer – and now to integrating the customer systematically. As its next move, marketing must permanently shed its reputation for hucksterism and image making and create an award for marketing much like the Malcolm Baldrige National Quality Award. In fact, companies that continue to see marketing as a bag of tricks will lose out in short order to companies that stress substance and real performance.

Marketing's ultimate assignment is to serve customers' real needs and to communicate the substance of the company – not to introduce the kinds of cosmetics that used to typify the auto industry's annual model changes. And because marketing in the 1990s is an expression of the company's character, it necessarily is a responsibility that belongs to the whole company.

The Goal of Marketing Is to Own the Market, Not Just to Sell the Product

U. S. companies typically make two kinds of mistakes. Some get caught up in the excitement and drive of making things, particularly new creations. Others become absorbed in the competition of selling things, particularly to increase their market share in a given product line.

Both approaches could prove fatal to a business. The problem with the first is that it leads to an internal focus. Companies can become so fixated on pursuing their R&D agendas that they forget about the customer, the market, the competition. They end up winning recognition as R&D pioneers but lack the more important capability – sustaining their performance and, sometimes, maintaining their independence. Genentech, for example, clearly emerged as the R&D pioneer in biotechnology, only to be acquired by Roche.

The problem with the second approach is that it leads to a market-share mentality, which inevitably translates into undershooting the market. A market-share mentality leads a company to think of its customers as "share points" and to use gimmicks, spiffs, and promotions to eke out a percentage-point gain. It pushes a company to look for incremental, sometimes even minuscule, growth out of existing products or to spend lavishly to launch a new product in a market where competitors enjoy a fat, dominant position. It turns marketing into an expensive fight over crumbs rather than a smart effort to own the whole pie.

The real goal of marketing is to own the market – not just to make or sell products. Smart marketing means defining what whole pie is yours. It means thinking of your company, your technology, your product in a fresh way, a way that begins by defining what you can lead. Because in marketing, what you lead, you own. Leadership is ownership.

When you own the market, you do different things and you do things differently, as do your suppliers and your customers. When you own the market, you develop your products to serve that market specifically; you define the standards in that market; you bring into your camp third parties who want to develop their own compatible products or offer you new features or add-ons to augment your product; you get the first look at new ideas that others are testing in that market; you attract the most talented people because of your acknowledged leadership position.

Owning a market can become a self-reinforcing spiral. Because you own the market, you become the dominant force in the field; because you dominate the field, you deepen your ownership of the market. Ultimately, you deepen your relationship with your customers as well, as they attribute more and more leadership qualities to a company that exhibits such an integrated performance.

To own the market, a company starts by thinking of a new way to define a market. Take, for instance, the case of Convex Computer. In 1984, Convex was looking to put a new computer on the market. Because of the existing market segmentation, Convex could have seen its only choice as competing for market share in the predefined markets: in supercomputers where Cray dominated or in minicomputers where Digital led. Determined to define a market it could own, Convex created the "mini-supercomputer" market by offering a product with a price/performance ratio between Cray's $5 million to $15 million supercomputers and Digital's $300,000 to $750,000 minicomputers. Convex's product, priced between $500,000 and $800,000, offered technological performance less than that of a full supercomputer and more than that of a minicomputer. Within this new market, Convex established itself as the leader.

Intel did the same thing with its microprocessor. The company defined its early products and market more as computers than semiconductors. Intel offered, in essence, a computer on a chip, creating a new category of products that it could own and lead.

Sometimes owning a market means broadening it; other times, narrowing it. Apple has managed to do both in efforts to create and own a market. Apple first broadened the category of small computers to achieve a leadership position. The market definition started out as hobby computers and had many small players. The next step was the home computer – a market that was also crowded and limiting. To own a market, Apple identified the personal computer, which expanded the market concept and made Apple the undeniable market leader.

In a later move, Apple did the opposite, redefining a market by narrowing its definition. Unquestionably, IBM owned the business market; for Apple, a market-share mentality in that arena would have been pointless. Instead, with technology alliances and marketing correctly defined, Apple created – and owned – a whole new market: desktop publishing. Once inside the corporate world with desktop publishing, Apple could deepen and broaden its relationships with the business customer.

Paradoxically, two important outcomes of owning a market are substantial earnings, which can replenish the company's R&D coffers, and a powerful market position, a beachhead from which a company can grow additional market share by expanding both its technological capabilities and its definition of the market. The greatest practitioners of this marketing approach are Japanese companies in industries like autos, commercial electronics, semiconductors, and computers and communications. Their primary goal is ownership of certain target markets. The *keiretsu* industrial structure allows them to use all of the market's infrastructure to achieve this; relationships in technology, information, politics, and distribution help the company assert its leadership.

The Japanese strategy is consistent. These companies begin by using basic research from the United States to jump-start new product development. From 1950 to 1978, for example, Japanese companies entered into 32,000 licensing arrangements to acquire foreign technology at an estimated cost of $9 billion. But the United States spent at least 50 times that much to do the original R&D. Next, these Japanese companies push out a variety of products to engage the market and to learn and then focus on dominating the market to force foreign competitors to retreat – leaving them to harvest substantial returns. These huge profits are recycled into a new spiral of R&D, innovation, market creation, and market dominance.

That model of competing, which links R&D, technology, innovation, production, and finance – integrated through marketing's drive to own a market – is the approach that all competitors will take to succeed in the 1990s.

Marketing Evolves as Technology Evolves

In a world of mass manufacturing, the counterpart was mass marketing. In a world of flexible manufacturing, the counterpart is flexible marketing. The technology comes first, the ability to market follows. The technology embodies adaptability, programmability, and customizability; now comes marketing that delivers on those qualities.

Today technology has created the promise of "any thing, any way, any time." Customers can have their own version of virtually any product, including one that appeals to mass identification rather than individuality, if they so desire. Think of a product or an industry where customization is not predominant. The telephone? Originally, Bell Telephone's goal was to place a simple, all-black phone in every home. Today there are more than 1,000 permutations and combinations available, with options running the gamut from different colors and portability to answering machines and programmability – as well as services. There is the further promise of optical fiber and the convergence of computers and communications into a unified industry with even greater technological choice.

How about a venerable product like the bicycle, which appeared originally as a sketch in Leonardo da Vinci's notebooks? According to a recent article in the *Washington Post*, the National Bicycle Industrial Company in Kokubu, Japan builds made-to-order bicycles on an assembly line. The bicycles, fitted to each customer's measurements, are delivered within two weeks of the order – and the company offers 11,231,862 variations on its models, at prices only 10% higher than ready-made models.

Even newspapers that report on this technology-led move to customization are themselves increasingly customized. Faced with stagnant circulation, the urban daily newspapers have begun to customize their news, advertising, and even editorial and sports pages to appeal to local suburban readers. The *Los Angeles Times*, for example, has seven zoned editions targeting each of the city's surrounding communities.

What is at work here is the predominant mathematical formula of today's marketing: variety plus service equals customization. For all of its bandying about as a marketing buzzword, customization is a remarkably direct concept – it is the capacity to deal with a customer in a unique way. Technology makes it increasingly possible to do that, but interestingly, marketing's version of the laws of physics makes it increasingly difficult.

According to quantum physics, things act differently at the micro level. Light is the classic example. When subjected to certain kinds of tests, light behaves like a wave, moving in much the way an ocean wave moves. But in other tests, light behaves more like a particle, moving as a single ball. So, scientists ask, is it a wave or a particle? And when is it which?

Markets and customers operate like light and energy. In fact, like light, the customer is more than one thing at the same time. Sometimes consumers behave as part of a group, fitting neatly into social and psychographic classifications. Other times, the consumer breaks loose and is iconoclastic. Customers make and break patterns: the senior citizen market is filled with older people who intensely wish to act youthful, and the upscale market must contend with wealthy people who hide their money behind the most utilitarian purchases.

Markets are subject to laws similar to those of quantum physics. Different markets have different levels of consumer energy, stages in the market's development where a product surges, is absorbed, dissipates, and dies. A fad, after all, is nothing more than a wave that dissipates and then becomes a particle. Take the much-discussed Yuppie market and its association with certain branded consumer products, like BMWs. After a stage of high customer energy and close identification, the wave has broken. Having been saturated and absorbed by the marketplace, the Yuppie association has faded, just as energy does in the physical world. Sensing the change, BMW no longer sells to the Yuppie lifestyle but now focuses on the technological capabilities of its machines. And Yuppies are no longer the wave they once were; as a market, they are more like particles as they look for more individualistic and personal expressions of their consumer energy.

Of course, since particles can also behave like waves again, it is likely that smart marketers will tap some new energy source, such as values, to recoalesce the young, affluent market into a wave. And technology gives marketers the tools they need, such as database marketing, to discern waves and particles and even to design programs that combine enough particles to form a powerful wave.

The lesson for marketers is much the same as that voiced by Buckminster Fuller for scientists: "Don't fight forces; use them." Marketers who follow and use technology, rather than oppose it, will discover that it creates and leads directly to new market forms and opportunities. Take audiocassettes, tapes, and compact discs. For years, record and tape companies jealously guarded their property. Knowing that home hackers pirated tapes and created their own composite cassettes, the music companies steadfastly resisted the forces of technology – until the Personics System realized that technology was making a legitimate market for authorized, high-quality customized composite cassettes and CDs.

Rather than treating the customer as a criminal, Personics saw a market. Today consumers can design personalized music tapes from the Personics System, a revved-up jukebox with a library of over 5,000 songs. For $1.10 per song, consumers tell the machine what to record. In about ten minutes, the system makes a customized tape and prints out a laser-quality label of the selections, complete with the customer's name and a personalized title for the tape. Launched in 1988, the system has already spread to more than 250 stores. Smart marketers have, once again, allowed technology to create the customizing relationship with the customer.

Marketing Moves from Monologue to Dialogue

We are witnessing the obsolescence of advertising. In the old model of marketing, it made sense as part of the whole formula: you sell mass-produced goods to a mass market through mass media. Marketing's job was to use advertising to deliver a message to the consumer in a one-way communication: "Buy this!" That message no longer works, and advertising is showing the effects. In 1989, newspaper advertising grew only 4%, compared with 6% in 1988 and 9% in 1987. According to a study by Syracuse University's John Philip Jones, ad spending in the major media has been stalled at 1.5% of GNP since 1984. Ad agency staffing, research, and profitability have been affected.

Three related factors explain the decline of advertising. First, advertising overkill has started to ricochet back on advertising itself. The proliferation of products has yielded a proliferation of messages: U.S. customers are hit with up to 3,000 marketing messages a day. In an effort to bombard the customer with yet one more advertisement, marketers are squeezing as many voices as they can into the space allotted to them. In 1988, for example, 38% of prime-time and 47% of weekday daytime television commercials were only 15 seconds in duration; in 1984, those figures were 6% and 11% respectively. As a result of the shift to 15-second commercials, the number of television commercials has skyrocketed; between 1984 and 1988, prime-time commercials increased by 25%, weekday daytime by 24%.

Predictably, however, a greater number of voices translates into a smaller impact. Customers simply are unable to remember which advertisement pitches which product, much less what qualities or attributes might differentiate one product from another. Very simply, it's a jumble out there.

Take the enormously clever and critically acclaimed series of advertisements for Eveready batteries, featuring a tireless marching rabbit. The ad was so successful that a survey conducted by Video Storyboard Tests Inc. named it one of the top commercials in 1990 – for Duracell, Eveready's top competitor. In fact, a full 40% of those who selected the ad as an outstanding commercial attributed it to Duracell. Partly as a consequence of this confusion, reports indicate that Duracell's market share has grown, while Eveready's may have shrunk slightly.

Batteries are not the only market in which more advertising succeeds in spreading more confusion. The same thing has happened in markets like athletic footwear and soda pop, where competing companies have signed up so many celebrity sponsors that consumers can no longer keep straight who is pitching what for whom. In 1989, for example, Coke, Diet Coke, Pepsi, and Diet Pepsi used nearly three dozen movie stars, athletes, musicians, and television personalities to tell consumers to buy more cola. But when the

smoke and mirrors had cleared, most consumers couldn't remember whether Joe Montana and Don Johnson drank Coke or Pepsi – or both. Or why it really mattered.

The second development in advertising's decline is an outgrowth of the first: as advertising has proliferated and become more obnoxiously insistent, consumers have gotten fed up. The more advertising seeks to intrude, the more people try to shut it out. Last year, Disney won the applause of commercial-weary customers when the company announced that it would not screen its films in theaters that showed commercials before the feature. A Disney executive was quoted as saying, "Movie theaters should be preserved as environments where consumers can escape from the pervasive onslaught of advertising." Buttressing its position, the company cited survey data obtained from moviegoers, 90% of whom said they did not want commercials shown in movie theaters and 95% of whom said they did want to see previews of coming attractions.

More recently, after a number of failed attempts, the U.S. Congress responded to the growing concerns of parents and educators over the commercial content of children's television. A new law limits the number of minutes of commercials and directs the Federal Communications Commission both to examine "program-length commercials" – cartoon shows linked to commercial product lines – and to make each television station's contribution to children's educational needs a condition for license renewal. This concern over advertising is mirrored in a variety of arenas – from public outcry over cigarette marketing plans targeted at blacks and women to calls for more environmentally sensitive packaging and products.

The underlying reason behind both of these factors is advertising's dirty little secret: it serves no useful purpose. In today's market, advertising simply misses the fundamental point of marketing – adaptability, flexibility, and responsiveness. The new marketing requires a feedback loop; it is this element that is missing from the monologue of advertising but that is built into the dialogue of marketing. The feedback loop, connecting company and customer, is central to the operating definition of a truly market-driven company: a company that adapts in a timely way to the changing needs of the customer.

Apple is one such company. Its Macintosh computer is regarded as a machine that launched a revolution. At its birth in 1984, industry analysts received it with praise and acclaim. But in retrospect, the first Macintosh had many weaknesses: it had limited, nonexpandable memory, virtually no applications software, and a black-and-white screen. For all those deficiencies, however, the Mac had two strengths that more than compensated: it was incredibly easy to use, and it had a user group that was prepared to praise Mac publicly at its launch and to advise Apple privately on how to improve it. In other words, it had a feedback loop. It was this feedback loop that brought about change in the Mac, which ultimately became an open, adaptable, and colorful computer. And it was changing the Mac that saved it.

Months before launching the Mac, Apple gave a sample of the product to 100 influential Americans to use and comment on. It signed up 100 third-party software suppliers who began to envision applications that could take advantage of the Mac's simplicity. It trained over 4,000 dealer salespeople and gave full-day, hands-on demonstrations of the Mac to industry insiders and analysts. Apple got two benefits from this network: educated Mac supporters who could legitimately praise the product to the press and invested consumers who could tell the company what the Mac needed. The dialogue with customers *and* media praise were worth more than any notice advertising could buy.

Apple's approach represents the new marketing model, a shift from monologue to dialogue. It is accomplished through experience-based marketing, where companies create opportunities for customers and potential customers to sample their products and then provide feedback. It is accomplished through beta sites, where a company can install a prelaunch product and study its use and needed refinements. Experienced-based marketing allows a company to work closely with a client to change a product, to adapt the technology – recognizing that no product is perfect when it comes from engineering. This interaction was precisely the approach taken by Xerox in developing its recently announced Docutech System. Seven months before launch, Xerox established 25 beta sites. From its prelaunch customers, Xerox learned what adjustments it should make, what service and support it should supply, and what enhancements and related new products it might next introduce.

The goal is adaptive marketing, marketing that stresses sensitivity, flexibility, and resiliency. Sensitivity comes from having a variety of modes and channels through which companies can read the environment, from user groups that offer live feedback to sophisticated consumer scanners that provide data on customer choice in real time. Flexibility comes from creating an organizational structure and operating style that permits the company to take advantage of new opportunities presented by customer feedback. Resiliency comes from learning from mistakes – marketing that listens and responds.

Marketing a Product Is Marketing a Service Is Marketing a Product

The line between products and services is fast eroding. What once appeared to be a rigid polarity now has become a hybrid: the servicization of products and the productization of services. When General Motors makes more money from lending its customers money to buy its cars than it makes from manufacturing the cars, is it marketing its products or its services? When IBM announces to all the world that it is now in the systems-integration business – the customer can buy any box from any vendor and IBM will supply the systems know-how to make the whole thing work together – is it marketing its products or its services? In fact, the computer business today is 75% services; it consists overwhelmingly of applications knowledge, systems analysis, systems engineering, systems integration, networking solutions, security, and maintenance.

The point applies just as well to less grandiose companies and to less expensive consumer products. Take the large corner drugstore that stocks thousands of products, from cosmetics to wristwatches. The products are for sale, but the store is actually marketing a service – the convenience of having so much variety collected and arrayed in one location. Or take any of the ordinary products found in the home, from boxes of cereal to table lamps to VCRs. All of them come with some form of information designed to perform a service: nutritional information to indicate the actual food value of the cereal to the health-conscious consumer; a United Laboratories label on the lamp as an assurance of testing; an operating manual to help the nontechnical VCR customer rig up the new unit. There is ample room to improve the quality of this information – to make it more useful, more convenient, or even more entertaining – but in almost every case, the service information is a critical component of the product.

On the other side of the hybrid, service providers are acknowledging the productization of services. Service providers, such as banks, insurance companies, consulting firms, even airlines and radio stations, are creating tangible events, repetitive and predictable exercises, standard and customizable packages that are product services. A frequent-flier or a frequent-listener club is a product service, as are regular audits performed by consulting firms or new loan packages assembled by banks to respond to changing economic conditions.

As products and services merge, it is critical for marketers to understand clearly what marketing the new hybrid is *not*. The service component is not satisfied by repairing a product if it breaks. Nor is it satisfied by an 800 number, a warranty, or a customer survey form. What customers want most from a product is often qualitative and intangible; it is the service that is integral to the product. Service is not an event; it is the process of creating a customer environment of information, assurance, and comfort.

Consider an experience that by now must have become commonplace for all of us as consumers. You go to an electronics store and buy an expensive piece of audio or video equipment, say, a CD player, a VCR, or a video camera. You take it home, and a few days later, you accidentally drop it. It breaks. It won't work. Now, as a customer, you have a decision to make. When you take it back to the store, do you say it was broken when you took it out of the box? Or do you tell the truth?

The answer, honestly, depends on how you think the store will respond. But just as honestly, most customers appreciate a store that encourages them to tell the truth by making good on all customer problems. Service is, ultimately, an environment that encourages honesty. The company that adopts a "we'll make good on it, no questions asked" policy in the face of adversity may win a customer for life.

Marketers who ignore the service component of their products focus on competitive differentiation and tools to penetrate markets. Marketers who appreciate the importance of the product-service hybrid focus on building loyal customer relationships.

Technology Markets Technology

Technology and marketing once may have looked like opposites. The cold, impersonal sameness of technology and the high-touch, human uniqueness of marketing seemed eternally at odds. Computers would only make marketing less personal; marketing could never learn to appreciate the look and feel of computers, databases, and the rest of the high-tech paraphernalia.

On the grounds of cost, a truce was eventually arranged. Very simply, marketers discovered that real savings could be gained by using technology to do what previously had required expensive, intensive, and often risky, people-directed field operations. For example, marketers learned that by matching a database with a marketing plan to simulate a new product launch on a computer, they could accomplish in 90 days and for $50,000 what otherwise would take as long as a year and cost at least several hundred thousand dollars.

But having moved beyond the simple automation-for-cost-saving stage, technology and marketing have now not only fused but also begun to feed back to each other. The result is the transformation of both technology and the product and the reshaping of both the customer and the company. Technology permits information to flow in both directions between the customer and the company. It creates the feedback loop that integrates the customer into the company, allows the company to own a market, permits customization, creates a dialogue, and turns a product into a service and a service into a product.

The direction in which Genentech has moved in its use of laptop and hand-held computers illustrates the transforming power of technology as it merges with marketing. Originally, the biotechnology company planned to have salespeople use laptops on their sales calls as a way to automate the sales function. Sales reps, working solely out of their homes, would use laptops to get and send electronic mail, file reports on computerized "templates," place orders, and receive company press releases and information updates. In addition, the laptops would enable sales reps to keep databases that would track customers' buying histories and company performance. That was the initial level of expectations – very low.

In fact, the technology-marketing marriage has dramatically altered the customer-company relationship and the job of the sales rep. Sales reps have emerged as marketing consultants. Armed with technical information generated and gathered by Genentech, sales reps can provide a valuable educational service to their customers, who are primarily pharmacists and physicians. For example, analysis of the largest study of children with a disease called short stature is available only through Genentech and its representatives. With this analysis, which is based on clinical studies of 6,000 patients between the ages of one month and 30 years, and with the help of an on-line "growth calculator," doctors can better judge when to use the growth hormone Protropin.

Genentech's system also includes a general educational component. Sales reps can use their laptops to access the latest articles or technical reports from medical conferences to help doctors keep up to date. The laptops also make it possible for doctors to use sales reps as research associates: Genentech has a staff of medical specialists who can answer highly technical questions posed through an on-line question-and-answer template. When sales reps enter a question on the template, the e-mail function immediately routes it to the appropriate specialist. For relatively simple questions, online answers come back to the sales rep within a day.

In the 1990s, Genentech's laptop system – and the hundreds of similar applications that sprang up in the 1980s to automate sales, marketing, service, and distribution – will seem like a rather obvious and primitive way to meld technology and marketing. The marketer will have available not only existing technologies but also their converging capabilities: personal computers, databases, CD-ROMs, graphic displays, multimedia, color terminals, computer-video technology, networking, a custom processor that can be built into anything anywhere to create intelligence on a countertop or a dashboard, scanners that read text, and networks that instantaneously create and distribute vast reaches of information.

As design and manufacturing technologies advance into "real time" processes, marketing will move to eliminate the gap between production and consumption. The result will be marketing workstations – the marketers' counterpart to CAD/CAM systems for engineers and product designers. The marketing workstation will draw on graphic, video, audio, and numeric information from a network of databases. The marketer will be able to look through windows on the workstation and manipulate data, simulate markets and products, bounce concepts off others in distant cities, write production orders for product designs and packaging concepts, and obtain costs, timetables, and distribution schedules.

Just as computer-comfortable children today think nothing of manipulating figures and playing fantastic games on the same color screens, marketers will use the workstation to play both designer and consumer. The workstation will allow marketers to integrate data on historic sales and cost figures, competitive trends, and consumer patterns. At the same time, marketers will be able to create and test advertisements and promotions, evaluate media options, and analyze viewer and readership data. And finally, marketers will be able to obtain instant feedback on concepts and plans and to move marketing plans rapidly into production.

The marriage of technology and marketing should bring with it a renaissance of marketing R&D – a new capability to explore new ideas, to test them against the reactions of real customers in real time, and to advance to experience-based leaps of faith. It should be the vehicle for bringing the customer inside the company and for putting marketing in the center of the company.

In the 1990s, the critical dimensions of the company – including all of the attributes that together define how the company does business – are ultimately the functions of marketing. That is why marketing is everyone's job, why marketing is everything and everything is marketing.

Reprint 91108

Marketers say they give people what they want. Critics say marketers get people to want what they don't need and often can't have. Something's wrong.

Marketing and Its Discontents

by Steven H. Star

Business sometimes has a bad name, and marketing is particularly singled out, especially advertising. Even businesspeople often hold marketing in deep suspicion. It is widely suspected of trying, with all the intelligence, technology, and cunning it can command, to get people to want what they don't need, of overpromising and exaggerating what can be delivered, and, worst, of exploiting people's vulnerabilities to get them to value, want, and expect the unattainable and undesirable. This criticism amounts to an attack on the ethics of marketing and, by extension, on business itself.

What makes this situation remarkable is the fact that for 30 years the driving theme in the practice of modern marketing has been the marketing concept, whose central principle is that business succeeds best when it tries to serve customers by giving them what they truly want. Something seems not right, and it is useful to try to understand what is going on and going wrong.

Actually, marketing and its practices, especially advertising and selling, have always been subjects of criticism and controversy. Some of these complaints go back as far as the Bible, Confucius, and classical Greek literature. More recently, the introduction of "personal deodorants" in the 1960s was highly controversial – both the idea of the product itself and the way it was advertised. Ten years ago, there was bitter criticism of "war toys," advertising aimed at children, and the promotion of baby formula in Africa. Today it's junk mail, the glorification to the young of hedonic lifestyles, the sheer abundance and intrusiveness of commercial communications.

Criticism of marketing focuses largely on two areas: its "excesses" and its "expertness." "Excesses" are about purposefully shoddy and objectionable products, inadequate warranties, deceptive or objectionable advertising, misleading packaging, questionable selling practices, and emphasis on tawdry values. These are the basis of what's broadly referred to as the "consumer movement," or "consumerism."

"Expertness" refers to the special ways marketing thinks about and approaches consumers. Most people define consumer needs or wants in terms of products and their functional attributes – what a product does, how it performs, tastes, or looks. Marketers do

Steven H. Star is editor-in-chief of the Sloan Management Review *and director of the Marketing Center at the MIT Sloan School of Management.*

the same, but lots more. They think also of how products perform in terms of consumers' psychological and psychosocial needs and wishes. These tend to be complex, subtle, and manipulatable. Individuals often don't perceive any need for particular products until they have been persuasively exposed to the possibility of having them – and it is marketing experts who expertly do the persuading. When an expert takes on an amateur, especially when money is involved, the general feeling is that it's unfair.

Remarkably, the debate about marketing has been silent about some of the mechanics of modern life that give rise to it, specifically, about the structure of modern media and audiences. Indeed, it can be argued that many of the social discontents, and even ethical issues, associated with marketing arise not from "excesses," "inappropriate" definitions of consumer wants and needs, or from greed or cunning but rather from functional limitations on the implementability of the marketing concept.

The true practitioner of the marketing concept is supposed to find out what consumers want or need and try to satisfy these needs – if that makes economic and strategic sense. Assuming for the moment that one wants to cater carefully to consumer wants and needs (and that's not always a justified assumption – there are charlatans and sharpshooters everywhere in all professions), if you think for a moment about the process of trying to practice the marketing concept carefully, you quickly see how things will necessarily go wrong.

First, the marketer identifies a market opportunity: an apparent consumer need – discovered by research, intuition, technological innovation, or some combination of these. Then the marketer determines its size, its intensity (how much the people who have the need would be willing to pay for its satisfaction), and whether the need could be satisfied at a profitable cost. In other words, would it be feasible and profitable for the marketer's company to seek to satisfy this particular consumer need?

Then there is target identification – the specific groups in the population that the necessary marketing effort (usually called "program") will go after – not just people with the indicated need but also with the wish, will, and money to try to satisfy it. Marketers identify potential consumers along demographic and, especially in consumer goods, psychosocial terms. If, for example, there are 500,000 potential consumers of the product, one wants to know specifically who they are – young or old, male or female, rich or poor, urban or rural, "with-it" or "square," active or passive, confident or concerned.

A basic thrust of behavioral research in marketing is to suggest that psychosocial factors are at least as

When an expert takes on an amateur, especially when money is involved, the feeling is that it's unfair.

DRAWINGS BY WALLOP MANYUM

important as demographic factors in defining a market segment. In other words, consumers who share a common set of attitudinal, perceptual, and sociological characteristics are more likely to share a particular set of needs than, say, consumers in the same age or income group.

These findings are useful for developing communications themes and other marketing efforts aimed at the target audience. Unfortunately, the efforts usually cannot be closely matched to the audiences. There are few media or channels of distribution that allow the marketer to direct a marketing program exclusively to an audience that has the highly specific behavioral or psychosocial characteristics of the targeted audience. No matter how specialized our media, how carefully computerized our audience data, how sophisticated the protocols of market analysis, there remain, as always, major misfits among products, audiences, messages, and media. As one marketing executive recently said, "This consumer and behavior research is interesting, but in the end we still tell our advertising agencies to cast a wide net, to go after middle-income housewives between 21 and 40."

Few media or distribution channels allow the marketer to hit only the target audience —and that spells trouble.

In the end, the marketer develops a program to coincide, to the greatest extent possible, with the attributes of the consumer target group. Unfortunately, the "greatest extent possible" is always full of disjunctions and static. Given the target group, marketers must make trade-offs regarding specific product features, packaging, personal selling, copy strategy, distribution channels, attendant services, price, advertising media, and much more. And while marketers typically view the "audience" for the selected program as a function of a media plan, it also depends on the choice of channels of distribution. Also, depending on how much personal selling is used either directly or through the distribution channels, it is a function of the "call instructions" given to the sales force.

This brief look at what's involved in the development of a marketing program allows us to identify three groups of consumers who are affected by that process, and how it works. First, there is the *market segment*—people with the need in question. Second, there is the *program target*—people in the segment with the "best fit" characteristics for the product and program. (Lots of people may need trousers, but only a few qualify as likely buyers of Giorgio Armani.) Finally, there is the *program audience*—all people who are actually exposed to the marketing program, without regard to whether they are in the segment of its best-fit component.

These three groups are rarely synonymous. The exception occurs occasionally in industrial products where customers for a particular product may be few and easily identifiable. Such customers, all sharing a particular need (a market segment), are likely to group themselves into a meaningful target (for example, all companies with a particular application of the product in question, such as high-speed filling of bottles at breweries). In such circumstances, direct selling is likely to be economically justified, and highly specialized trade media exist to help expose the members of the program target (and *only* the members of the program target) to the marketing program. Under these circumstances, the marketing segment, program target, and program audience often will be virtually identical.[1]

Most consumer goods markets are significantly different. Typically, there are many rather than few potential customers. Each represents a relatively small amount of potential sales. Rarely do members of a particular market segment group themselves neatly into a meaningful program target. There are substantial differences among households or individual consumers with similar demographic characteristics.[2] Even with all the past decade's advances in information technology, in microsegmentation of consumers, in communications, and in specialized media and distribution systems, the economic feasibility of direct selling of consumer goods is rare. Mass marketing remains the predominant mode.

The continued existence in consumer goods of significant differences between market segments and program targets and between program targets and program audiences is obvious enough. Assume that a market segment of one million household buyers has been determined to have a particular need—say for a heavy-duty laundry detergent. Seventy percent of these buyers share a particular set of demographic characteristics—they have small children who frequently play outdoors in muddy fields. The remaining 30% have demographic characteristics that are randomly distributed throughout the rest of the population—the households include adults who work as auto mechanics. Under these conditions, if the program target is democratically defined in terms of families with small children, it will include only 70% of the market segment.

Moreover, the set of demographic characteristics that provides a best-fit description of the market segment almost certainly also describes a group of consumers who are not members of the market segment (they do not have the need in question because, say, their children don't play in muddy fields). If, for example, the small-children households total 1,500,000, then members of the muddy-fields market segment represent less than 50% of the members of the program target. The misfit is enormous.

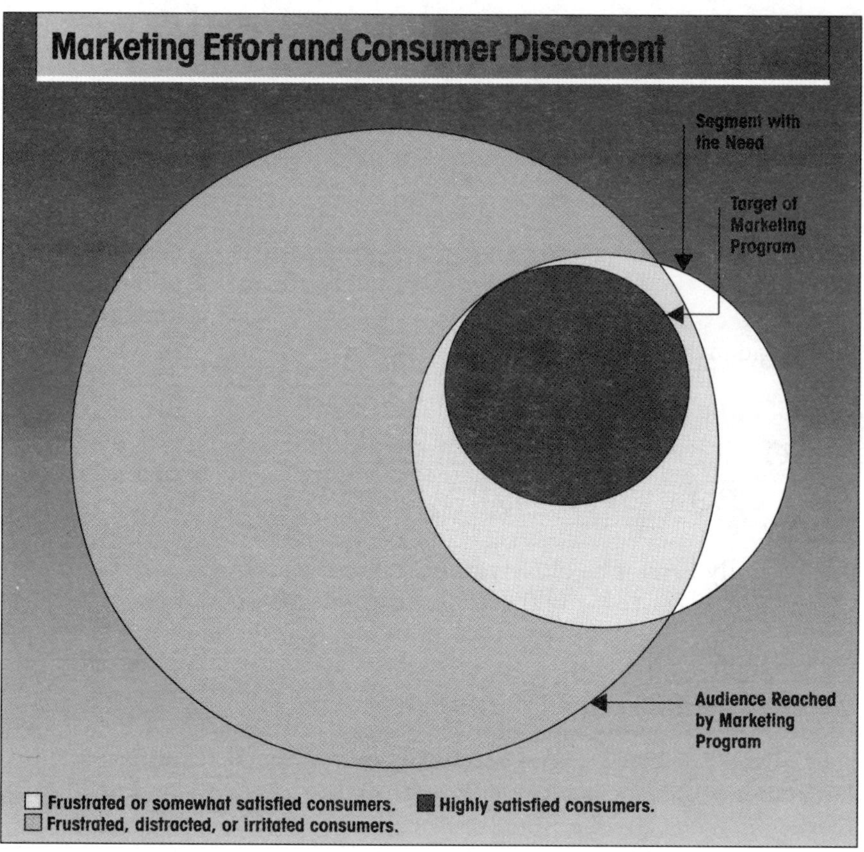

Similar misfits accompany the translation of a program target into a program audience. The usual objective is to maximize advertising exposure of the program target for a particular budgetary expenditure. The most efficient media schedule will rarely reach all members of the program target. But it will almost certainly reach people who are not in the program target. The same kinds of misfits will almost certainly occur in distribution channels. From the marketer's perspective, these inefficiencies are unfortunate but totally unavoidable.

Thus marketing programs generate three partially overlapping groups of consumers–the market segment, the program target, and the program audience. Largely, these divide into six meaningful clusters:

1. Segment, target, and audience.
2. Segment and audience.
3. Target and audience.
4. Audience.
5. Segment and target.
6. Segment.[3]

The relative size of each of these clusters for a particular marketing program is a function of the level of congruence between the market segment, the program target, and the program audience (as shown in the illustration, "Marketing Effort and Consumer Discontent").

Cluster 1 (segment, target, *and* audience) represents the social value of the marketing concept. Consumers in this cluster have had their needs identified, have had a marketing program designed specifically around their characteristics, and have been exposed to the marketing program. The marketing program has satisfied the needs of these consumers.

Cluster 2 (segment *and* audience) consists of consumers whose needs have been identified, have had a product made available to them in the market, and have been exposed to the marketing program. But unfortunately, neither the product nor the program has been designed with their particular characteristics in mind. The product may be too expensive, sold through inconvenient channels (outlets that exist only in large urban centers), or the copy strategy may make them feel uncomfortable (a youth theme when they are of advanced years). Members of this cluster may be partially satisfied (if they purchase the product though it doesn't quite fill their needs) or frustrated (if, for example, they can't afford the product).

Consumers in Cluster 3 (target *and* audience) are exposed to the marketing program even though they have no interest in it (they don't feel the need to which it is addressed). The marketing program is likely to be distracting or even irritating, especially since it has been designed (copy, media, channels) to appeal to consumers with their particular characteristics.[4] Cluster 4 (audience *only*) is quite similar except that the marketing program is likely to be somewhat less distracting since it was not designed to appeal to members of this cluster (they are not members of the program target).

Clusters 5 (segment *and* target) and 6 (segment *only*) consist of consumers who have a need that a marketer has attempted to fill, but they are not aware of the product's availability because they are not members of the program audience. They've not heard or seen the message. They are the "dropped outs" of the marketing process. The marketing concept is not working for them. Behaviorally, these consumers are frustrated.[5]

It is obvious that the number of possible mismatches are from three to six times greater than possible close matches. (For a summary of the clusters, see the chart, "Marketing Clusters and Consumer Reactions.") The possibilities of disaffection are abundant, not because of carelessness, indifference, irresponsibility, ineptitude, or cupidity, but because the world is imperfect.

While a well-conceived marketing program certainly provides satisfaction to some consumers (Clusters 1 and some of Cluster 2), it most likely will also distract some consumers (Clusters 3 and 4) and frustrate others (Clusters 5 and 6 and some members of Cluster 2). And it is these consumers who almost surely give rise to much (though not all) of the criticism of marketing in our intensely commercial times.

It is quite possible that the effects of segment-target incongruence would be of little importance if they were randomly distributed through the population. A certain amount of dissatisfaction, distraction, and frustration seems inherent in the human condition, and–according to some psychologists–may even be a necessary condition of psychological health. Unfortunately, certain segments of society probably encounter disproportionately large amounts of distraction and frustration. In particular, people whose needs differ significantly from others who have their particular demographic characteristics are likely to experience an unusually large amount of distraction. They get exposed to a great deal of marketing effort (mostly via mass communications) that is not intended for them. And so they get mad.

This possibility was documented over 20 years ago in the Harvard Business School study, *Advertising in America*.[6] Users of products who encountered advertisements for those products had more favorable (or fewer unfavorable) attitudes toward those advertisements than nonusers. And users of particular brands of those articles had even better attitudes toward ads featuring those brands than users of other brands. Getting irritated or mad depends, as they say, on "where you're coming from."

The likelihood of getting mad is almost surely greater in the better educated sectors and among the professional commentators of our society. They fall disproportionately into Cluster 3 (target and audience, but not segment), where they probably share many of the demographic characteristics of the dominant middle class (age, income, location) but differ significantly in values and perceived needs. This subgroup may be exposed to a great many marketing programs in which it has little interest, or which it perceives as alien to its values. It probably also has disproportionately greater access to the institutions

People get exposed to a great deal of marketing effort that is not intended for them. And so they get irritated, frustrated, or mad.

and instruments of public commentary (via lectures, news reports, columns, and articles) and is likely therefore to make a disproportionately large amount of critical noise about modern marketing.

Marketing Clusters and Consumer Reactions

Clusters	Reactions
1. Segment, target, and audience	Highly satisfied
2. Segment and audience	Somewhat satisfied or frustrated
3. Target and audience	Highly distracted or irritated
4. Audience	Somewhat distracted
5. Segment and target	Frustrated
6. Segment	Frustrated

Another group of consumers who are exposed to marketing programs that bother them are those who have the needs that the programs address but not the demographic characteristics of the best-fit program targets. They may have, for example, a strong desire for a high-performance sports car or expensive toys for their children (as advertised on Saturday morning TV) but not the resources to pay for them. Such consumers are likely to experience an unusual amount of frustration. The same is also true of variously disadvantaged members of society–falling disproportionately into Clusters 6 (segment only) and 2 (segment and audience).

Although their needs may be recognized and they may be exposed to relevant marketing communications, such consumers are rarely targets of the particular marketing programs. The marketing programs are rarely tailored specifically to their circumstances (low income, lack of "normal" credit, limited physical or psychological mobility), and so they are likely to be extremely frustrated. Presumably, this frustration would be higher for the segment-audience cluster (the urban disadvantaged) than for the segment-only cluster (the rural disadvantaged), but this is only conjecture. Nor is this to suggest that the frustrations of the disadvantaged are attributable to the marketing process. Clearly the causes are far more basic. But it does suggest some of the reasons why the practice of the marketing concept and the operations of the marketing process at least do not prevent, avoid, or minimize frustrations.

The marketing concept, like all good things that seem to make good sense, is burdened by process constraints that limit, in implementation, the achievement of its promises. In particular, the lack of congruence among segments, targets, and audiences seems a significant cause of consumer distraction and frustration. Marketing programs that produce social goods (consumer satisfaction) will almost surely also have dysfunctional social effects.

This line of reasoning takes us into the old, and not very reassuring, subject of welfare economics–a method of analysis that, like so much else in the rhetoric of the social sciences, suffers deeply from analysis paralysis. If a particular marketing program has both functional and dysfunctional effects, how does one make a trade-off between them? If a given program could be shown to have satisfied 1 million consumers, distracted 500,000, and increased the frustration of 300,000, would its net effect on society be negative or positive? While the relative intensity of these several social effects would certainly have to be an important part of the equation, even this information would leave the question unanswered, since reasonable people would surely continue to dispute the social importance of a unit of satisfaction as compared with a unit of frustration.

The social effects of the marketing process must, like all social phenomena, be looked at in some sort of trade-off matrix. While there may never be agreement on the proper trade-offs among social effects, it would be useful to have a better picture of what these effects are. This would make it possible to determine the relative magnitudes of the effects occasioned by various marketing programs in each of the six clusters, to measure the intensity of the hypothesized behavioral effects of such clusterings, and to determine whether selected subgroups of society fall into particular clusters to a disproportionate degree. It should also be possible to identify specific points at which technical improvements in the marketing process would have significant social payoffs.

> If a marketing program satisfies a million people, distracts 500,000, and frustrates 300,000, what is the net effect?

Of course, the analysis suggested here regarding marketing's sometimes bad reputation is independent of corrupt business practices, such as calculated duplicity, conscious misrepresentation, distortion, trickery, shoddiness, and the like–none of which is, in any case, unique to modern times. But at all times there will be misfits between products, segments, targets, and audiences. It is useful to understand their innocent origins and inevitability.

Still, any such understanding should not prevent asking what real problems are being missed because we argue about the wrong things. An explanation of a phenomenon is not its justification. Do we fail to exercise the self-restraint that civilized life requires? Do we get so intent in fighting our critics that we fail honestly to confront critical issues while avoiding the necessity to be honestly self-critical? Have we tried honestly to fix some of the misfits and alleviate some of the discontents?

References

1. The overwhelming success of IBM in the computer mainframe business, from roughly 1957 to 1980, was based largely on the congruence of its market segments, program targets, and audiences. It divided its data-processing business into 16 major segments, most of which were further divided into subsegments. In general, these segments were defined by applications commonality: the "distribution" segment, for example, included all companies for which inventory and physical distribution costs represented a major component of controllable expense. A separate program was developed for each segment (or subsegment), and individual salespeople and sales offices specialized in those segments. Every potential purchaser of data-processing equipment in the United States was assigned to an IBM salesperson who was expected to tailor marketing programs to the potential customer's specific needs. As a result, IBM achieved a high degree of congruence among segments, targets, and audiences, despite the fact that its market was highly varied. See E. Raymond Corey and Steven H. Star, *Organization Strategy: A Marketing Approach* (Cambridge: Harvard University Press, 1971), pp. 108-155.

2. In theoretical terms, a consumer market segment consists of individuals who share psychological, sociological, and demographic characteristics, which–together–are likely to lead to a particular purchase act. In implementing a marketing program, however, it is frequently necessary to treat demographics as the sole variable of interest (except in copy formulation). Thus, while behavioral research in marketing helps explain the reasons for program-target incongruence, it has made remarkably little headway in helping marketers reduce the incongruence.

3. A separate "target" cluster is also possible but is not relevant for this present purpose.

4. Actually, a consumer who had the need but has satisfied it would also fall into this cluster. For example, a consumer who may have needed information prior to purchasing a watch may find such information distracting after he has made the purchase, especially if it makes him question his purchase. Conversely, he may find advertising of the product he purchased useful in reducing postpurchase cognitive dissonance, as would seem to be the case with automobiles.

5. Of course, segment-audience incongruence is not the only (or even major) source of consumer frustration. In many cases, consumer needs will not be satisfied because of (1) technological constraints–it can't be done; (2) economic constraints–it isn't profitable; (3) strategic constraints–companies choose not to do it; or (4) information constraints–companies have simply not yet identified the need. In this context, we may view segment-audience incongruence as a *process constraint* on consumer satisfaction.

6. Raymond A. Bauer and Stephen A. Greyser, *Advertising in America: The Consumer View*, Division of Research, Graduate School of Business Administration, Harvard University, Boston, 1968.

Reprint 89612

"However, under another accounting procedure."

It's far more than the cliché "getting close to the customer."

What the Hell Is 'Market Oriented'?

by Benson P. Shapiro

The air hung heavy in French Lick, Indiana. A tornado watch was in effect that morning, and the sky was black. In a meeting room in one of the local resort hotels, where top management of the Wolverine Controller Company had gathered, the atmosphere matched the weather. Recent results had been poor for the Indianapolis-based producer of flow controllers for process industries like chemicals, paper, and food. Sales were off, but earnings were off even more. Market share was down in all product lines.

As the president called the meeting to order he had fire in his eyes. "The situation can't get much more serious," he proclaimed. "As you all know, over the past couple of years everything has gone to hell in a handbasket. We're in deep trouble, with both domestic and foreign competition preempting us at every turn. The only way to get out of this mess is for us to become customer driven or market oriented. I'm not even sure what that means, but I'm damn sure that we want to be there. I don't even know whether there's a difference between being market driven and customer oriented or customer driven and market oriented or whatever. We've just got to do a hell of a lot better."

"I couldn't agree with you more, Frank," the marketing vice president put in. "I've been saying all along that we've got to be more marketing oriented. The marketing department has to be more involved in everything that goes on because we represent the customer and we've got an integrated view of the company."

It's OK to push your own functional goals–to a point.

The CEO scowled at him. "I said *market* oriented, not marketing oriented! It's unclear to me what we get for all the overhead we have in marketing. Those sexy brochures of yours sure haven't been doing the job."

There followed a lively, often acrimonious discussion of what was wrong and what was needed. Each vice president defended his or her function or unit and set out solutions from that particular standpoint. I will draw a curtain over their heedless and profane bickering, but here are paraphrases of their positions:

Benson P. Shapiro is a professor and senior associate dean for publications at the Harvard Business School. Currently he is researching the relationships among the management of a company's product line, the selection and nurturing of its most strategic accounts, and how its functional departments and divisions can work together to support these accounts.

Sales VP: "We need more salespeople. *We're* the ones who are close to the customers. We have to have more call capacity in the sales force so we can provide better service and get new product ideas into the company faster."

Manufacturing VP: "We all know that our customers want quality. We need more automated machinery so we can work to closer tolerances and give them better quality. Also, we ought to send our whole manufacturing team to Crosby's Quality College."

Research and development VP: "Clearly we could do much better at both making and selling our products. But the fundamental problem is a lack of *new* products. They're the heart of our business. Our technology is getting old because we aren't investing enough in R&D."

Finance VP: "The problem isn't not enough resources; it's too many resources misspent. We've got too much overhead. Our variable costs are out of control. Our marketing and sales expenses are unreasonable. And we spend too much on R&D. We don't need more, we need less."

The general manager of the Electronic Flow Controls Division: "We aren't organized in the right way—that's the fundamental problem. If each division had its own sales force, we would have better coordination between sales and the other functions."

Her counterpart in the Pneumatic Controls Division: "We don't need our own sales forces anywhere near as much as we need our own engineering group so we can develop designs tailored to our customers. As long as we have a central R&D group that owns all the engineers, the divisions can't do their jobs."

As the group adjourned for lunch, the president interjected a last word. "You all put in a lot of time talking past each other and defending your own turf.

> Knowledge of "the trade" has to permeate every corporate unit.

Some of that's all right. You're supposed to represent your own departments and sell your own perspectives. If you didn't work hard for your own organizations, you wouldn't have lasted long at Wolverine, and you couldn't have made the contributions that you have.

"But enough is enough! You aren't just representatives of your own shops. You're the corporate executives at Wolverine and you have to take a more integrated, global view. It's my job to get all of you coordinated, but it's also the job of each of you. I don't have the knowledge, and nothing can replace direct, lateral communication across departments. Let's figure out how to do that after we get some lunch."

All Right, What Is It?

Leaving the Wolverine bunch to its meal, I want to make a start in dispelling the president's uncertainty. After years of research, I'm convinced that the term "market oriented" represents a set of processes touching on all aspects of the company. It's a great deal more than the cliché "getting close to the customer." Since most companies sell to a variety of customers with varying and even conflicting desires and needs, the goal of getting close to the customer is meaningless. I've also found no meaningful difference between "market driven" and "customer oriented," so I use the phrases interchangeably. In my view, three characteristics make a company market driven.

Information on all important buying influences permeates every corporate function. A company can be market oriented only if it completely understands its markets and the people who decide whether to buy its products or services.

In some industries, wholesalers, retailers, and other parts of the distribution channels have a profound influence on the choices customers make. So it's important to understand "the trade." In other markets, nonbuying influences specify the product, although they neither purchase it nor use it. These include architects, consulting engineers, and doctors. In still other markets, one person may buy the product and another may use it; family situations are an obvious illustration. In commercial and industrial marketplaces, a professional procurement organization may actually purchase the product, while a manufacturing or operational function uses it.

To be of greatest use, customer information must move beyond the market research, sales, and marketing functions and "permeate every corporate function"—the R&D scientists and engineers, the manufacturing people, and the field-service specialists. When the technologists, for example, get unvarnished feedback on the way customers use the product, they can better develop improvements on the product and the production processes. If, on the other hand, market research or marketing people predigest the information, technologists may miss opportunities.

Of course, regular cross-functional meetings to discuss customer needs and to analyze feedback from buying influences are very important. At least once a year, the top functional officers should spend a full day or more to consider what is happening with key buying influences.

Corporate officers and functions should have access to all useful market research reports. If company staff appends summaries to regular customer surveys, like the Greenwich commercial and investment banking reports or the numerous consumer package-goods industry sales analyses, top officers are more likely to study them. That approach lets top management get the sales and marketing departments' opinions as well as those of less-biased observers.

Some companies that have customer response phones—toll-free 800 numbers that consumers or distributors call to ask questions or make comments—distribute selected cassette recordings of calls to a wide range of executives, line and staff. The cassettes stimulate new ideas for products, product improvements, packaging, and service.

Reports to read and cassettes to hear are useful—but insufficient. High-level executives need to make visits to important customers to see them using their industrial and commercial products, consuming their services, or retailing their consumer goods. When, say, top manufacturing executives understand how a customer factory uses their products, they will have a more solid appreciation of customer needs for quality and close tolerances. Trade show visits provide valuable opportunities for operations and technical people to talk with customers and visit competitors' booths (if allowed by industry custom and show rules).

In my statement on the first characteristic, I referred to "important" buying influences. Because different customers have different needs, a marketer cannot effectively satisfy a wide range of them equally. The most important strategic decision is to choose the important customers. All customers are important, but invariably some are more important to the company than others. Collaboration among the various functions is important when pinpointing the key target accounts and market segments. Then the salespeople know whom to call on first and most often, the people who schedule production runs know who gets favored treatment, and those who make service calls know who rates special attention. If the priorities are not clear in the calm of planning meetings, they certainly won't be when the sales, production scheduling, and service dispatching processes get hectic.

The choice of customers influences the way decisions are made. During a marketing meeting at Wolverine Controller, one senior marketing person said, "Sales and marketing will pick out the customers they want to do business with, and then we'll sit down with the manufacturing and technical people and manage the product mix." Too late! Once you have a certain group of customers, the product mix is pretty much set; you must make the types of products they want. If sales and marketing choose the customers, they have undue power over decisions. Customer selection must involve all operating functions.

Strategic and tactical decisions are made interfunctionally and interdivisionally. Functions and divisions will inevitably have conflicting objectives that mirror distinctions in cultures and in modes of operation. The glimpse into the meeting at French Lick demonstrates that. The customer-oriented company possesses mechanisms to get these differences out on the table for candid discussion and to make

trade-offs that reconcile the various points of view. Each function and division must have the ear of the others and must be encouraged to lay out its ideas and requirements honestly and vigorously.

To make wise decisions, functions and units must recognize their differences. A big part of being market driven is the way different jurisdictions deal with one another. The marketing department may ask the R&D department to develop a product with a certain specification by a certain date. If R&D thinks the request is unreasonable but doesn't say so, it may develop a phony plan that the company will never achieve. Or R&D may make changes in the specifications and the delivery date without talking to marketing. The result: a missed deadline and an overrun budget. If, on the other hand, the two functions get together, they are in a position to make intelligent technological and marketing trade-offs. They can change a specification or extend a delivery date with the benefit of both points of view.

Barriers had arisen among Wolverine's functional departments...

An alternative to integrated decision making, of course, is to kick the decision upstairs to the CEO or at least the division general manager. But though the higher executives have unbiased views, they lack the close knowledge of the specialists. An open decision-making process gets the best of both worlds, exploiting the evenhandedness of the general manager and the functional skills of the specialists.

Divisions and functions make well-coordinated decisions and execute them with a sense of commitment. An open dialogue on strategic and tactical trade-offs is the best way to engender commitment to meet goals. When the implementers also do the planning, the commitment will be strong and clear.

The depth of the biases revealed at the French Lick gathering demonstrates the difficulty of implementing cross-functional programs. But there's nothing wrong with that. In fact, the strength of those biases had a lot to do with Wolverine's past success. If the R&D vice president thought like the financial vice president, she wouldn't be effective in her job. On the other hand, if each function is marching to its own drum, implementation will be weak regardless of the competence and devotion of each function.

Serial communication, when one function passes an idea or request to another routinely without interaction—like tossing a brick with a message tied to it over the wall—can't build the commitment needed in the customer-driven company. Successful new products don't, for example, emerge out of a process in which marketing sends a set of specifications to R&D, which sends finished blueprints and designs to manufacturing. But joint opportunity analysis, in which functional and divisional people share ideas and discuss alternative solutions and approaches, leverages the different strengths of each party. Powerful internal connections make communication clear, coordination strong, and commitment high.

Poor coordination leads to misapplication of resources and failure to make the most of market opportunities. At one point in the meeting at French Lick, the vice president for human resources spoke up in this fashion: "Remember how impressed everyone was in '86 with the new pulp-bleaching control we developed? Not just us, but the whole industry—especially with our fast response rate. Even though the technology was the best, the product flopped. Why? Because the industry changed its process so that the response rate was less important than the ability to handle tough operating conditions and higher temperatures and pressures. Plus we couldn't manufacture to the tight tolerances the industry needed. We wasted a lot of talent on the wrong problem."

Probably the salespeople, and perhaps the technical service people, knew about the evolving customer needs. By working together, manufacturing and R&D could have designed a manufacturable product. But the company lacked the coordination that a focused market orientation stimulates.

Action at Wolverine

Just about every company thinks of itself as market oriented. It's confident it has the strength to compete with the wolf pack, but in reality it's often weak and tends to follow the shepherd. In marketing efforts, businesses are particularly vulnerable to this delusion. Let's return to French Lick to hear of such a sheep in wolf's clothing.

"Look at Mutton Machinery," the vice president of manufacturing was saying. "They've done worse than we have. And their ads and brochures brag about them being customer oriented! At the trade show last year, they had a huge booth with the theme 'The

Customer is King.' They had a sales contest that sent a salesperson and customer to tour the major castles of Europe."

The sales vice president piped up. "They should send their salespeople for technical training, not to look at castles. We interviewed two of their better people, and they didn't measure up technically. The glitzy trade show stuff and the sexy contest don't make them customer oriented."

No, slogans and glossy programs don't give a company a market orientation. It takes a philosophy and a culture that go deep in the organization. Let's take a look at Wolverine's approach.

It's unlikely that any company ever became market oriented with a bottom-up approach; to make it happen, you need the commitment and power of those at the top. In gathering everybody who mattered at French Lick, Wolverine was taking the right step at the start. And from what we have heard, clearly they were not sugarcoating their concerns.

...Each was on its own little island.

By the end of the first day, the executives had decided that they knew too little about their own industry, particularly customers and competitors. After a mostly social dinner meeting and a good night's sleep, they began at breakfast on day two to develop a plan to learn more. They listed 20 major customers they wanted to understand better. They designated each of the ten executives at the meeting (CEO, six functional heads, and three division general managers) to visit the customers in pairs in the next two months; the sales force would coordinate the visits. All ten agreed to attend the next big trade show.

They assigned the marketing vice president to prepare dossiers on the 20 customers plus another 10, as well as prospects selected by the group. Besides data on the customer or prospect, each dossier was to include an examination of Wolverine's relationship with it.

Finally, the group singled out seven competitors for close scrutiny. The marketing vice president agreed to gather market data on them. The R&D vice president committed herself to drawing up technical reviews of them, and the financial vice president was to prepare analyses of financial performance. The seven remaining executives each agreed to analyze the relative strengths and weaknesses of one competitor.

Spurred by the president, the group concluded on day two that barriers had arisen among Wolverine's functional departments. Each was on its own little island. The human resources vice president took on the responsibility of scrutinizing cross-functional communication and identifying ways to improve it.

Back at headquarters in Indianapolis, the top brass did another smart thing: it involved all functional leadership so that line as well as staff chieftains would contribute to the effort. Top management quickly pinpointed the management information system as a major point of leverage for shaping a more integrated company view. Therefore, the president invited the MIS director to join the team.

Top management also decided that the bonus plan encouraged each function to pursue its own objectives instead of corporate-wide goals. So the controller teamed up with the human resources vice president to devise a better plan, which won the approval of top management.

As a new interest in communication and cooperation developed, the president perceived the need to make changes in structure and process. Chief among these were the establishment of a process engineering department to help production and R&D move new products from design into manufacturing and the redesign of managerial reports to emphasize the total company perspective.

The management group, more sensitive now to the ways people deal with each other, awoke to the power of informal social systems. To make the salespeople more accessible to headquarters staff, the sales office at a nearby location moved to headquarters (over the objections of the vice president of sales). The effort to promote interfunctional teamwork even extended to the restructuring of the bowling league. Wolverine had divided its teams by function or division. Now, however, each team had members from various functions. Some old-timers snorted that that was taking the new market orientation too far. But in a conversation during a bowling league party, the head of technical field service and a customer-service manager came up with an idea for a program to improve customer responsiveness. Then even the skeptics began to understand.

The analyses of customers and competitors identified an important market opportunity for Wolverine. The management group diverted resources to it, and under the direction of the Pneumatic Controls Division general manager, a multifunctional task force launched an effort to exploit it. Top management viewed this undertaking as a laboratory for the

development of new approaches and as a showcase to demonstrate the company's new philosophy and culture. Headquarters maintained an intense interest in the project.

As the project gained momentum, support for the underlying philosophy grew. Gradually, the tone of interfunctional relationships changed. People evinced more trust in each other and were much more willing to admit responsibility for mistakes and to expose shortcomings.

Unfortunately, some people found it difficult to change. The sales vice president resisted the idea that a big part of his job was bringing customers and data about them into the company as well as encouraging all functions to deal with customers. He became irate when the vice president of manufacturing worked directly with several major customers, and he told the president that he wouldn't stand for other people dealing with *his* customers. His colleagues couldn't alter his attitude, so the president replaced him.

Wolverine's sales and earnings slowly began to improve. The market price of its stock edged upward. Internally, decision making became more integrative. Some early victories helped build momentum. Implementation improved through cooperation very low in the ranks, where most of the real work was done.

Imitate Larry Bird

A year after Wolverine's first meeting in the French Lick hotel, the management group gathered there again. A new sales vice president was present, and the newly promoted MIS vice president/controller was also there.

This time the executives focused on two concerns. The first was how to handle the inordinate demands on the company resulting from the new push to satisfy important customers. The second was how to maintain Wolverine's momentum toward achieving a market orientation.

Attacking the first item, the group agreed to set major customer priorities. At hand was the information gathered during the year via industry analysis and executives' visits to top accounts. Available to the executives also were several frameworks for analysis.[1] Some accounts fit together in unexpected ways. In some situations, a series of accounts used similar products similarly. In others, the accounts competed for Wolverine's resources.

> For a successful marketer, complacency is the implacable enemy.

It took several meetings to set priorities on customers. The hardest part was resolving a dispute over whether to raise prices drastically on the custom products made for the third largest account. Wolverine was losing money on these. "Maybe not all business is good business," the R&D vice president suggested. That notion was pretty hard for the team to accept. But the CEO pushed hard for a decision. Ultimately, the group agreed to drop the account if it did not accede to price increases within the next six to eight months.

1. They used the account profitability matrix described by Benson P. Shapiro, V. Kasturi Rangan, Rowland T. Moriarty, and Elliot B. Ross in "Manage Customers for Profits (Not Just Sales)," HBR September-October 1987, p. 101.

Self-Examination Checklist

1. **Are we easy to do business with?**
   Easy to contact?
   Fast to provide information?
   Easy to order from?
   Make reasonable promises?

2. **Do we keep our promises?**
   On product performance?
   Delivery?
   Installation?
   Training?
   Service?

3. **Do we meet the standards we set?**
   Specifics?
   General tone?
   Do we even know the standards?

4. **Are we responsive?**
   Do we listen?
   Do we follow up?
   Do we ask "why not," not "why"?
   Do we treat customers as individual companies and individual people?

5. **Do we work together?**
   Share blame?
   Share information?
   Make joint decisions?
   Provide satisfaction?

On the second matter, the management group decided it needed a way to measure the company's progress. The approach, everybody understood, had to be grounded in unrelieved emphasis on information gathering, on interfunctional decision making, and on a vigorous sense of commitment throughout the organization. They recognized how easy it is to get complacent and lose detachment when examining one's own performance. Nevertheless, the executives drew up a checklist of customer-focused questions for the organization to ask itself. It appears in the insert.

Two years after the company changed its direction, a major customer asked the president about his impressions of Wolverine's efforts to become market oriented. Here is his response:

"It's proved to be harder than I had imagined. I had to really drive people to think about customers and the corporation as a whole, not just what's good for their own departments. It's also proved to be more worthwhile. We have a different tone in our outlook and a different way of dealing with each other.

"We use all kinds of customer data and bring it into all functions. We do much more interfunctional decision making. The hardest part of all was account selection, and that really paid off for us. It also had the most impact. Our implementation has improved through what we call the three Cs, communication, coordination, and commitment. We're getting smooth, but we sure aren't flawless yet.

"Last night I watched the Pacers play the Boston Celtics on TV. The Celtics won. Sure they've got more talent, but the real edge the Celtics have is their teamwork. At one point in the game, the Indiana team got impatient with each other. They seemed to forget that the Celtics were the competition.

"That's the way we used to be too—each department competing with each other. A few years ago we had a meeting down at French Lick where everything came to a head, and I was feeling pretty desperate. There's a real irony here because French Lick is the hometown of Larry Bird.

"When I think about the Celtics and Bird, what working together means becomes clear. If each Wolverine manager only helps his or her department do its job well, we're going to lose. Back when the company was small, products were simple, competition was unsophisticated, and customers were less demanding, we could afford to work separately. But now, our individual best isn't good enough; we've got to work as a unit. Bird is the epitome. He subverts his own interest and ego for the sake of the team. That's what I want to see at Wolverine."

Reprint 88610

People, production, and patriotism made Samsung a world-class competitor.

Fast Heat: How Korea Won the Microwave War

by Ira C. Magaziner and Mark Patinkin

The microwave oven, invented in the United States 40 years ago, recently became the best-selling major appliance in the world – a multibillion-dollar industry that has spawned tens of thousands of jobs. Yet if you were to buy a microwave oven in the United States today, the odds are one in three that it was built 10,000 miles away, in Korea. The odds are one in five that it was designed by a 43-year-old engineer named Yun Soo Chu and made by Samsung, the world's leading microwave-oven producer. But it wasn't until 1979, when the United States was already making millions of microwave ovens, that Samsung set up its first crude assembly line. That year the company made only a few dozen a week. Today it makes over 80,000 a week. How Samsung succeeded illustrates the growing sophistication of our competitors in developing nations.

On my first visit to Samsung's Suwŏn complex, the headquarters of the company's electronics and appliance division was even more Third World than I expected. The factory floors were bare concrete. People hand-wheeled parts to and from the production line. The research lab reminded me of a

Ira C. Magaziner is the founder and president of Telesis, an international consulting firm. His books include Minding America's Business *(Random House, 1983) and* Japanese Industrial Policy *(University of California-Berkeley Press, 1981). Mark Patinkin is a nationally syndicated columnist for the* Providence Journal-Bulletin. *"Fast Heat" is adapted from their forthcoming book,* The Silent War: Inside the Global Business Battles Shaping America's Future, *to be published in March by Random House.*

dilapidated high-school science classroom. But the work going on at Suwŏn–what they were doing with televisions, for example–was intriguing. At the time, there wasn't a single TV station in Korea that could broadcast in color. But Samsung's engineers had gathered color televisions from every leading company in the world–RCA, GE,

Before Korea had a TV station that could broadcast in color, Samsung had designed its first color set.

Hitachi–and were using them to design a model of their own.

I spoke with the chief engineer, a young graduate of a U.S. university. I asked him about Samsung's color television strategy, telling him I presumed the company planned to buy parts overseas and do only assembly in Korea. Not at all, he replied. The company was going to make everything itself, even the color picture tube. They'd already picked the best foreign models and signed agreements for technical assistance. Soon, he said, Samsung would be exporting around the globe. I wasn't convinced. Maybe in 10 or 15 years, I thought, but not much sooner. To be a world player, you need world-class engineers, and that was something Korea was short on.

What I didn't realize was that Samsung's chairman, Lee Byung Chull, was investing not just in better technology but in better minds as well. Slowly he was building what was soon to become the biggest company engineering pool in any developing country. Had I looked in all the corners of the Samsung lab that day in 1977, I might have seen Yun Soo Chu, one of those engineers, just beginning work on a microwave oven prototype.

When Chu joined Samsung in 1973, the company had just taken on a manufacturing challenge decades old for America but new to Korea: making home appliances. Chu started by designing washing machines, then moved to electric skillets. In 1976, he received an unexpected assignment. That year, on a visit to the United States, a Samsung vice president named J.U. Chung had become intrigued by a new kind of oven, heated not by electricity or gas but by microwaves. Chung knew there was no way he could market such an oven at home–few Koreans could afford it. But that wasn't a concern. In Korea, when a company considers a new product, the first question is, can we export it?

Knowing that Americans like convenience, Chung thought the microwave oven was perfect for that

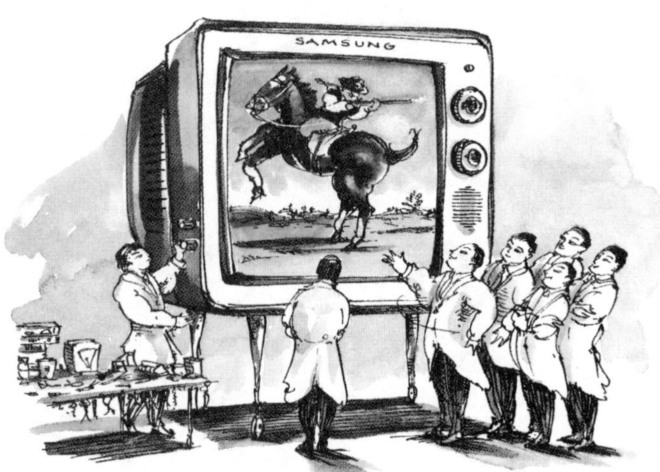

market, the world's largest. When he got back to Korea, he asked Chu to form a team to design a Samsung microwave. Chu knew his company was starting well behind Japanese and U.S. producers, but he felt Samsung had two advantages: low-wage workers and a willingness to wait for a payback. The company's first priority, he knew, wasn't high profits but high production. And Samsung was especially interested in modern products. For Korean industry, that was almost unprecedented.

Traditionally, low-wage countries have been content to let their factories lag a decade behind countries like the United States. They make bicycles in the age of the automobile, black-and-white televisions in the age of color. Samsung was one of the first Third World companies to take a new approach, to compete directly in modern products.

Chu began by ordering the Jet 230, a new microwave model made by General Electric, America's leading appliance company. Before long, he was looking at his first microwave oven. Chu took it apart but still had no idea how it worked. The plastic cavity seemed simple enough, as did the door assembly and some of the wiring. But there were several complex parts, especially the device that generated the microwaves–the magnetron tube. To build it, he knew, required expertise Samsung lacked. He began to tinker anyway.

Chu's team was given 15 square feet in the corner of an old lab. The lab served the company's entire electronics division, which at the time consisted of three Quonset-hut factories. It seemed absurd that such a place could consider challenging giant U.S. and Japanese corporations, and Chu knew it. But he also knew Samsung's senior managers cared little at the moment about marketing. They'd told him they wanted only one thing–production. They'd worry about selling the oven later.

Soon, Chu had gathered a number of the world's top models and was choosing the best parts of each for his prototype. One thing that drove him was his failure in his last assignment, designing an electric skillet. He just hadn't been able to make it work right. This time, he told himself, he had to succeed.

Samsung didn't have all the manufacturing equipment he needed, so Chu began visiting press vendors, plastic vendors, toolmakers. When he couldn't find anyone in Korea to do the kind of welding he wanted, he decided to seal the oven prototype with caulking instead. Slowly, it came together–brackets, outer panel, door. But when he got to the magnetron tube, he was lost. There was no way Samsung could make or subcontract it locally. At the time, only three manufacturers in the world had that ability, two in Japan, one in Rhode Island. Chu decided to buy the magnetron tube outright–to source it–from Japan.

As the months passed, he drove himself even harder, often working in the lab all night. It took him a year of 80-hour weeks to finish the prototype, but finally he was ready to test it. He pushed the "on" button. In front of his eyes, the plastic in the cavity melted. So much for a year's work.

Chu spent more 80-hour weeks rebuilding his prototype, readjusting it, redesigning it. Again he turned it on. This time the stir shaft melted. Even his wife began to question his obsessiveness. "You must be mad," she'd tell him. At times, he agreed with her. The Japanese and Americans, he knew, were now selling over 4 million microwave ovens a year, and he couldn't even get a single prototype to work.

After a year of 80-hour work weeks, Chu pushed the "on" button. The microwave melted.

Microwave-oven technology was pioneered in the late 1940s by a U.S. defense contractor, Raytheon. While experimenting with radar microwaves, a Raytheon researcher noticed that a candy bar in his pocket melted when exposed to the waves. That led to the idea of an oven. Raytheon and another defense-oriented company, Litton, tried to sell the product in the United States without much success. Few U.S. appliance makers saw promise in it. Even though it was the first new major appliance in a generation, it seemed unnecessary. Most U.S. households already had an oven. Who would want two?

The product seemed ideal for Japan, however, a nation of small houses and small kitchens. Moreover, Japanese cooking relied heavily on reheating, a strong point of microwaves. But even though a few U.S. companies saw the microwave's sales potential in Japan, they weren't interested. Exporting to distant markets wasn't worth the trouble.

That's how the Japanese became the first big manufacturers of microwave ovens. They seized the technology, began perfecting it, and soon went beyond their backyard. They saw export as an opportunity, not a burden. They pushed the product overseas, harvesting a windfall when the world market took off, going from 600,000 ovens in 1970 to 2.2 million in 1975. Finally, in the late 1970s, U.S. appliance makers like GE began investing seriously in microwave ovens. But they paid a price for being late. By 1979, when the U.S. market finally eclipsed Japan's, Japanese companies already controlled over 25% of it.

June 1978–and in the corner of his Suwŏn lab, Chu finally finished another prototype. Ready for the worst, he turned it on for a test. This time, nothing melted. His bosses were encouraged. They knew Chu's oven was still too crude to compete in the world market, but they told him to make more anyway. Chu himself had few global hopes. At best, he thought, Samsung would find a small, low-priced niche in the United States. But that didn't discourage him. The company's preeminent goal was production.

Samsung management sent out a few salespeople with the prototypes. They didn't have much success, but headquarters decided to put together a makeshift production line anyway. Management wanted to be ready in case an order came. It was one of the company's rules: never, ever keep a customer waiting.

The production team began making one oven a day, then two. Soon, it was up to five. By mid-1979, when over 5 million ovens were sold around the world, Samsung had finished making only 1,460 of them. That's when the company decided to try its first real sales push. It chose to focus on the local market. Unfortunately, its low scale meant high prices—an exorbitant $600 per oven—half the yearly income of an average Korean family. Almost no one bought. Still, management was upbeat. The machines worked. Having no sales was no reason to stop development.

With the domestic push a washout, Samsung's salespeople began to look abroad. They sent out brochures and hired distributors in dozens of countries. They offered to cut the price and were ready to fill the smallest order. The first came from Panama—for 240 ovens. By the time it had shipped them, Samsung had lost money. But there was celebration in Suwŏn. They'd broken through. And besides, this would be a good way to learn what customers wanted. They could refine the product in a few small markets before trying big ones.

The Panama sales gave Samsung the confidence to apply for the Underwriters' Laboratory approval needed for exports to the United States. Late in 1979 they got it. For Samsung, America wasn't a totally foreign market. Many of the company's managers had gone to school there; they knew the country, knew English. And Samsung was ready to do something few U.S. manufacturers were doing: tailor its product to foreign tastes. If that meant retooling production back in Suwŏn, it would spend the money. Instead of planning on a single line of ovens for the world, its strategy was to make unique models for unique markets.

> In 1980, Samsung got its first big break—an order from J.C. Penney for a few thousand $299 ovens.

Microwave ovens were then selling for $350 to $400 each in the United States. One of the country's biggest retailers, J.C. Penney, had been searching for a cheaper model, but hadn't had any luck in either Japan or the United States. Then Penney heard about Samsung and saw an opportunity—a low-wage country capable of building a high-tech product. In 1980, the retailer asked Samsung if it could build a microwave oven to sell in the United States for $299.

By then, world sales were up to 4.7 million units a year. Samsung was being asked for a few thousand ovens only. On top of that, Penney's order would mean designing a whole new oven and taking heavy losses, all in the name of gaining a fraction of 1% of the U.S. market. But in Suwŏn, Samsung's managers were ecstatic. They promised Penney anything it wanted. To deliver, they promised Chu any investment he needed. They still put no pressure on him for profits. All they wanted was production and a doorway into a major foreign market.

Penney's technical people would help Chu with product quality, but Chu knew the greatest burden would be on Samsung. The challenge now was to turn a still-primitive assembly room into an efficient factory almost overnight. And he and his team would have to get it right the first time. This wasn't another Panama. The machines would be going to Americans, the most sophisticated consumers in the world.

Chu's boss was a quiet mechanical engineer named Kyung Pal Park. Ask him why he chose manufacturing, and he'll tell you about U.S. soldiers during the Korean War. Everything about them suggested wealth: their clothes, their equipment, their vehicles. How, Park wondered, had the United States achieved that? In time, he saw that production was the answer. America was wealthy because it made things. Park wanted that for Korea too—a nation not of rice paddies, but factories. In 1969 he joined Samsung. In 1980, at the age of 39, he was named head of home appliances. Delivering the Penney order was his responsibility.

Soon, Park came up with his plan for organizing a team. In the United States, product designers would normally head such a team; factory engineers would come second. At Samsung, production is king. So Park merged his product and factory people, stressing that design should be done with manufacturing in mind. He gave the team one unbreakable rule: no matter what, it would deliver on every deadline, not a day later. The responsibility for following through would fall to Park's chief lieutenant, I.J. Jang, a production engineer just transferred from Samsung's motor division.

Before his transfer, Jang had managed the production of millions of motors a year on four separate lines. Now he found himself in a division making five or six ovens a day. He didn't see it as a demotion. "There is one thing more valued at Samsung than high production," he explains, "the potential of high production." The best engineers aren't placed with boom products but with products yet to take off.

Jang immersed himself in learning the product, spending hours talking with designers like Chu, then journeying overseas to Matsushita, Sanyo, and GE.

Once he'd learned world standards, he began to make sure Samsung was living up to them. He studied the prototype test results, pausing on the high microwave leakage numbers. He asked if they could be fixed and was told the seal design made it hard to get a better weld. So Jang, one of Samsung's most senior production managers, went to the welding vendor to help him upgrade his process. Of the 100 outside vendors working on the project, Jang ended up visiting 30 of them himself.

Then he turned his attention to building the assembly line. He started with an empty factory room and a delivery date only months away. His senior people often began at dawn, worked until 10:30 P.M., then took a brief nap, and went back to work for the rest of the night. Even Jang's boss, Park–one of the highest executives at Suwŏn–kept the same hours. There was only one sign of privilege–a few cots scattered around the factory. The executives got those–the others grabbed their naps in chairs.

The line took shape and production began; inevitably, there were bugs. They couldn't afford to lose production, however, so they manufactured by day, then ran the line all night to fine-tune it. Production improved to 10 ovens a day, then 15. Soon they were making 1,500 a month, enough to meet Penney's order of several thousand.

Penney liked the ovens and soon asked for more. Could Samsung deliver 5,000 in another month? The company made that deadline too, but there wasn't time for celebration. Now Penney wanted another 7,000. There was only work. "Like a cow," Jang would say later.

The production team thought it wise to install more assembly lines and asked management for the money. "It was no problem," Jang said. By the end of 1981, Samsung had increased microwave production a hundredfold over the previous year, from just over 1,000 to over 100,000. Still, that was only a fraction of the world market. And almost none of the giants in the United States or Japan noticed. They still couldn't see Korea as a serious competitor in such sophisticated technology. But they were overlooking a crucial factor: the role the Korean government was playing in the country's development.

Around this time, in 1981, I returned to Korea and spent several days meeting with both corporate managers and government economic planners. Korea's progress, I found, was driven by government, the key player being the Economic Development Board. Its job was to think about where Korea's economy should be headed and give incentives to help companies get there. The board built industrial parks, subsidized utilities, provided tax rebates for export, and made low-cost loans for investment in selected new products. The incentives were particularly helpful to big companies like Samsung, whose managers met frequently with government officials, plotting strategy, trading ideas, and discussing projects.

> Jang began work with an empty factory room and a delivery date only months away.

Both business and government understood the country couldn't depend on low-wage industries for long, not with even cheaper labor in countries next door. Just as the United States had lost thousands of jobs in the apparel industry to Korea, soon, the Koreans knew, they would lose such jobs to Malaysia and China. To prepare, the government consulted with companies and developed incentives for investing in new industries. By 1980, the country had gone beyond textiles into steel and ships. Now it was making automobiles. And it had begun moving toward world-class electronics. Korea was developing faster than I had expected.

Samsung's microwave production in 1982 topped 200,000, double what it had produced the previous year. But Park and his team didn't think it was enough. They knew that, in microwaves, Samsung was still a global afterthought. U.S. manufacturers were making over 2 million ovens a year and the Japanese were making even more–2.3 million at home and another 820,000 in their U.S. plants. Matsushita had 17% of the world market. Sanyo had 15%.

Moreover, the big producers were bringing their prices down, narrowing Samsung's key advantage. If Samsung were to keep growing, it had to lower its own prices even more. Samsung's managers pored over their cost structure. The highest item was the magnetron tube, which they were still buying from the Japanese. Could they make it themselves? It would mean millions of dollars of investment for a new, highly complex factory. They approached Japan's magnetron producers for technical assistance but were turned down. That left only one other company to approach–Amperex, the Rhode Island company that was America's sole manufacturer. But that plant, Samsung found, was going out of business. It had been unable to compete with Japan.

That same year in Louisville, Kentucky, Bruce Enders–the head marketing manager for GE Appliances–was beginning to see warning signs in his microwave-oven division. Because GE had come into microwave ovens so late, it had not yet made money on them. Now the losses began to get worse; the Japanese were chipping away at GE's U.S. share, pushing it down from over 16% in 1980 to 14% in 1982. No one at GE was thinking about conceding ground, though. Japan's wage rates were no lower than GE's, and GE was just completing a multimillion dollar modernization at its microwave-oven factory in Columbia, Maryland. Just as important, Enders knew that his company understood the U.S. consumer better than any other appliance maker. GE had just scored a tremendous success with the Spacemaker, for example, the industry's first under-the-shelf model. If the Maryland modernization could make GE cost-competitive, he knew that they could make the business profitable.

But in late 1982, the Japanese began to export a new midsize line of ovens at an alarmingly low price—even below GE's cost at its modernized plant. Enders' manufacturing people insisted that the Japanese must be dumping. Enders wanted to know for sure. He asked me to do a study.

The study was supposed to focus on Japan, so I spent three weeks there. But I knew Samsung had begun to make microwaves, so before coming home, I flew to Korea for a two-day visit. It was my first glimpse of Samsung since 1977. It was soon clear that there had been big changes.

In Suwŏn, the three Quonset huts had been replaced by a dozen new buildings. I was taken on a tour, which began in the basement of the microwave building where the machining was done. That wasn't so impressive. Most of the equipment was old. Then my guides took me to the second floor where the microwaves were being assembled. It was a little better but still backward. Samsung's wage rates, I thought, could perhaps outcompete GE, but its technology couldn't.

Then my guides invited me to see the TV plant. The old one, I remembered, had long lines of women plugging in parts by hand. But this was different—

> A truck pulled up at the Suwŏn complex. Workers began unloading America's last magnetron plant.

as automated as any TV plant I'd seen in the United States. Next, they invited me to see the new television-tube factory. It was much larger and more modern than I'd expected. The biggest surprise was a highly complex TV-glass plant being put up in partnership with America's Corning Glass Works. Clearly Samsung had been serious about producing every color television part by itself.

Finally I went to the R&D lab. It had gone from an old high-school science room to a large modern operation. Instead of a handful of engineers, there were 500. Everything Samsung had said in 1977 that it would do, it had done. I understood they weren't showing me all this out of pride alone. Management knew I was doing a study for GE and hoped I'd bring back a message: Samsung could do in microwaves what it had done in TVs.

As I was leaving Suwŏn, I saw a truck pull up and men begin to unload equipment. I looked at it, then looked closer. Months before, I'd visited Amperex, America's last magnetron plant. Now, here in Korea, Amperex's equipment was coming off the truck. Park and the others had decided to build their own magnetrons after all. In an almost disturbingly symbolic strategy, they were going to transplant a U.S. factory that could no longer compete, and sell its goods—now made in Korea—back to U.S. consumers.

Early in 1983, I gave my initial impressions to GE. The Japanese weren't dumping. Their plants and product designs were so efficient they could indeed land microwave ovens in the United States cheaper than those coming off GE's new assembly line. Moreover, GE's share was falling even as the world market grew. Global sales had gone from 5 million in 1980 to 7 million in 1983, but GE's U.S. market share had shrunk to 12%. Other U.S. producers had declined even more. The shift had almost all gone to the Japanese.

GE had two options. One was to invest, as the Japanese had, in hundreds of engineers. But GE was already pouring enormous investment into refrigerators and dishwashers, products in which it was a leader. Microwaves were a lower priority. That brought us to the second option—get product from overseas through sourcing or a joint venture.

While I was finishing my final report, GE decided to explore a joint-venture factory with the Japanese to be built in the United States. Its hope was to work with Matsushita, the biggest producer. Enders traveled to Japan to negotiate and seemed to be getting close. He even got Samsung's management to agree that a co-venture would be highly profitable for both. But in the end, Matsushita declined because it would mean losing some of the U.S. market to GE. Foreign market share is a key priority, one of the company's key executives explained. "Enders-san," he said, "you have to understand. In Japan, it's our destiny to export. If we don't export, we don't survive."

That left GE with one other option: sourcing—buy Japanese products and put the GE label on them. No one in Louisville was ready to shut down the new Maryland plant, but maybe it made sense to source a few lines.

In April 1983, I finished my full report. In it, I raised a Korean option. If GE sourced only with Matsushita, it would be at the mercy of a direct competitor. Korean costs, however, were potentially low enough to undercut the Japanese. And because the Koreans were anxious for volume, it would be easier to negotiate a good deal with them.

Louisville was skeptical. The Koreans? Perhaps they were making a few ovens for Penney, but they were a Third World country. A high-quality company like GE–selling a million ovens–couldn't risk depending on Korea.

But then we looked at the cost differences. In 1983, it cost GE $218 to make a typical microwave oven. It cost Korea's Samsung only $155. Then we broke the costs down: assembly labor cost GE $8 per oven; Samsung, only 63 cents. The differences in overhead labor–supervision, maintenance, setup–were even more astounding: for GE it was $30 per oven; for Samsung, 73 cents. GE was spending $4 on materials handling for each oven; Samsung, 12 cents. The biggest area of difference was in GE's line and central management–that came to $10 per oven. At Samsung, it was 2 cents. What the companies got for their money was the most disturbing figure of all. Samsung workers were paid less but delivered more. GE got four units per person each day. Samsung got nine. And once their volume increased, Korean costs could go even lower.

The GE managers continued to waver. Japanese costs, though not at Korean levels, were better than those at GE. And Japan's products were clearly high quality. Many thought it was more prudent to source there. To explore the option further, Enders decided to go to Korea himself. At the end of his first day, he asked Samsung's managers for a proposal, including a cost breakdown, a delivery schedule, and a description of how they would build the GE ovens. In the United States, it takes companies four to six weeks to develop that kind of plan. The next morning, Enders had a final breakfast meeting with Samsung executives.

"A group of engineers came in," Enders recalls, "and they gave us their proposal. Their hair was messed up–their eyes were bloodshot. Those guys had worked all night. And it met our target. I couldn't believe it."

A few weeks later, Roger Schipke, the head of GE Appliances, decided to go to Korea. He was walking down a Samsung corridor with his hosts when a crowd of white coats came bustling the other way. He had to stand against the wall to let them by. There were dozens of them, all very young. When they'd passed, he asked who they were. "Those are our new microwave-oven engineers," his host told him. There were more of them than Schipke had working in his whole microwave division, and these were just Samsung's newest hires. Louisville, he realized, was probably outengineered ten to one. He asked where the new hirees were trained. The answer came back: Purdue, the University of Southern California, the University of Washington.

> Could a high-quality company like GE risk depending on a Third World country like Korea?

"I'm a simple guy," Schipke would say later. "I just looked around. And I said, 'Wow, I'm not getting into that game.' "

Louisville decided in June 1983 to begin sourcing small and midsize microwave ovens from the Far East. GE would continue to make the full-size models in the United States. The biggest order went to Japan. But GE did give Samsung a much smaller order–only about 15,000. It wanted to see whether the Koreans could deliver high-quality goods at a price America's biggest appliance maker could no longer match.

General Electric sent technical people to Korea to outline its standards for the ovens. From GE's perspective, this was simply quality control for a second-rate supplier. But in Suwŏn, Kyung Pal Park, head of home appliances, saw things differently. If he was a good student, he would learn world-class skills. Once again, there was one unbreakable rule: every deadline had to be met. To make it, he knew he would have to depend on his foot soldiers as well as his lieutenants–the disciplined workers who give 70-hour weeks. Who exactly are they?

At the Suwŏn complex, more than half the basic assemblers are women. Most stay four or five years, arriving with high-school educations and leaving with husbands. Jo Yon Hwang and Jang Mee Hur are in their early twenties. Both applied to Samsung because of its reputation for being good to its workers. They were among the one-third of all applicants accepted. Upon arrival, they were given blue uniforms and two weeks of training. Then they were put to work on the microwave line, 11 hours a day, 27 days a month. Everyone, even the senior people, works the same schedule. The two women say it's why they feel so committed to the company–their bosses make the same sacrifices they do. In 1988, their base wage was just over $350 a month—a little over $1.20 an hour. Male assembly workers are paid the same. Medical services are free, so is lunch. Dinner and breakfast, offered in company dining areas, cost 15 cents each. The workers receive gifts several times a year: clothes, shoes, hiking bags, tape recorders. The recorders are made by Samsung.

Hwang and Hur get five days off in winter and another five in summer, which they can spend at a beach camp on the coast run by Samsung. Like most of Suwŏn's female employees, Hwang lives free in a company dormitory. There are 15 such dormitories, housing 420 women each, 6 to a room. Hur lives outside the complex, in an apartment with a girlfriend. Rent is not a problem: Samsung loaned her $2,000, which she gave to the landlord who invested it and keeps whatever interest it yields. Hur, meanwhile, pays Samsung 10% interest on the loan. When she leaves, she'll give the $2,000 back to the company. Hur and Hwang usually get up at 6 A.M. and have breakfast at 7 A.M. Hwang walks to her factory; Hur comes by company bus. At day's end, Hwang has to be back in the dorm by 9:30 P.M., even on the three Sundays a month she is off.

> If you own a GE Spacemaker, chances are Jo Yon Hwang attached the label.

The subject both women are most enthusiastic about is quality. Hwang is convinced no workers in the world pay as close attention to products as workers at Samsung. She checks her own work one last time even after an inspector has double-checked it. Her task is to attach serial numbers and name-brand labels to microwave ovens. If you own a GE Spacemaker, chances are that Hwang attached the label. She puts on 1,200 GE labels a day. Hur attaches microwave doors, also about 1,200 a day. It's the same simple function, hour after hour, but they see their jobs as a challenge to personal discipline, even integrity. Doing it perfectly each time is a way of teaching themselves excellence. "I put my spirit, my soul, in this product," explains Hwang.

Like everyone, they would love higher salaries, but they also see themselves as planting seeds for both company and country. They still remember a Korea of dirt roads, few cars, and many slums, and though they can't analyze all the reasons for the change, they know manufacturing has been a big one. As factory workers, they feel they're part of that, part of something historic.

Suwŏn's second biggest regiment is its engineers. The company has hundreds, all working the same 68 hours a week. S.D. Lee is typical—a smart, energetic young man who's committed to staying with Samsung. He knows if he works hard, his managers will promote him when he's ready. Although he's a junior engineer, Samsung has already schooled him with extra knowledge. The company has given him 20 days of full-time quality control instruction and once sent him to Japan for two weeks to learn technology from Toshiba. Before that trip, he was given three months of Japanese language training. "Three years after college," he explains, "you forget what you learned. Reeducation is needed."

What are Samsung's most lasting lessons? Two things, Lee says. First, management by target. Set a goal, then meet it no matter what—even if it means working through the night for a week. Second, always think several years ahead; ask where things will be next decade. The assignment Lee himself has illustrates that philosophy. Although Samsung's

microwave ovens have the lowest cost in the world, Lee is working on factory automation to make them lower still.

Does he know that Americans work only eight hours a day, five days a week? He smiles. He is envious of that. So why is it worth working so much harder, for less money? Because you don't measure by money alone, he says, you measure by life-style. And his is rising faster than he ever expected. His father could never afford a car. He plans to buy one soon. He sees even greater promise for his children. "If our generation doesn't work hard," he says, "the next generation will suffer."

At first, Samsung's ovens were not up to GE standards. But with the help of GE's quality engineers, things soon got better. Bruce Enders grew more and more impressed and eventually put in another order. Sales steadily improved. It was the GE label customers reached for but Korean workmanship that satisfied them. On his next trip to Suwŏn, Enders was surprised at the changes. The assembly line had gone from roller conveyors to automatic transfer mechanisms. Clearly, Samsung had the capacity to deliver more than GE had been asking for. Enders put in a bigger order. Sales kept improving. Around that time, in mid-1983, the Suwŏn workers hit a milestone. They shipped their five-hundred thousandth oven. For the first time since they'd begun four years before, Park said it was time to celebrate. They paused for a brief party. When the party was over, they went back to work.

By the end of 1983, Samsung's annual microwave production topped 750,000. By 1984 it passed one million. The factory expanded as well. In four years, it had gone from a few prototypes to ten mass-production lines. The product that had begun with melted plastic in an old lab was becoming a major performer in America's market. But for Samsung, that wasn't good enough.

The company had grown concerned over some new market projections. From 1982 to 1986, U.S. microwave sales were expected to keep growing at a healthy rate, but for the four years after that, things would slow. It was time to seek out other markets. The European market, expected to grow by 20% a year, offered the most promise. Among those assigned to the new market was a young executive named J.K. Kim, soon to be named head of appliance export sales.

Like many Samsung executives, Kim is fluent in foreign languages. Like many, he graduated from a U.S. university. Although his parents had little money, they found the means to send him to Berkeley. In Korea, he will tell you, education and family come before everything. Even in the poorer sections of the countryside, over 95% of the population is literate—far higher than in the United States. Kim still remembers arriving in California for school. The size of America's cities, the number of cars, the wealth of the people—all of it astounded him. He returned to Korea determined to help build his own country.

With his prestigious degree, Kim had many career options. Although it paid far less than banking or law,

> The United States taught Kim what not to do.

he chose manufacturing. "I thought it could help more the totality of Korea," he explains. "If I work for a lawyer's office, I can get my job and my secretary's job. In Samsung, I can contribute 10,000 jobs."

Kim found Samsung an ideal home. The hours were long, to be sure, but he liked the idea of working for Korea's biggest company. Part of it was the three weeks of training he got each year; another was the company's willingness to invest. Samsung seemed to blend the risk-taking mentality of a startup with the resources of a great corporation. Most of all, Kim liked the company's drive to be a world player. Now, with the European strategy, he was being asked to be part of that.

Curiously, the United States had taught Kim how to succeed abroad. It taught him what not to do. As most Koreans know, U.S. manufacturers rarely customize. "They just send us products made for Americans and say, 'Why don't you Koreans buy them?' " he says. So when Kim began to focus on Europe, he looked at how it differs from America. Europeans, he found, like colder dishes. And they prefer fish to meat and chicken. This information was fed back to Suwŏn's design division. Soon it began designing new European models. In 1983, Samsung microwaves broke into Germany and Norway. In 1984, they added France, Finland, Australia, and Belgium. And, all along, they kept pushing for a bigger piece of the United States.

In most companies, only the sales force travels. Samsung, like many foreign companies, sends engineers abroad to learn buyers' habits too. That's why Jang, head of production, was sent on regular marketing trips to the United States. Jang remembers flying in with a dozen other engineers from Suwŏn for an electronics show in Las Vegas. At one point, he took a side trip on his own, visiting stores such as Sears and talking to salespeople. He asked what models were most popular, what features attracted consumers. Spotting a woman buyer, he asked her what she looked for in a microwave oven.

Why couldn't he rely on Samsung's marketing people? An engineer has to see some things for himself, he explains. You can't describe color by phone or fax. Being told to make a model red isn't enough. He wants to know what kind of red. What size, exactly, the knobs on an oven should be. He seeks more than technical knowledge–something subtler, a feel for America's tastes, its character, its people.

General Electric began shifting more of its orders to Samsung. Soon, GE's Korean models were selling as well as those GE itself made in the United States, and at a much higher profit. Some in Louisville began to wonder whether it was time to source everything. Before going that far, Enders asked if the Columbia, Maryland factory could be further streamlined. The plant's defenders delivered an impressive proposal. They were able to get much lower costs than Enders expected. Still, even if the company went through with the plan, its costs would remain far higher than those in Korea. Management had little choice. In May 1985, GE publicly announced it would stop U.S. production of microwave ovens. From now on, GE would be doing the sales and service side of the product; Samsung, the manufacturing. Soon, the people in Suwŏn would be the biggest makers of microwave ovens in the world.

> Samsung's vision is to emerge as another GE.

In deciding to source, GE made a prudent choice. The company had discovered the potential for microwave ovens too late. By the time it invested, the Japanese were way ahead. Going to the Koreans was a good way to leap past the Japanese and fight back. It could have been different, though. If GE or other U.S. appliance companies had acted earlier, not at the height of market demand but ahead of it, they could have built enough scale to afford more product research and factory investment when competition got intense. Dollar-an-hour countries can be beaten. U.S. technology can often overwhelm low wages. But only if we're among the first in the arena. We can no longer afford to spend years analyzing new products. Too many other nations, like Korea, are willing to seize them immediately.

Often, those nations do it with our help. Samsung would have had a hard time succeeding so quickly in microwave ovens without Penney and GE. The Americans helped bring Samsung world-class design, quality, scale, and legitimacy with other world customers, and GE got a good deal in return. But how long can a U.S. company thrive by sourcing? And how long will Samsung be content to be a supplier? Its final vision, as with all great corporations, is to emerge as another General Electric, to become a household name. In some ways, that's already happening. Most luggage carts in West Germany's Frankfurt airport bear an advertisement for Samsung. Drivers on New York's Broadway, Chicago's Loop, London's M1, and even Tokyo's Keio Highway are beginning to see billboards with the same name–Samsung. Someday, Korea will no longer need to market its products through U.S. labels; it will sell them directly, as Hyundai now does its cars.

Back in Suwŏn, it's hard for Yun Soo Chu, Samsung's microwave-oven designer, to sit still for an interview. He'd rather be working. His office is no longer the corner of a primitive lab, it's a vast room filled with dozens of desks. Another dozen rooms for research and testing surround it. Behind his desk are five clocks, each marking the time at Samsung offices: LA, Chicago/Mexico, London/Madrid, Frankfurt/Paris, NYC/Miami. At the moment, Chu has a map of Sweden on his desk. Samsung began exporting there last year. He is organizing trips to Sweden for his staff–not marketing staff but engineers. He wants them to go there as often as possible, to know their customers.

Ask Yun Soo Chu what he works for, and he will tell you his highest goal is to give his children a better standard of living than his own. So each morning, he dons his company jacket, stands for the company song, and then goes back to work, designing the next line of microwave ovens for the modern world's kitchens. On most nights he is likely to be at the office very late.

Reprint 89114

Investments in technology and people can keep jobs and profits in the United States.

Cold Competition: GE Wages the Refrigerator War

by Ira C. Magaziner and Mark Patinkin

Fifty miles south of Nashville, outside the city of Columbia, where the restaurants offer Bar-B-Q and catfish, is an unlikely piece of smokestack America. There, nestled amid the pine and hardwood of rural Tennessee, is one of the world's most automated factories. Had it not been built, U.S. households might soon have had yet another product–the refrigerator–stamped "Made in Japan." Instead, here in the heartland, General Electric found a way to build products better and cheaper than those made by foreign workers paid one-tenth American wages. The going has not been easy, but GE's struggle shows the challenges the United States must and can meet if it is to regain world manufacturing leadership.

Tom Blunt still remembers the day in 1979 that he first stepped into Building 4, the plant in Louisville, Kentucky where compressors for GE's refrigerators were made. The compressor–the pump that creates cold air–is by far the most expensive part of the product. It is also the refrigerator's heart, as important as an engine in a car. You'd have never guessed that by looking at Building 4.

The plant was a loud, dirty operation built with 1950s technology: old grinders, old furnaces, too many people. Finishing a single piston took 220 steps. Even the simplest functions had to be done by hand. Workers loaded machines, unloaded machines, carried parts from one machine to the next. The scrap rate was ten times higher than it should have been; 30% of everything the plant made was thrown out. There was only one thing Blunt liked about Building 4. He liked the thought of beating it–changing it, rebuilding it. But it wasn't his place to suggest that. He had only recently joined GE's Major Appliance Business Group (MABG) as chief manufacturing engineer for ranges. He was too new to start pushing for major projects–especially projects in someone else's department. Besides, he thought management would never pour huge dollars into redoing a whole factory. He'd come to realize that MABG preferred cosmetics–bells and whistles–to engineering. In Louisville, the money was all on the marketing side.

> Ten years before, sourcing would have been a sacrilege. Now it looked like salvation.

Over the next 18 months, however, others at GE also began to worry about Building 4. A series of warning signals started to wake Louisville up. The group's profits were off. Market share was falling. Competitors were pushing hard on several fronts. Matsushita was manufacturing better, cheaper compressors in Singapore–and selling them to GE's Canadian subsidiary. Mitsubishi was experimenting with rotary compressors–a technology that GE had invented but used only in its air conditioners. Most disturbing, Whirlpool, GE's chief competitor, was moving its compressor manufacturing to Brazil. While Louisville had been focusing on bells and whistles, Whirlpool had looked overseas, glimpsed the future, and acted.

Then, the threat got even closer to home. In the fall of 1981, both Matsushita and Necchi, an Italian manufacturer, approached MABG itself, offering lower priced compressors that were indeed fine machines. Had that happened ten years earlier, there would have been one response: fight back. No one would have thought of buying from the competition. Even to whisper the word "sourcing" would have been sacrilege. MABG manufactured at home–in the United States. Its factories were unequaled. But things had changed. Now many in Louisville began to wonder if Japan could be their deliverance. People began talking about a new strategy–sourcing.

Tom Blunt didn't appreciate that kind of talk. By now he'd been named head of advanced manufacturing for refrigerators, MABG's biggest product. Few things put him in a worse mood than a decision to close a plant. "Sourcing makes sense in some circumstances," he says, "but you can't source everything. My instinct is always–always–to *make* things." Colleagues told him it was time to face the truth: there are certain areas, certain products that the United States can't compete in anymore. "Bull," he would say. "All we have to do is find a way to make it faster, cheaper, better."

John Truscott, MABG's chief engineer, agreed. "The compressor is the heart of the refrigerator," he says. "The refrigerator is the heart of this group. I didn't want to give away our heart." Actually, no one was quite ready to go that far yet. Sourcing was a compelling idea, but it was still a new one. MABG needed more information. My consulting firm was asked to supply it.

My research began in Japan. I found that Matsushita had built a plant in Singapore that planned to produce millions of low-cost reciprocating compressors for world markets. Both Toshiba and Mitsubishi were making rotary compressors that were cheaper, quieter, and more efficient than the reciprocating compressors all other refrigerator manufacturers used. Sanyo was planning to move into rotaries as well. None of this was a fluke. Obsessive exporters, the Japanese had spent the last few years traveling to the United States, probing the appliance market in search of a weakness–and found it. Now they were anxious to show off their plants. They knew that GE was considering sourcing compressors, and they all wanted to sell.

Next I went to Italy; Necchi turned out to be as great a threat as the Japanese manufacturers. Its new compressor plant was far more automated than Building 4. Finally, I visited Embraco, the new Whirlpool plant in Brazil. GE itself had a subsidiary nearby, making refrigerators for the regional market just as it did in Canada. This plant, too, wanted to buy a rival's compressors–Embraco's.

I returned to Louisville and gave my interim report. The numbers were daunting. It cost MABG over $48 to make each compressor. It cost Necchi and Mitsubishi between $32 and $38. Sanyo, Hitachi, and Toshiba were designing plants that would make com-

Ira C. Magaziner is the founder and president of Telesis, an international consulting firm that is now a division of Cresap, a Towers Perrin company. He has published a number of books and articles, including Minding America's Business: The Decline and Rise of the American Economy *(Random House, 1983) and* Japanese Industrial Policy *(University of California-Berkeley Press, 1981). Mark Patinkin is a nationally syndicated columnist for the* Providence Journal-Bulletin. *"Cold Competition" is adapted from their book,* The Silent War: Inside the Global Business Battles Shaping America's Future *(Random House, 1989).*

pressors for under $30. Embraco and Matsushita's Singapore plant were aiming at $24–almost half GE's cost. One reason was labor. GE was paying over $17 an hour, including benefits–compared with Matsushita's $1.70 in Singapore and Embraco's $1.40 in Brazil. Even more astounding was the difference in productivity. It took GE 65 minutes of labor to make a compressor. It took 48 minutes in Singapore, 35 minutes in Brazil, and under 25 minutes in Japan and Italy. A company that's paying higher wages for lower efficiency doesn't have much of a chance.

The competition's export plans were equally daunting. Embraco was already shipping 10,000 compressors a month to the United States and aiming for ten times that amount within four years. Meanwhile, Necchi had just boosted exports to a million a year, and Matsushita would soon be in the multimillions. Overnight, foreign companies had gone from a small percent of the U.S market to a full 20%. And the real invasion had yet to begin.

> Overnight, foreign companies had claimed 20% of the U.S. market. And the real invasion had yet to begin.

MABG's biggest product was in jeopardy. If management didn't act soon, it could be disastrous for the whole group. The options? One possibility was to source. Another was to build a factory overseas in a low-wage country, perhaps in a joint venture. The third possibility was to invest in a new, more efficient factory here at home. It was clear which way Louisville was leaning.

"If they're that far ahead of us," one executive said, "how can we possibly catch up?" "We ought to just go for the source," someone else added. Even John Truscott, the group's head of engineering, wavered, shocked by the difference in labor costs. Most felt it was a shame that GE was being outcompeted and a bigger shame to think about closing a factory; but a company's first mission is to survive.

Although this was only an initial overview, for many it was enough. The sourcing bandwagon began to roll. Don Awbrey, a Louisville general manager who had been put in charge of the compressor project, decided to speed up plans for a sourcing option. It was a good idea. Even if GE built a new plant, it would take years to get it up and running. Meanwhile, they'd need a bridge.

Compelling as sourcing was, however, there were still good arguments against it. Once you shut your plants, you're in danger of being hostage to your suppliers, many of whom, in this case, were also potential competitors. To source a product when you're a second-level producer to begin with–as GE did with microwave ovens–is one thing. To source the heart of your biggest product when you're the market leader is a much larger risk. The tide in Louisville was moving toward sourcing, but was it the right direction?

The ideal alternative would be to build a new U.S. plant that could make compressors cheap enough to undercut those built by the dollar-an-hour people abroad. Could a high-wage country do that? Theoretically, yes–through automation. But not with the same product design as the competition–in this case, reciprocating compressors. Brazil's Embraco had automated the recips about as far as they could go–and with low-wage workers. GE's only hope was a new design–the rotary. Because it had fewer parts, there seemed a good chance of making it quicker, boosting productivity. That was what Toshiba was planning to do with its rotary. Could MABG do even better on its own? I doubted it. It's hard to become the leader in a new technology that a competitor has already started to run with. True, GE had invented the rotary for air conditioners, but refrigerators were different; they worked a compressor much harder. But there was no need to do it alone. If GE could get Toshiba to help with either a joint venture or a technology license, it would have a better chance with less of a gamble. At least it was an alternative. But proposing it to GE headquarters in Connecticut would take more than rhetoric. It would take a detailed plan.

To explore the rotary option, I made an appointment with Tom Blunt. He wasn't pleased to see me. He'd heard about my interim presentation–and the way the sourcing bandwagon was rolling. He was sure the decision had already been made. But I explained about the rotary and asked if he could put together a plan for a factory. He nodded. That's what he did for a living–it wouldn't be a problem. I told him he needn't design it from the ground up. Instead, GE could work with Toshiba or another Japanese producer. Blunt's response matched his name. He didn't want to do it that way. If we gave his guys a chance, he said, they could outperform the Japanese. But he doubted management would let them try. A new factory wouldn't be cheap, and back then, it was almost unheard-of for a U.S. smokestack company to fight foreign competitors with a big plant investment. Still, he said he wanted to do it–even though he didn't think anything would come of it. I agreed to back him. We'd propose building a new plant without the Japanese.

John Truscott was also intrigued. Before coming to Louisville, he'd pushed technology forward at each step of his career, first on an aerospace team involved in breaking the sound barrier, then when he'd helped perfect medical CAT scanning. Now he saw that same promise in the challenge of automating smokestack America. It was time to show that the United States could still be a world leader in manufacturing.

Truscott spent some time studying the rotary with an engineer's eye. He found it could indeed be made simpler than the old-fashioned reciprocating compressors. He also found that even the Toshibas were far from perfect. There was room to take this technology beyond the competition. He assembled a team to create a new design. The challenge was to make the compressor as simple as possible, with low noise, high efficiency, and–hardest of all–durability. At the same time, it couldn't be loaded up with too much metal or it would cost too much.

After a few months of work, the engineers came up with a model they were convinced could be made more cheaply than the one the Japanese were producing in Singapore. There was only one problem: the design required the key parts to work together at a friction point of fifty-millionths of an inch–about one-hundredth the width of a human hair. No product on earth had ever been mass-produced at such an extreme tolerance. Most engineers thought technology hadn't advanced far enough even to try. Tom Blunt knew some machines operated at those tolerances–jet engines, for example. But their parts had to be tooled one at a time, over long hours. Was it possible to get such precision in a plant that made 3,000 pumps a day? Everyone they talked to doubted it could be done. The design engineers took the idea to Truscott anyway. "It looks possible," Truscott said. He told Blunt to gather the people necessary to plan a factory. Blunt knew he'd just bargained himself into an obsessive few months. Designing a new factory is an enormously complex job with 100 new headaches a day. But that's why he likes doing it, he says. "Because it's hard."

Blunt knew this would be a first–one of the world's most automated factories. To design it, he'd need 40 people. Many GE colleagues advised him to go outside. To pioneer new technology, they said, you have to find designers who are already on technology's edge. But Blunt decided to stay with his own people. He gathered many from an unlikely place–Building 4. "We didn't go out and get a bunch of Star Wars guys," he would say later. "Most of these people came from one of the most nonautomated places you've ever seen in your life."

Why did he risk that? Blunt is convinced that American industry doesn't have to recruit experts for breakthrough projects. Most seasoned engineers can do it, he says. All they need is the backing–and confidence. At MABG, he knew his people had neither. "Some of the engineers here were the brightest people I had ever seen," he recalls. "They had degrees coming out of their ears. But they'd never been allowed to do anything." For years they'd been free to innovate on gadgetry but not on basic manufacturing. That left most of the engineers in a deep malaise. What made it worse, said Blunt, was that they were treated like second-class citizens. "A lot of people thought that we couldn't walk and chew gum at the same time."

If the engineers were to come up with a world-class breakthrough, they had to believe they could do it. So Blunt started by working on morale. As the engineers began their work, he pep-talked them. The reason he'd plucked them from Building 4 was that he needed people who knew factories–and still believed in them. He was convinced that they could design a better plant than anyone in Japan or Korea. True, no one had ever built a factory that could mass-produce parts of this precision–or achieve interchangeability at fifty-millionths of an inch. But none of that mattered. Here in America, in Louisville, they'd be the first. One of Blunt's favorite approaches was to remind his team that few outsiders would understand why they built factories for a living. You get no credit for it, he'd say, even though it's about the most difficult thing there is to do. But that's why they'd picked it, because of the challenge. And then he'd deliver the clincher: "*Anyone* can source," he'd say. Gradually, his people began to feel more confident than they had in years.

> It was time to show that the sun wasn't setting on U.S. manufacturing.

The problem with most manufacturing, Blunt felt, was that the factories were designed around products. This time, he and Truscott decided to design the process and product together, adjusting each as they went. They began by moving the product engineers and the manufacturing engineers across the hall from each other. Day by day, more and more people crossed the linoleum. Gradually, they fine-tuned the pump down to the most automatable model–a stationary vane rotary. With fewer than 20 parts, it was also the simplest. The computer simulation said it would work, but only if the machining went far beyond anything the Japanese were doing with their plants. To help find a way to do that, Blunt brought in specialists from GE's jet-engine division. He brought in computer modeling engineers he'd met at Ford. He brought in the head of the Swiss Institute of Technology and consultants from the Structural Dynamics Research Corporation. But they were just for advice. He still relied mostly on his own people, the people from Building 4.

Blunt's main rule was never to allow someone to say it couldn't be done. "We figured it was the way to drive our people beyond state of the art," he says. "If you say it can't be done, you won't do it. But if you say, 'We don't care that it's never been done, we're going to be the first,' then you have a shot."

> Tom Blunt's other rule: "Every piece of equipment must be made in the United States."

Slowly, week by week, the plan came together. "There weren't great 'eureka' breakthroughs," recalls Blunt. "It doesn't work that way. The whole thing was block-and-tackle grunt work." As he expected, there were 100 headaches a day. Constant frustration. Late nights. Blunt hadn't enjoyed work this much since he'd come to Louisville.

The factory began to take shape on paper. Each time they finished roughing out a new piece of it, they taped it into a matrix unfolding along a corridor wall. The matrix soon took up a quarter block of space. To keep it going, they had to find empty offices and extend the paper in there. They spent a lot of time just sitting, drinking coffee, and looking at it. How to integrate the grinding and the gauging? The loading and the material handling? They moved around pages, deciding what to automate and what to do with workers.

And then it was done. "But that still didn't mean anything," says Blunt. "It was just a bunch of sheets of paper. Anybody can do that." Now came the second stage. Could they design machines that would make the parts the paper called for?

Blunt had one other rule. He wanted every piece of equipment in this plant to be U.S.-made. His stated reason was that it's too hard to deal with vendors 12,000 miles away. But there was another reason. He wanted to show that the United States could outdo the world using only its own resources.

One of Blunt's chief engineers was Dave Heimedinger. Under his direction, a team of engineers began to negotiate with suppliers of grinding and gauging machines. The vendors would look over the plan to mass-produce parts at jet-engine precision, and then they'd shake their heads.

"You can't do that," one vendor said.

"We think we can," said Heimedinger.

"Well," said the vendor, "it's our equipment, and we don't think it'll do that."

"We think we can find a way to make it do it."

"Well," said the vendor, "all right. We'll sell it to you. But it won't do that."

One manufacturer insisted on putting a clause into the sales agreement saying the purchasers had been warned they would not be able to get the tolerances they hoped for. He also added a no-return clause. Heimedinger bought the grinding machine anyway.

Blunt's theory of how to make machines do something they weren't built to do was simple enough. "We played around with them." Heimedinger and his team began experimenting with combinations that had never been tried. Often people would come by

GE asked workers to sacrifice 120 to 400 training hours without pay. Workers lined up.

and ask Blunt why he was bothering. MABG is in trouble, they told him. Why gamble on a new factory? Let's just source and get on with it. Blunt smiles at the memory. "I just put my head down and said, 'Well, we're working on the damn thing.' "

The first prototype machines began to deliver parts the manufacturers had said they couldn't produce. Blunt knew it wasn't final proof. Test machining is a good guide, but when you're building an unprecedented manufacturing process, the only real test is the plant itself. "A first-of-its-kind factory is its own prototype," Blunt says.

On one hand, he considered that a welcome risk, a sign of limitless potential. If they could have proved the plant would work, it would have meant they weren't breaking new ground. On the other hand, it made for sleepless nights. Until it was done, and the switch was thrown, there was no way of knowing whether they'd succeed. Blunt did, however, have two tests he used to gauge whether each of the new ideas would work. One he calls the eye test. "If you look into an engineer's eyes," he explains, "you can see whether he feels good about something, or whether he's afraid of it." The other is the "I'll try" test. "If you hear an engineer say, 'I'll try,' " he says, "you better look real close, because he's afraid it's impossible." When they'd finally finished their plan, no one was saying, "I'll try."

One thing made Blunt more nervous than the technical question—the financial question. Would this plant make cheaper compressors than anyone else in the world? It was up to me to make those first projections. Both Blunt and I knew that if they didn't add up, it wouldn't matter how brilliant the design was. Headquarters couldn't possibly go ahead with it.

There was no getting around the fact that the costs were enormous. The plant itself would cost $120 million. And it would take tens of millions more to redesign the refrigerator so the new compressor would fit it. That would make it one of the biggest single investments GE had ever made in a factory. It was a lot to gamble on the hope that GE could produce cheaper goods—with $17-an-hour labor—than rival factories paying less than $2.

> When you're building an unprecedented manufacturing process, the only real test is the factory itself.

The risk was beginning to loom as almost unacceptable. Then GE's engineers came up with a way to reduce it. GE had a Columbia, Tennessee plant that made air-conditioning compressors—rotary models. Instead of going from nothing to the prototype factory in a single leap, they could begin by adapting the machinery already there. It would let them move into rotaries faster and work out the bugs while the new factory was being completed. The numbers on that proposal looked better. Even at ten times the wages, the new factory would still be the lowest cost compressor plant on earth. At least on paper.

Blunt knew this was no guarantee that GE's Connecticut headquarters would back the proposal. Fairfield was wary of huge capital investments, especially since GE had recently lost money on a failed washing-machine plan. How could MABG convince management to invest an even bigger amount on an even riskier venture? Especially when it could source for almost nothing?

I finished my calculations and called Blunt. He asked what I thought. Until now, I'd not come down firmly on either side. Now I said I'd weighed the two options carefully and had decided to recommend that GE invest the $120 million. "You really are a crazy son of a bitch," he said.

I went to Don Awbrey, head of compressors. After a thorough discussion, he called his people together and told them he was prepared to go with the factory. But he wanted an airtight proposal. So did Jim Lehman, a finance man who had been with GE for 30 years. Like all good finance people, he treated requests as if the money would come from his own pocket. At first he was doubtful. He made us recompute the numbers with every possible risk factored in. But finally, everything seemed to add up.

That's when the completed plan went to Roger Schipke, the new head of MABG. In his prior post as head of dishwashers, Schipke had successfully managed one of the few MABG projects in a decade that went beyond bells and whistles—a factory and product redesign that cut costs, improved quality, and doubled market share. This didn't mean that Schipke favored big investments, though. Conservative by nature, he had come up through sales, knew the importance of profit, and, like most in Louisville, had gone beyond the early 1970s mind-set about manufacturing everything in America. But one of Schipke's priorities was to get rid of the Louisville malaise. When a division becomes lackluster, people tend to turn on each other—Schipke was working hard to change that, getting rival managers to work together and stressing cooperation with the unions. Slowly, MABG was becoming more cohesive.

And now Schipke had been handed this proposal. The compressor team had numbers proving the new factory would be more than ten times as productive as any other. Because the plant was so automated, labor costs weren't nearly as big a factor as Schipke had expected. He said it was time to take the proposal to Jack Welch, GE's chairman.

Schipke, Truscott, and Blunt flew to Connecticut to make the final pitch. Later, Blunt would recall the plane ride. The betting was that they wouldn't get approval. A few years before, management had been almost haughty about the Japanese; they could never touch GE's quality or technology. That had changed. The attitude now was that the Japanese had become manufacturing geniuses. Why try to beat them when you can borrow from them? Or buy?

It was Blunt's first time in the Fairfield boardroom. The room was nearly empty as he filed in with the Louisville team. Then a half dozen executives from headquarters, including Jack Welch, came in. The Louisville people made their case.

"Jack poked at us three or four times," remembers Blunt. Then the chairman asked his colleagues their opinions. A few said that they doubted it could be done. Welch looked at Blunt. "Why should I believe you people can build a factory to do this?" he asked. "You've never done anything like this before."

"No one ever asked us to," said Blunt. "And I believe we can do it."

Welch nodded and turned to Ed Hood, a vice chairman of GE and one of his most trusted technical advisers. Blunt watched as he drew out Hood's comfort level. Blunt was counting on three things. Welch, he thought, had faith in Schipke's new management team. He'd seen the numbers showing the plant could do it—if the technology worked. Finally, the chairman wanted to keep major appliances as a core business for GE and was concerned enough about Louisville's slide to know that only big investments could turn things around.

Welch turned back to Schipke, Truscott, and Blunt. "Okay," he said. "Go ahead."

Keith Moore, recently transferred from GE's lighting business in Cleveland, was in charge of the startup. That first meant retrofitting the old Columbia, Tennessee air-conditioner-compressor factory with the new processes developed by Blunt's engineers.

Moore's people soon found that it's easier to design a new process than to make it work. The suppliers' warnings proved true. At first, GE couldn't make the equipment do what Blunt's engineers wanted. It took endless hours of debugging and hundreds of changes on each machine. The required tolerances were so extreme that even the tiniest slippage could throw a whole process off. Ultimately, GE had to develop new gauging and sensing systems to get the machines to readjust instantaneously as they worked.

Machinery deliveries were 2 months late at the start and up to 14 months late at the end. Management found it hard to shepherd the process from Louisville, 200 miles away, so GE rented 22 apartments in Columbia to house engineers. The company even started a daily air shuttle between the two cities so that the lab results could be flown in from Louisville and test observations could be flown back from Columbia. By October 1985, GE had finally begun Phase One. The old factory started producing the new compressor—first 5 per day, then 10, then 100. By month five, it was up to volume production, with the quality holding just fine.

> A few years before, GE management had been almost haughty about the Japanese. That had changed.

But if GE were to succeed at Phase Two—making the new fully automated plant work—it would have to face another challenge just as important as improving its hardware: improving its people.

A high-wage country can't compete with better technology alone; its other weapon has to be a better trained work force. Could MABG create that in a place like Columbia, Tennessee, where the biggest annual celebration is Mule Day? GE knew it would have to try. Hiring high-salary technicians from around the country was too expensive. At $17 an hour—benefits included—the new plant could still beat the competition, but not at $25 or $30 an hour. So GE planned to staff the new factory with the assembly people already there at its Columbia air-conditioner complex. Most were unskilled. Few had more than a high school education.

GE decided to make yet another big investment: it would build one of the most sophisticated blue-collar training centers ever put in a U.S. factory. The cost would be more than $2 million, which would have been difficult had GE not gotten help from a welcome partner—the state of Tennessee gave the company a training grant. But MABG still couldn't afford to pay workers for the hundreds of extra hours it would take to train them. So GE asked workers to sacrifice 120 to 400 hours in classrooms, labs, and computer stations without pay and with no guarantee of promotion—that would depend on how they performed. All GE could offer were new skills.

Paul Varner, who'd been named to help run the training center, thought the whole idea was a bad mistake. He'd worked on the Columbia assembly line and knew that most of the people there were conservative souls, wary of anything new. They already had secure jobs; what would be the point of sacrificing up to a year of nights and weekends for no pay? His guess was that almost no one would volunteer. "It took me two weeks to realize I was totally wrong," Varner says today. "I ate crow."

Workers lined up for the training. Partly, it was because of the prestige GE gave it. Those who made it through got diplomas and graduation dinners. But there was another draw as well, the same one that had prompted Varner to apply for a training-center job himself. He saw that plants throughout America were closing and knew it was a matter of time before distant forces put him out of work too. Columbia's old equipment was antiquated. They couldn't hope to beat 1980s rivals with a 1960s factory.

So when GE announced its new plant, Varner wanted to be part of it. He didn't mind unpaid nights and weekends in the training center. For him, joining the future was incentive enough. And, as it turned out, it was enough for hundreds of others too. Clayton Russell was among the first.

Russell had been hired in 1974 for an unskilled assembly job. "That's all we had then," he says. His job was to put four screws into the rear case of an air conditioner—712 times a day. Gloria Anthony began

Standing before their computer terminals, the line people are symbols of the new American blue-collar worker.

the same year, also on the line. "A monotonous job," she says. "Over and over and over." Then construction began on the new plant. To be a part of it, they'd have to put in hundreds of hours of training, all on their own time. It didn't matter. They attended training sessions mornings, nights, weekends. "Whenever we had a chance," says Russell.

Dan Edlin, another line worker, put in 400 hours. Like the others, he was motivated by more than the chance of a bigger paycheck. "I wanted the opportunity to be in on something totally brand new," he says. "This is where business is going–automation." Was there resentment that automation would cost jobs? "Machines aren't taking people's jobs," he says. "Machines are making new jobs. Anyone who wants to get off his duff and train can have one."

In the center's first year, the workers of GE Columbia spent over 50,000 hours learning new skills. Paul Varner learned a lesson: give American workers an opportunity and they'll sacrifice for it. "From Welch on down, they were saying, 'You can do it,'" says Varner. "We wanted to prove their faith in us."

Soon Keith Moore was facing his next challenge: moving manufacturing from the converted air-conditioner plant into the new factory. He knew that making the just-completed factory perfect would mean thousands of adjustments. He also knew that his floor workers would be best able to spot many of those adjustments. So, right from the start, he held meetings with workers and engineers sitting shoulder to shoulder to discuss getting better quality and efficiency. Moore was just as likely to reorganize a part of the plant at an assembly worker's suggestion as at an engineer's. And he soon got an unexpected payback from spreading responsibility through the ranks. In the past, if even a small thing went wrong, line workers had to call a supervisor to solve it. Now they fixed it themselves. Part of it, says Moore, is the training: they know what to do. But they also feel like they own their part of the factory–making it run is on them, not their bosses.

Moore also got workers involved in writing training manuals for the equipment. He figured that if they had to teach the techniques, they'd learn them better themselves.

Finally, he forbade finger pointing. Moore had seen before how workers blamed each other when things went wrong. So he announced that any failure would be considered the fault of the whole team. That way, Moore hoped, if one worker was having trouble, everyone else would rally. They did.

Looking back, Moore realizes how important it was to keep up camaraderie. Frustrations could have easily gotten out of hand. Late deliveries backed up the timetable. Processes that worked in the lab often failed on the factory floor. There were late nights and occasional 7 A.M. Sunday morning meetings. But they made it; the plant opened on schedule, in March 1986. Both production and quality went smoothly, though inevitably there were bugs. Having the older plant to occasionally fall back on was a blessing. GE admits it had to pour in more investment than expected–that happens when you're pushing technology's edge. But the factory is working, exceeding quality and cost targets. Ask Moore to point to one thing that did it and he won't mention hardware; he says it's the freedom he gave his workers. "We provided people with the tools to run their own businesses on the factory floor."

The celebration was short-lived. In January 1988, 22 months after the first compressor rolled out of the new factory, a problem surfaced. Some of the larger compressors–those in GE's bigger refrigerators–began to fail. It was only a small percentage of the plant's total production, but for a consumer product like this, reliability is essential and so is customer satisfaction. Schipke immediately formed a team of design engineers to find what was going wrong. The team worked for weeks, often through the night. The fact that only a small portion of the compressors had actually failed made the job especially difficult. But based on those few, the engineers went into a massive testing program and found that others could fail too.

Before long, the team discovered what was wrong: a lubrication problem was causing one of the compressor's smaller parts to wear more quickly than expected. The problem mostly affected the compressors that had to work the hardest, but some others were failing too. Eventually Schipke would learn that GE wasn't alone. Japanese companies using rotaries were having similar problems. But that was no comfort.

> In the past, line workers called supervisors to solve even the smallest problem. Now they'd fix it themselves.

Now that the cause had been isolated, finding a fix became Louisville's obsession. Truscott and some corporate engineers led a new team that worked on the problem for months. Finally, the team came up with a better design and showed it to Schipke. He was confident it would work and told the team to go ahead. Meanwhile, he approved a plan to replace immediately any compressor that broke down—service people would be dispatched to customers' homes at GE's expense.

Still Schipke faced a serious dilemma. While projections showed that only a small percent of the compressors would fail, redesigning the lubrication device would take months. He didn't want to risk GE's reputation by shipping refrigerators that might develop problems. To be as safe as possible, he made a painful choice. In the spring of 1988, he decided that MABG would start to source reciprocating compressors from abroad while the engineering team put the fix into place. It would mean a layoff at the old plant in the Columbia complex. And it would mean a high cost burden, since GE had to pay top dollar for the sourced recips and take longer contracts than it needed. Schipke knew it would probably cost GE far less to stay with its rotaries and just replace those that eventually broke down. But every failure, he feared, would hurt the company's reputation. That was more important than today's money.

Despite problems, the payoff stands: GE's compressors are 20% cheaper than those of its dollar-an-hour competitors.

He took some comfort in knowing he could let the new factory keep making rotaries for many GE refrigerators. He was also relieved that the group would be back to full production within a few years. But it was—and is still—a painful time. The compressor problem has drawn hard criticism from both the competition and the press. Some at GE are embarrassed because they had to source. Others are irritated at how much money the problem has cost: MABG's 1988 profits were way down because of the compressor problem, which has eaten up years of savings from the rotary program. Still others are angry because it was potentially avoidable. Early lab tests showed the compressors would last 20 years, but obviously, the truest test is performance in the field. Looking back, many MABG executives see a lesson. When using a brand-new technology, it may be wiser to introduce it gradually, working out the bugs over a few years, than to convert your entire production to it immediately.

The irony is that over 90% of GE's compressor investment—and risk—was tied up in the factory, by far the most complex technological challenge. And the factory works perfectly. A relatively simple part of the product design itself caused the crisis.

As GE knows, occasional product recalls are part of the price of gambling on new technologies. It happened with fuel-injected car engines, electric shavers, and microwave ovens when they were first introduced, and now it has happened with rotary refrigerator compressors. The cost to GE is high. But the payoff still stands: here in America, GE continues to make compressors that are 20% cheaper than any made by dollar-an-hour competition.

Clayton Russell, who used to put four screws into the rear case of an air conditioner 712 times each day, now runs a $700,000 synchronous machine with 12 different stations. Gloria Anthony is now a skilled controlperson who can operate machines by computer, adjusting them whenever the terminal tells her there's a slight problem. "I never thought I'd go this high," she says. "When I began, I was just sweeping the floor." Both are proud to be part of a plant that makes twice as many compressors as the old one, with less than a quarter the people. Productivity, they say, is the only way America can compete. "We got production," says Russell. "That's a feeling of pride."

Edward Fite, director of the training center, guides visitors around the automated Columbia plant with the pride of someone showing off a new home. Overhead, compressor pieces roll down long, winding chutes into machines that stamp, cut, and refine; computers direct the pieces from one machine to the next, warning that they're on the way. The machines work and work, never stopping. Grinders, welders, testers, and robots do their drilling, milling, tapping, and gauging. There may be no other mass-production factory in the world that makes goods this precisely. Most of the line people stand before computer terminals: they're symbols of the new American blue-collar worker, equipped with tools to outcompete the world.

At 36, Fite himself has come from stuffing wires to teaching workers how to run a high-technology plant. He sees people like himself as the final mission of a factory like this—it gives common people a standard of living beyond what they ever hoped for.

Tom Blunt will always be a figure from an earlier America. "I like the gritty stuff," he says. His father was a toolmaker, and he proudly traces his ancestry back through 11 generations of factory mechanics. But he knows the United States can lead the world in factories only by building a new kind. At his desk in Louisville, he leans over a computer terminal and punches a few keys. A moving diagram appears on the screen. He explains that he is monitoring the Columbia factory. Sitting in Louisville, 200 miles away, he can peer by computer into the guts of any machine he wants—judging how it's working, how many parts have been made correctly, how many had to be set aside for rework.

"Let me show you something interesting," Blunt says. He punches a few more keys, then leans back, clasping his hands behind his head. "Since 7 A.M.," he says, "we've made 3,413 pumps." He pushes an update button. "Sorry," he says, "3,415." He pushes the update button again. "3,417. So far," he says, "we've had only five defective parts today." He pushes another button and nods; the computer is showing him a diagram of the day's tolerances for one of the machined parts. "The problem was with one of the grinders that went down," he says. "It's fixed now." Is there any other plant in the world that has this automated an information system?

"There isn't," says Blunt.

Building 4 still stands a few hundred yards from Tom Blunt's office. Only now, it's half empty. Even if Columbia hadn't been built, it would have been dead by now. The choice was simple: it would either be replaced by a foreign plant or by an American plant; a foreign payroll or an American one. Despite the setbacks, GE is proud it chose to go with this side of the ocean.

Reprint 89211

Getting the Job Done

Productivity gets a lift from information technology.

Automation to Boost Sales and Marketing

by Rowland T. Moriarty and Gordon S. Swartz

In the rush to automate, the marketing and sales function is the next frontier. As everybody knows, over the past decade information systems have been making great inroads in engineering and manufacturing. Automation has cut direct labor to a small fraction of production costs – an average of 8% to 12% in manufacturing companies. Therefore, wringing yet more cost reductions from production labor is increasingly difficult. In such technically advanced industries as computers, semiconductors, airframes, metalworking, and autos, incremental investments are now garnering diminishing returns.

> By automating the sales and marketing functions, companies have increased sales anywhere from 10% to more than 30%.

On the other hand, investments in marketing and sales automation systems hold tremendous potential for productivity improvements. Marketing and sales costs average 15% to 35% of total corporate costs (not just production costs). So a focus on marketing and sales provides a welcome lever for boosting productivity. Moreover, the importance of marketing and sales services is growing. According to the U.S. trade representative and the National Association of Accountants, manufacturers' service activities account for 75% to 85% of all value added.[1] This means that the price a product can command is less a reflection of raw materials and labor than of marketing-related services like selecting appropriate product features, determining the product mix, and ensuring product availability and delivery.

In cases we have reviewed, sales increases arising from advanced marketing and sales information technology have ranged from 10% to more than 30%, and investment returns have often exceeded 100%. These returns may sound like the proverbial free lunch, but they are real.

Because of the complexity of their marketing organizations, large companies are good prospects for what we call marketing and sales productivity (MSP) systems. Tangles of national account management, direct sales, telemarketing, direct mail, literature fulfillment, advertising, customer service, dealers, and

Rowland T. Moriarty is an associate professor of business administration at the Harvard Business School, where he currently conducts a course on creative marketing strategy. Before entering teaching, he held sales management and marketing positions at Xerox and IBM. Gordon S. Swartz is a research associate at the Harvard Business School and was formerly research director at the Competitive Assessment Center, a computer industry research company.

distributors all offer opportunities for efficiency improvements. But even small companies that adopt MSP systems can expect impressive results.

Marketing automation investments by a $7 billion electronics manufacturer and an $8 million custom printing company each produced a first-year return of more than 100%. The electronics concern installed a sales support system for more than 500 salespeople. Sales rose 33%, sales force productivity rose 31%, and sales force attrition dropped 40%. The reduced attrition alone produced savings in recruiting and training costs that paid for the company's $2.5 million investment in less than 12 months. At the custom printer, an $80,000 investment in a minicomputer and telemarketing software returned a 25% increase in sales and attained payback in less than 6 months.

Increasing marketing productivity even a small amount can have a great impact on the bottom line. MSP systems have a double punch because they can reduce fixed costs and variable costs. Lower fixed costs mean lower breakeven points. So a given percentage increase in sales produces a correspondingly larger increase in operating profits, as the chart on the next page shows. Meanwhile, lower variable costs mean that every sale contributes more to the bottom line. Indeed, because lower variable costs make the slope of the new contribution curve steeper, the absolute size of the financial advantage continues to grow as sales rise.

Despite the proven worth of this technology, few companies have automated any part of their marketing and sales functions. Even fewer appear to understand the significant strategic benefits that can accrue from marketing and sales automation; most early adopters have automated as a matter of faith rather than as part of a strategy for gaining competitive advantage. A better approach begins with an understanding of what marketing and sales automation can do, how it works, and how it can be implemented.

What the Systems Do

Distinct from general office automation systems, MSP networks are of course specific to marketing and sales. They support more intense product or service differentiation, improved customer service, reduced operating costs, and more streamlined operations. Here are some MSP systems and the tasks for which they are customarily used:

Salesperson productivity tools–Planning and reporting of sales calls, reporting of expenses, entering orders, checking inventory and order status, managing distributors, tracking leads, and managing accounts.

Direct mail and fulfillment–Merging, cleaning, and maintaining mailing lists; subsetting lists (or markets); tracking and forwarding leads; customizing letters, envelopes, and labels; generating "picking lists" for literature packages; and managing literature inventory.

Telemarketing–Merging, cleaning, and maintaining calling lists; subsetting lists (or markets); tracking and forwarding leads; ranking prospects; and prompting scripts (sales, customer service, and support).

Sales and marketing management–Providing automated sales management reports (sales forecasts, sales activity, forecasts versus actuals, and so on); designing and managing sales territories; and analyzing marketing and sales programs by such criteria as market, territory, product, customer type, price, and channel.

MSP systems can automate the work of a single salesperson, a single marketing activity like direct mail, or a company's entire marketing and sales operation. MSP systems also cut across every type of information technology from single-user PCs to networks of PCs, minicomputers, and mainframes serving thousands of users.

A simple system meets the needs of one fast-growing $25 million producer of data communications equipment that sells its products through 65 distributors. To cut down on paperwork in handling sales leads, the company adopted a PC-based MSP system. (See the flow chart showing its operation.) Compare this with the networks supporting the more than 5,000 direct salespeople of a major office automation vendor. (See the "map" showing its operation.) This vendor's system combines direct selling, distributor relationships, telemarketing, and direct mail to: generate, qualify, rank-order, distribute, and track sales leads; fill prospects' requests for product and price information; update customer and prospect files; provide sales and technical product support by telephone; and automate order entry and sales reporting.

While the scales of these two networks are obviously vastly different, both of them collect, organize, and update information about every lead generated, every sales task performed, and every customer or

1. James Brian Quinn, Jordan J. Baruch, and Penny Cushman Paquette, "Technology in Services," *Scientific American*, December 1987, p. 50.

Authors' note: We thank Professor Thomas V. Bonoma of the Harvard Business School and Charles A. Khuen, president of Adelie Corporation, for helpful comments on early drafts of this article.

prospect closed or terminated. What is less obvious, but no less important, is the basis both systems provide for improving marketing and sales executives' decision making.

Most MSP data bases contain essential information on customers, prospects, products, marketing programs, and marketing channels. Some systems supplement the essentials with industry data (growth rates, entries, exits, and regulatory trends) and data on competitors (products, pricing, sales trends, and market shares). For most businesses, the information incorporates a subtle but important shift from other data bases. Rather than focusing on products (What was the cost to produce each unit? How many units were made, sold, and shipped?), the MSP data base is customer driven.

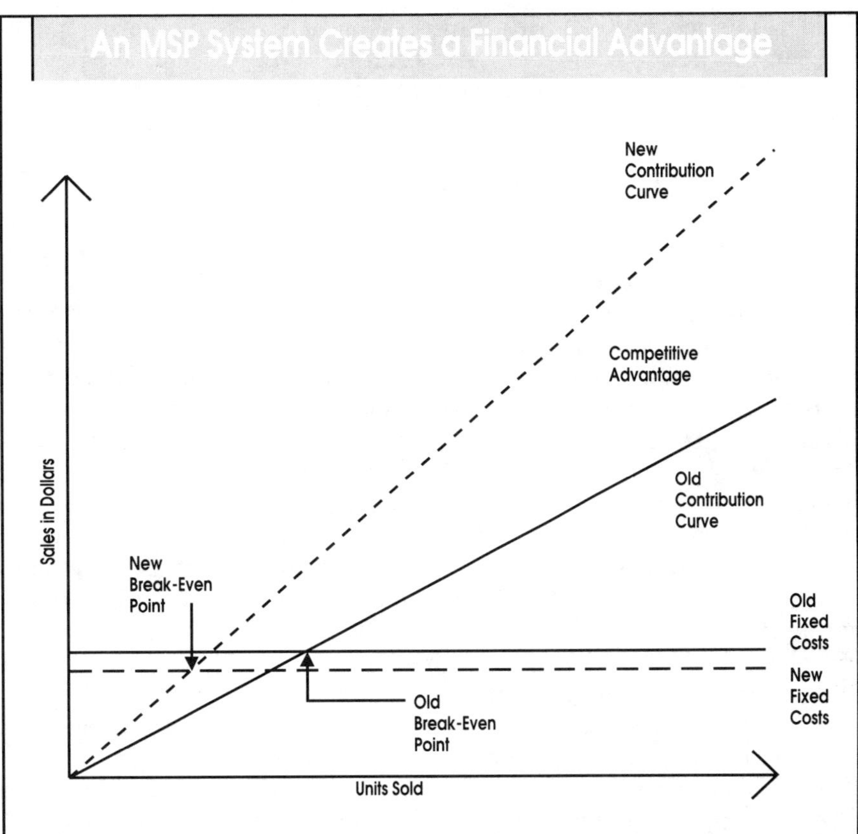

Whenever marketing or sales activities are performed, the data base captures information that answers questions about customers and their needs. Who were the prospects? What were their interests? How were these interests generated? Which sales or marketing personnel performed which tasks? When were the tasks performed? Which follow-up tasks are required and when? Did any sales result? Gradually the data base becomes a rich source of marketing and sales information, enabling management to track marketing activities and measure the results of marketing programs.

How They Aid Productivity

MSP systems improve productivity in two ways. First, automation of selling and direct marketing support tasks boosts the efficiency of the sales and marketing staff. Second, automating the collection and analysis of marketing information improves the timeliness and quality of marketing and sales executives' decision making.

These networks make direct sales and direct marketing more efficient by automating highly repetitive support tasks, like answering requests for product literature and writing letters, and by reducing the time salespeople spend on nonselling tasks, like scheduling sales calls, compiling sales reports, generating proposals and bids, and entering orders. In 1985, Xerox installed an internally developed MSP system in its southern region. Xerox credits the system with a 10% to 20% gain in sales force productivity and with trimming $3 million off the company's 1987 marketing support and overhead budget. By automating sales administration and support tasks, Xerox has given its salespeople more time to sell.[2]

MSP systems for direct marketing also hone the efficiency of customer contacts. For example, a system for the telemarketing function can schedule and dial calls based on the prospect's priority, prompt the telemarketer with a sales script, and automatically update customer files. At Aratex Services, a $500 million uniform supply company based in Encino, California, telemarketers using the company's old manual system each made 35 to 40 calls per day and about one sale per month. Working with an automated system, each telemarketer now makes 50 or 60 calls daily and lands three or four sales per month.[3]

Automated networks also elevate the impact of each sales communication. Access to the central data base gives salespeople and direct marketers information to improve the quality of the contact, whether it is by mail, by telephone, or in person. A large financial services concern uses a telemarketing system to handle account inquiries. While responding to a customer's request or query, the telemarketer is prompted by the system to update the customer's profile information and to cross-sell other financial products.

At a division of Vanity Fair that makes women's and children's apparel, salespeople use laptop PCs to access the corporate data base for up-to-date inventory and order status information on 2,000 stock-keeping units. This step has trimmed the company's order cycle from more than two weeks to just three days. It also has made ordering more accurate, resulting in greater customer satisfaction, reduced order cancellations, and a 10% increase in sales.

In companies with many channels, MSP systems upgrade efficiency by using the central data base to track and coordinate all marketing activity. Without this coordination, independent marketing groups often unwittingly pursue conflicting goals. At one multibillion-dollar office automation company, a direct salesperson had just nailed down a big order by giving a key account the "maximum" price discount. Before the deal was signed, however, the telemarketing group reached this customer and undercut the salesperson's price by 10%. Aside from the damage to its reputation, this vendor lost much of its expected margin on the sale.

This company is now installing an MSP system that will collect and organize information on all marketing programs and activities, including: (1) all customer contacts, whether by mail, phone, direct salesperson, or national account manager; (2) the status of all sales efforts; (3) the origins of all leads; (4) all leads that are being qualified internally and by whom, and all leads that have been forwarded to distributors; (5) all customers who decided to buy; (6) what and when they purchased; and (7) any incentives or promotions that helped close the deal. Coordination of information through this system is expected to prevent further embarrassments.

A Management Tool

Creation of an MSP data base is an investment in astute management. The data base chronicles every one of a company's marketing and sales activities, from advertising that generates leads to direct mail and telephone qualification of the leads to closing the first sale—all the way through the life of each account. It enables marketing and sales management to relate marketing actions with marketplace results.

At the $25 million data communications company whose lead-handling system we diagrammed, marketing managers use this system to evaluate media placements on the basis of sales closed. Before this procedure was in place, the company had no way to link information on leads to sales and evaluated media placements solely on the number of leads generated, not closed.

MSP systems also reduce marketing inertia because they streamline the implementation of marketing programs. For example, after designing an in-house system to organize and manage its customer/prospect files, one $2.5 million industrial manufacturer let 70 manufacturer's agents go and replaced them with in-house direct mail and telemarketing functions. The results? The company raised its accounts by 50% and cut marketing costs from 18% of sales to 13%.

Systems for sales force automation also drive the rapid implementation of less drastic changes in marketing programs. By using telecommunications software and laptop PCs, Du Pont's Remington Arms division has trimmed the time requirement for a national rollout of pricing and promotional programs from two weeks to less than two days.

As marketing managers become accustomed to these systems, they find new uses for them, like analyzing and modeling the buying behavior of prospects and customers. The data base at Excelan, a $39 million marketer of circuit boards and software in San Jose, California, was essential in identifying a shift in customers' buying behavior from a very technical product focus to an office automation orientation. This discovery has influenced the marketing and sales managers' decisions about hiring and training employees as well as about selecting and developing new target markets.

Account histories also improve management's ability to devise and implement account management policies based on profits. By linking orders, services delivered, and prices paid with the actual costs of lead generation, preselling, closing, distribution, and postsale support, MSP systems furnish the tools for analyzing and adjusting the marketing mix. Grede Foundries, a Milwaukee producer of castings for original equipment manufacturers, has used the MSP system to develop a "perceived quality index" that yields a more complete and more accurate measure of customers' reactions than simply tracking returned goods. The system also provides pricing support. By tracking quoted prices and final selling prices, the system gives management a better idea of the price that will win a particular job.[4]

2. Thayer C. Taylor, "Xerox: Who Says You Can't Be Big and Fast?," *Sales & Marketing Management*, November 1987, p. 63.

3. Kate Bertrand, "Converting Leads with Computerized Telemarketing," *Business Marketing*, May 1988, p. 58.

4. Louis A. Wallis, *Computers and the Sales Effort* (New York: Conference Board, 1986).

Economies of Scale?

Small businesses may gain an initial competitive edge from MSP systems because they often can adopt these systems much faster than their big counterparts. With fewer levels of management, small companies are faster on their feet in making decisions. They also tend to have simpler marketing organizations, usually relying on a single-method, single-channel selling system like a small direct sales force.

Large companies face two imposing barriers. First, they generally have both multiple layers of administration and cross-functional decision-making groups. When analyzing, evaluating, and adopting MSP systems, large companies draw in not only marketing and sales but also the accounting, finance, and MIS functions. Second–as a glance at the flow chart and map shows–their marketing organizations customarily rely on complex arrangements of communications methods and selling channels. Accordingly, their MSP systems require great sophistication and customization.

In large companies, marketing and sales automation is a high-stakes decision needing the support of many parties. In a major telecommunications company, the evaluation and selection of an MSP system called for: (1) initial screening presentations by three software vendors; (2) detailed presentations to 15 senior executives; (3) a visit by eight managers to a company with an operating MSP system; and (4) at least nine internal follow-up meetings, including presentations to the vice presidents of marketing and sales, the general managers of the ten operating companies, the directors of the MIS and MIS-procurement groups, several financial analysts, and several senior salespeople. More than 40 people had a hand in the decision. All this work occurred in a period of more than nine months after the corporate decision to automate marketing and sales.

But the story doesn't end there. Once the company had selected a $200,000 off-the-shelf system, it spent 18 months and $250,000 more installing and customizing the software. During the next two years, functional additions to the system and training of the end users added more than $1 million to the cost.

Moreover, automated networks coordinate and direct sales resources–including salespeople, distributors and agents, direct mailers, telemarketers, and manufacturers' representatives–toward the highest priority prospects and customers. Hewlett-Packard's Qualified Lead Tracking System (QUILTS) electronically transmits inquiries to a telemarketing center, which qualifies and ranks them and electronically returns them to H-P headquarters. The company has trimmed the turnaround time for leads from as much as 14 weeks to as little as 48 hours. "Hot" leads are handled even faster; they are telephoned to the field sales force from the telemarketing center.[5] Similarly, field salespeople in Chevron Chemical's fertilizer division in San Francisco use laptop PCs to access rank-ordered prospect lists in the company's mainframe. At any time, the salespeople have access to leads that are only 24 hours old. Before automation, new prospect lists were printed at headquarters and mailed to the field reps, which took one to two weeks.

> Early adopters of marketing and sales productivity systems have erected impressive competitive barriers.

Finally, the MSP data base is a management tool for making better use of marketing resources–that is, ensuring that they are employed to further corporate goals rather than the goals of individual marketing or sales groups. While this may sound like something management does without effort, our research shows that optimizing marketing resources is much more easily said than done. In several companies we've looked at, salespeople routinely discard hundreds or even thousands of sales leads, making little or no effort to evaluate or review them. In essence, they are dissipating the resources that generated these leads–budgets for advertising, trade shows, public relations, and other communications media.

In their defense, the salespeople complain that pursuing raw leads is a waste of time. And they are generally right. In one of these companies, salespeople who followed up the raw leads averaged only one or two sales per month, while those who followed their "instincts" averaged more than three. The cost of pursuing the raw leads was at least one lost sale per salesperson per month. To the salespeople, ignoring the leads was common sense. On the other hand, the advertising group, which was evaluated on the number of leads generated, was increasing its budgets to generate more and more leads. One company has solved this problem by implementing an MSP system that will use telemarketing to qualify leads before sending them to the salespeople. The system will also close the loop, allowing management to evaluate both the company's advertising placements and its sales efforts on the basis of their contributions to revenues and earnings.

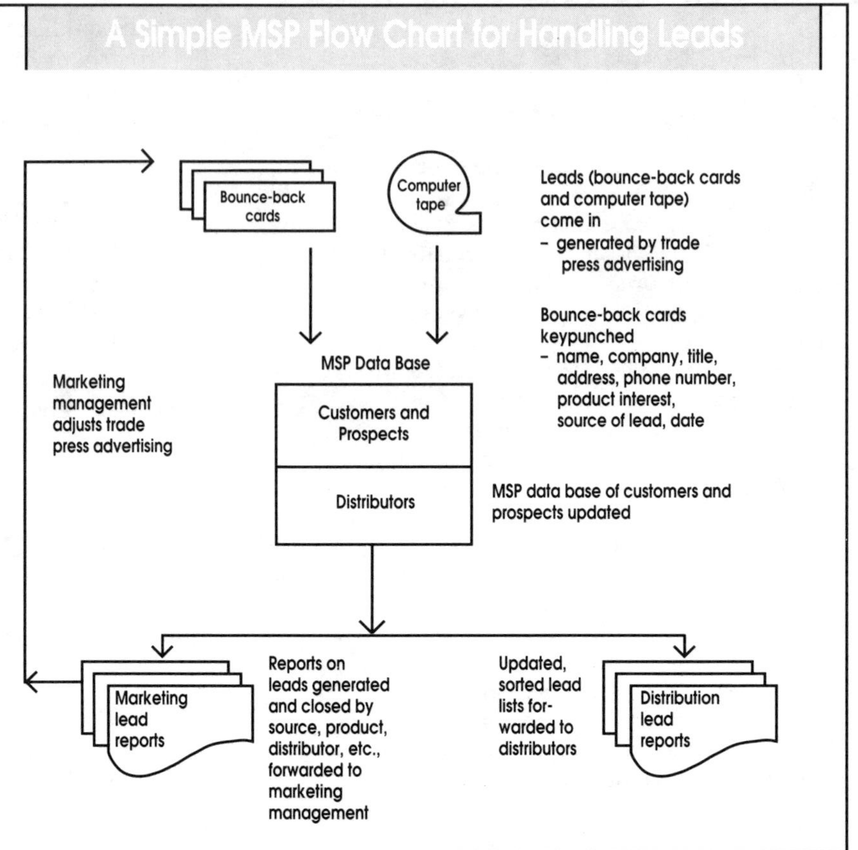

Efficiencies gained through task automation and improved marketing management are interdependent and reinforcing. Task automation drives the collection of more complete customer and marketplace information, and more informed decision making targets marketing and sales activities where they are most effective. In this way, marketers get a bigger payoff from low-cost, low-impact selling methods, like direct mail and catalogs, as data bases customize the timing and content of mass-marketing campaigns. At the same time, high-cost, high-impact selling methods, like personal selling and national account management, become more efficient as MSP systems perform routine sales support tasks, reduce nonselling time, and synchronize the use of these resources.

When you combine low-cost, low-impact methods with high-cost, high-impact approaches to gain just the right amount of stimulus at just the right time, you can obtain hefty impact at minimum cost. Hewlett-Packard, for one, has taken advantage of this synergy and has discovered the savings made possible by orchestrating direct mail, telemarketing, and personal selling.

How to Get from Here to There

The cases we have reviewed show that companies implementing MSP systems encounter many of the same barriers they would confront adopting any new technology.[6] From our observation, the process can be streamlined by following six guiding principles.

1. *Clarify the scale of the project as well as potential additions.* An audit of the marketing and sales tasks will yield these categories: those that must be automated now, those that will or may be automated later, and those that will not be automated. This simple exercise will identify marketing and sales activities that must be coordinated and focus the automation effort on getting measurable results without sacrificing flexibility.

It is important to view the project not from the perspective of the marketing groups but from a corporate perspective. With a corporate view, the company can build a "battleship"—a system that takes advantage of information-sharing and task-coordination synergies. Without this strategic perspective, independent marketing groups are more likely to invest in a number of incompatible and wasteful "rowboats." And even a rowboat can cause problems. At a big high-tech manufacturer, eight salespeople had their own PC-based sales force automation system installed. By raising issues of compatibility, data entry, and "file structure definitions," they delayed the start-up of a companywide, 300-salesperson MSP system for more than a year.

2. *Concentrate on tasks that can add value for the customer.* As in other corporate activities, marketers can get competitive advantage in two ways: by lowering costs and by enhancing the differentiation of the product or service offering. At the custom printer we referred to, streamlined job-costing and order-entry processes enable customers to price and place orders with one phone call. The "real-time" order-entry and order-tracking capabilities of the Vanity

5. Karen Blue, "Closing the Loop: Hewlett-Packard's New Lead Management System," *Business Marketing*, October 1987, p. 74.
6. Dorothy Leonard-Barton and William A. Kraus, "Implementing New Technology," HBR November-December 1985, p. 102.

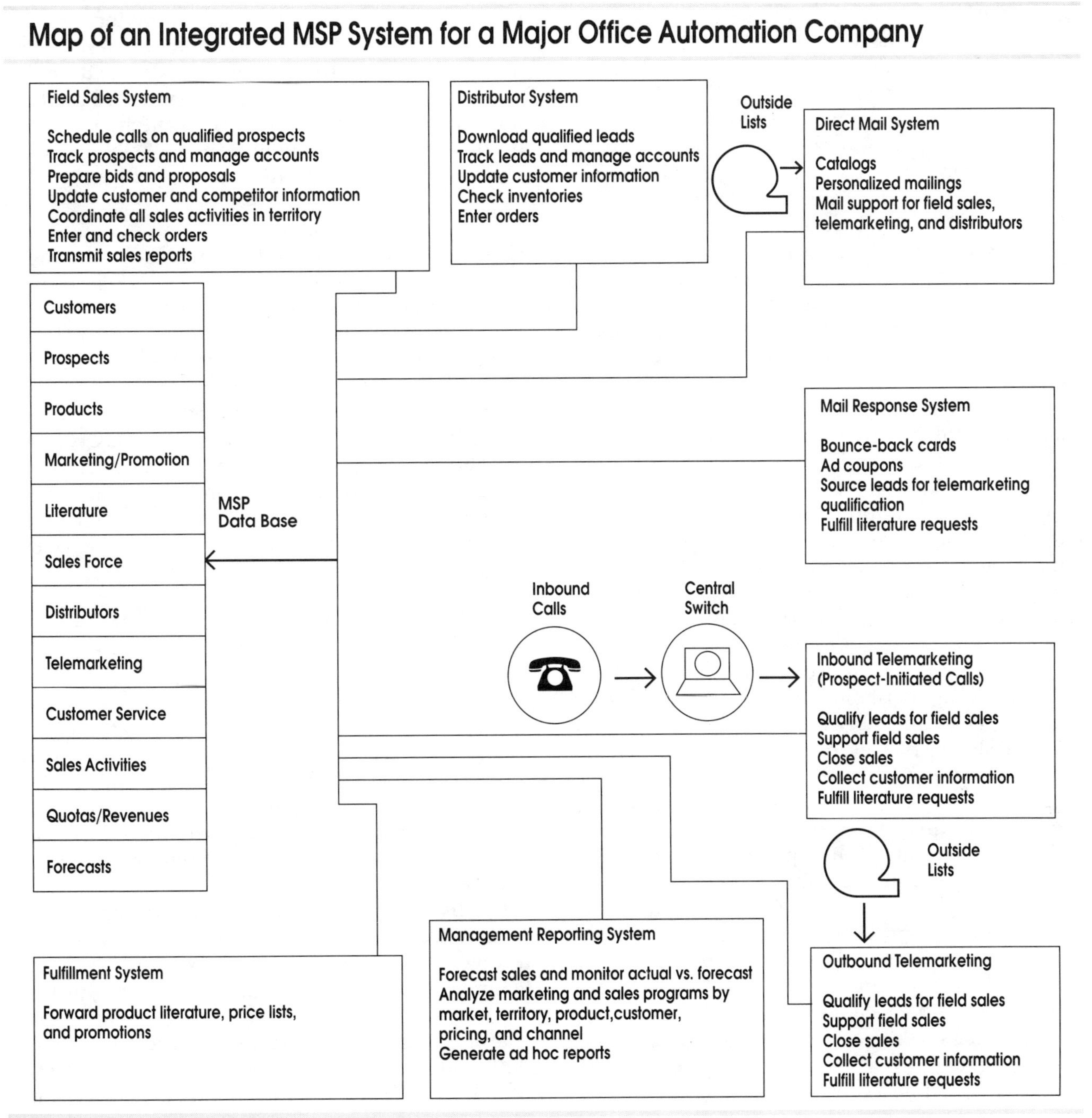

Fair unit's salespeople have upgraded its customer service. In both cases, customers benefit from better service, and sellers benefit from lower costs.

Other companies add value by using automation to improve the exchange of information during sales calls. The 22 salespeople in Hercules's Fragrance and Food Ingredient Group use their laptop PCs and a computer program called Flavor Briefs to consult with prospects on applications. Otherwise, Hercules salespeople would be unable to provide such detailed advice on their product line's many applications. The system saves the customer and the salesperson time and also furnishes a valuable service.

3. *In the budget process, account for hidden costs and intangible benefits.* Budgeting for an MSP system entails overcoming three principal obstacles: high perceived financial risk, poorly understood benefits, and biased capital budgeting systems.

First, automating marketing and sales is costly. A typical hardware and software outlay per salesperson ranges from $4,000 to $7,000–so automating the tasks of 100 field salespeople can cost between $400,000 and $700,000. In addition, if the MSP system must communicate with other corporate information systems, it is likely to require the development of specialized minicomputer, mainframe, or communications networking software.

Department-level telemarketing or direct mail systems range in price from $30,000 to more than $100,000. Sales or marketing management software may up the price another $30,000 to $100,000. Of course, the cost of tying all these pieces together depends on how many pieces there are, where they are located, and how they communicate. It would not be unusual for a company with 500 salespeople as well as telemarketing, fulfillment, and direct mail operations to spend between $3 million and $5 million on integrated MSP hardware and software.

But the budget process must anticipate and account for hidden costs too. In a number of cases we studied, in-house information was so scattered and communications equipment so incompatible that simply preparing a customer list required a major effort. Other hidden costs include system customization, expert consulting, and end-user training. Depending on the circumstances, these services can double or even triple the overall cost.

Because malfunctioning of an automated marketing system can threaten a business's revenue stream, it's advisable to budget for the cost of two systems – automated and manual – until the network has proved out. Naturally, all these expenses ratchet up the perceived financial risk of MSP automation.

On the other side of the equation, estimating the full financial benefit of an MSP system is extremely difficult. Tangible productivity gains, like increases in selling time and cost reductions on telephone campaigns, can be gauged fairly accurately. But intangible productivity gains, like better marketing decision making, more responsive customer service, and deeper understanding of customers, are much more difficult to track.

Still, it would be a mistake to ignore them, especially since capital budgeting processes are often biased against intangible productivity investments. Furthermore, few marketing managers and even fewer sales managers know much about their companies' capital budgeting processes – especially when huge investments in information technology are at stake. Senior executives have to take care that the process remains flexible enough to give MSP automation a reasonable evaluation.

An MSP system is a strategic investment for the whole corporation. But unlike other assets that are consumed over time, the more it is used, the more valuable it becomes. So it should be viewed as a long-term asset, not as the expense of a functional group. And, needless to say, senior management must match the scale of the company's investment to the scale of the project. Otherwise, fragmented marketing budgets will foster fragmented automation. The result, as noted above, may be many MSP rowboats with little or no coordination or compatibility.

4. *Make any tests realistic.* Because launching a full-scale network can be tremendously risky, most companies hedge their bets first by piloting automation on small portions of their marketing operations. A single function, like telemarketing or personal selling, is usually the test site. If this pilot is successful, the company adds more functions.

This ramp-up strategy, however, has serious drawbacks. It permits no insight into the complexity of coordinating multiple marketing and sales activities. Though single-function solutions may yield gratifying returns, evidence of their true worth may also stay hidden until they are combined into a system that demonstrates synergy. Consequently, estimates of financial returns based on single-function pilots may be negatively biased.

> Field salespeople use laptop PCs to tap their company's data base – and trim the order cycle from more than two weeks to three days.

Finally, critical performance limitations may remain hidden unless the complexity and scale of the test parallel the system's actual use. One big manufacturer's telemarketing pilot ran flawlessly, providing the telemarketers with a steady stream of calls and instant access to customer profiles and scripts. But eventual integration of telemarketing with other MSP networks seriously degraded the performance of the overall system. Every time the telemarketers asked for new information during a call, they were confronted by blank computer screens for more than 40 seconds. As the business manager put it, "That's a long time to talk about baseball."

A company with a multichannel, multimethod marketing system is better off with a pilot plan that automates a multifunctional subset of the marketing organization. In this type of pilot, an integrated system, encompassing all marketing and sales functions, is installed for a single division, region, product line, or customer group. This experience is likely to be more realistic than the single-function approach.

5. *Pinpoint the roles and responsibilities of those selecting, designing, and operating the system.* Even standard MSP systems, though they may be touted as off-the-shelf products, require extensive customization. This necessity complicates the selection or design process in a number of ways.

□ The process requires expertise in technology (computers, data communications, and software) as well as in marketing and sales.

□ Naturally, a company's existing MIS systems are likely to constrain the choice (or development) of an MSP system.

□ Marketing professionals and MIS professionals rarely speak a common language, and they often approach marketing automation projects with different perspectives. While marketing thinks about functionality (e.g., Will the system help perform marketing and sales tasks?), MIS people often focus on technical considerations (e.g., Will the system interact with other corporate information systems? Who is responsible for ensuring the integrity of corporate data bases?).

It's senior management's job to make sure that the MIS and marketing professionals talk to each other and work together. It's not easy. An MIS group may automate its conception of marketing and sales only to discover later that the automated system does not actually work. Everybody knows of cases in which the MIS department loads the sales force down with reams of report forms to complete and return to headquarters. Of course, much of the requested information is irrelevant from the salespeople's standpoint, and the report forms end up in the same round file as the old lead cards.

> The more you use the system, the more valuable it becomes.

During the long, complex process of designing and implementing a major MSP system, responsibilities sometimes become diffuse and project accountability gets blurred. In one case we know of, poorly defined responsibilities for MIS and marketing have caused big headaches. Bickering over cost allocations and data-base controls has made the company's $1 million MSP system useless. The MIS group will not allow marketing to access the corporation's data bases. But the marketing group's computer budget is too low to keep the marketing data base up-to-date. (Not surprisingly, headquarters viewed the entire MSP development process as a marketing expense instead of a corporate investment.)

6. *Modify the technology and the organization to support the system.* As in every instance in which management implements new technology, it must pay close attention to the attitudes of people in the organization. In successful MSP implementations that we have seen, both the organization and the MSP system have gone through an interactive process of change–altering the technology to fit the marketing and sales environment, then altering the environment to fit the technology.

To be useful, for example, the MSP data base obviously must contain accurate, up-to-date information. Because obtaining this information requires salespeople to use the system and to support the information collection process, they have to become adept at using the new technology. Problems can result, however, if the end-users lack computer skills or if they are uninterested in using the system.

Training can overcome skill problems (if enough money is budgeted and enough time set aside), but lack of interest is harder to deal with. Experience suggests that the best way to sell the sales staff on the network is to demonstrate that it can give every user something back. That is, by helping salespeople or telemarketers work more productively, MSP systems can boost not only the company's sales but also *their* sales and *their* compensation.

For many companies, postponement of automation of the marketing function may seem to be a good way of skirting a difficult decision, but this do-nothing posture condemns the organization to being a marketing laggard. It may also be a costly mistake. Early adopters of MSP systems have gained superior competitive advantage. Compared with their "manual" competitors, they perform selling tasks with greater economy and impact. They know their customers better and can tailor their sales communications to supply just the right amount of sales stimulus at just the right time. Overall, they craft and control their marketing programs more intelligently. In the long run, the competitive barriers they establish may change the nature of marketing in their industries.

In view of this impressive record, some marketers about to embark on automation may embrace unrealistically high expectations. But MSP systems cannot work miracles. They will not offset a poorly conceived or poorly executed marketing strategy. They will not compensate for an inferior sales force, and they will not sell inferior products. Complex MSP systems are difficult to implement, and the associated returns, like any other lasting accomplishment, have to be earned.

Reprint 89105

No-quibble guarantees are self-fulfilling – they promise quality and produce it.

The Power of Unconditional Service Guarantees

by CHRISTOPHER W.L. HART

When you buy a car, a camera, or a toaster oven, you receive a warranty, a guarantee that the product will work. How often do you receive a warranty for auto repair, wedding photography, or a catered dinner? Virtually never. Yet it is here, in buying services, that the assurance of a guarantee would presumably count most.

Many business executives believe that, by definition, services simply can't be guaranteed. Services are generally delivered by human beings, who are known to be less predictable than machines, and they are usually produced at the same time they are consumed. It is one thing to guarantee a camera, which can be inspected before a customer sets eyes on it and which can be returned to the factory for repairs. But how can you preinspect a car tune-up or send an unsuccessful legal argument or bad haircut back for repair? Obviously you can't.

Al Burger *started* with an unconditional guarantee and built his company around it.

But that doesn't mean customer satisfaction can't be guaranteed. Consider the guarantee offered by "Bugs" Burger Bug Killers (BBBK), a Miami-based pest-extermination company that is owned by S.C. Johnson & Son.

Most of BBBK's competitors claim that they will reduce pests to "acceptable levels"; BBBK promises to eliminate them entirely. Its service guarantee to hotel and restaurant clients promises:

- You don't owe one penny until all pests on your premises have been eradicated.
- If you are ever dissatisfied with BBBK's service, you will receive a refund for up to 12 months of the company's services – plus fees for another exterminator of your choice for the next year.
- If a guest spots a pest on your premises, BBBK will pay for the guest's meal or room, send a letter of apology, and pay for a future meal or stay.
- If your facility is closed down due to the presence of roaches or rodents, BBBK will pay any fines, as well as all lost profits, *plus* $5,000.

In short, BBBK says, "If we don't satisfy you 100%, we don't take your money."

Christopher W.L. Hart is an assistant professor at the Harvard Business School, where he teaches a course on service management. As a researcher and consultant, he helps companies design and implement service-guarantee and quality-improvement programs.

How successful is this guarantee? The company, which operates throughout the United States, charges up to ten times more than its competitors and yet has a disproportionately high market share in its operating areas. Its service quality is so outstanding that the company rarely needs to make good on its guarantee (in 1986 it paid out only $120,000 on sales of $33 million—just enough to prove that its promises aren't empty ones).

A main reason that the "Bugs" Burger guarantee is a strong model for the service industry is that its founder, Al Burger, began with the concept of the unconditional guarantee and worked backward, designing his entire organization to support the no-pests guarantee—in short, he started with a vision of error-free service. In this article, I will explain why the service guarantee can help your organization institutionalize superlative performance.

What a Good Service Guarantee Is

Would you be willing to offer a guarantee of 100% customer satisfaction—to pay your dissatisfied customer to use a competitor's service, for example? Or do you believe that promising error-free service is a crazy idea?

Not only is it not crazy, but *committing* to error-free service can help force a company to *provide* it. It's a little like skiing. You've got to lean over your skis as you go down the hill, as if willing yourself to fall. But if you edge properly, you don't fall or plunge wildly; you gain control while you pick up speed.

Similarly, a strong service guarantee that puts the customer first doesn't necessarily lead to chaos and failure. If designed and implemented properly, it enables you to get control over your organization—with clear goals and an information network that gives you the data you need to improve performance. BBBK and other service companies show that a service guarantee is not only possible—it's a boon to performance and profits and can be a vehicle to market dominance.

Most existing service guarantees don't really do the job: they are limited in scope and difficult to use. Lufthansa guarantees that its customers will make their connecting flights *if* there are no delays due to weather or air-traffic control problems. Yet these two factors cause fully 95% of all flight delays. Bank of America will refund up to six months of checking-account fees if a customer is dissatisfied with any aspect of its checking-account service. However, the customer must close the account to collect the modest $5 or $6 per month fee. This guarantee won't win any prizes for fostering repeat business—a primary objective of a good guarantee.

A service guarantee loses power in direct proportion to the number of conditions it contains. How effective is a restaurant's guarantee of prompt service *except* when it's busy? A housing inspector's guarantee to identify all potential problems in a house *except for* those not readily apparent? Squaw Valley in California guarantees "your money back" to any skier who has to wait more than ten minutes in a lift line. But it's not that easy: the skier must first pay $1 and register at the lodge as a beginner, intermediate, or expert; the guarantee is operative only if *all* lifts at the skier's skill level exceed the ten minutes in any half-hour period; and skiers must check with a "ski hostess" at the end of the day to "win" a refund. A Squaw Valley spokesperson said the resort had made just one payout under the guarantee in a year and a half. No wonder!

What is a good service guarantee? It is (1) unconditional, (2) easy to understand and communicate, (3) meaningful, (4) easy (and painless) to invoke, and (5) easy and quick to collect on.

Unconditional. The best service guarantee promises customer satisfaction unconditionally, without exceptions. Like that of L.L. Bean, the Freeport, Maine retail store and mail-order house: "100% satisfaction in every way...." An L.L. Bean customer can return a product at any time and get, at his or her option, a replacement, a refund, or a credit. Reputedly, if a customer returns a pair of L.L. Bean boots after ten years, the company will replace them with new boots and no questions. Talk about customer assurance!

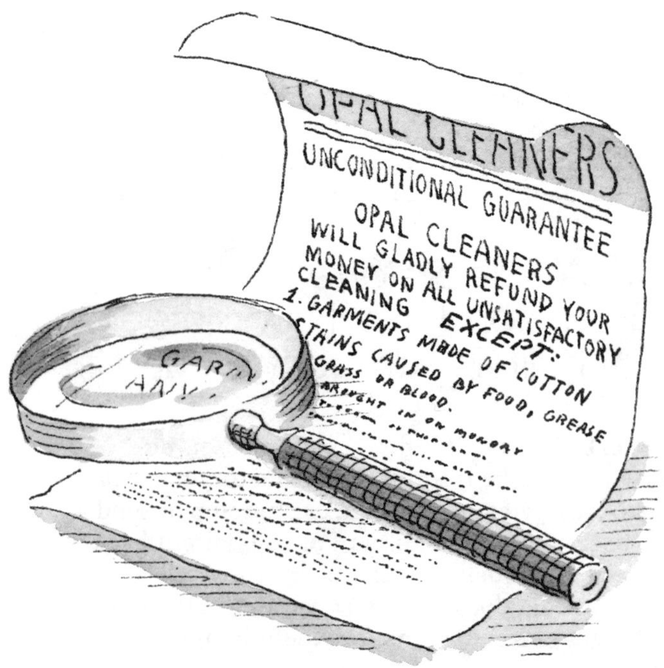

Customers shouldn't need a lawyer to explain the "ifs, ands, and buts" of a guarantee—because ideally there shouldn't be any conditions; a customer is either satisfied or not.

If a company cannot guarantee all elements of its service unconditionally, it should unconditionally guarantee the elements that it can control. Lufthansa cannot promise on-time arrival, for example, but it could guarantee that passengers will be satisfied with its airport waiting areas, its service on the ground and in the air, and its food quality—or simply guarantee overall satisfaction.

Easy to Understand and Communicate. A guarantee should be written in simple, concise language that pinpoints the promise. Customers then know precisely what they can expect and employees know precisely what's expected of them. "Five-minute" lunch service, rather than "prompt" service, creates clear expectations, as does "no pests," rather than "pest control."

Meaningful. A good service guarantee is meaningful in two respects. First, it guarantees those aspects of your service that are important to your customers. It may be speedy delivery. Bennigan's, a restaurant chain, promises 15-minute service (or you get a free meal) at lunch, when many customers are in a hurry to get back to the office, but not at dinner, when fast service is not considered a priority to most patrons.

In other cases, price may be the most important element, especially with relatively undifferentiated commodities like rental cars or commercial air travel. By promising the lowest prices in town, stereo shops assuage customers' fears that if they don't go to every outlet in the area they'll pay more than they ought to.

L.L. Bean will replace its boots—even after ten years' use.

Second, a good guarantee is meaningful financially; it calls for a significant payout when the promise is not kept. What should it be—a full refund? An offer of free service the next time? A trip to Monte Carlo? The answer depends on factors like the cost of the service, the seriousness of the failure, and customers' perception of what's fair. A money-back payout should be large enough to give customers an incentive to invoke the guarantee if dissatisfied. The adage "Let the punishment fit the crime" is an appropriate guide. At one point, Domino's Pizza (which is based in Ann Arbor, Michigan but operates worldwide) promised "delivery within 30 minutes or the pizza is free." Management found that customers considered this too generous; they felt uncomfortable accepting a free pizza for a mere 5- or 15-minute delay and didn't always take advantage of the guarantee. Consequently, Domino's adjusted its guarantee to "delivery within 30 minutes or $3 off," and customers appear to consider this commitment reasonable.

Easy to Invoke. A customer who is already dissatisfied should not have to jump through hoops to invoke a guarantee; the dissatisfaction is only exacerbated when the customer has to talk to three different people, fill out five forms, go to a different location, make two telephone calls, send in written proof of purchase with a full description of the events, wait for a written reply, go somewhere else to see someone to verify all the preceding facts, and so on.

Traveler's Advantage—a division of CUC International—has, in principle, a great idea: to guarantee the lowest price on the accommodations it books. But to invoke the guarantee, customers must prove the lower competing price by booking with another agency. That's unpleasant work. Cititravel, a subsidiary of Citicorp, has a better approach. A customer who knows of a lower price can call a toll-free number and speak with an agent, as I did recently. The agent told me that if I didn't have proof of the lower fare, she'd check competing airfares on her computer screen. If the lower fare was there, I'd get that price. If not, she would call the competing airline. If the price was confirmed, she said, "We'll refund your money so fast, you won't believe it—because we want you to be our customer." That's the right attitude if you're offering a guarantee.

Similarly, customers should not be made to feel guilty about invoking the guarantee—no questioning, no raised eyebrows, or "Why me, Lord?" looks. A company should encourage unhappy customers to invoke its guarantee, not put up roadblocks to keep them from speaking up.

Easy to Collect. Customers shouldn't have to work hard to collect a payout, either. The procedure should be easy and, equally important, quick—on the spot, if possible. Dissatisfaction with a Manpower temporary worker, for instance, results in an immediate credit to your bill.

What you should *not* do in your guarantee: don't promise something your customers already expect; don't shroud a guarantee in so many conditions that it loses its point; and don't offer a guarantee so mild

1. See British Airways study cited in Karl Albrecht and Ron Zemke, *Service America!* (Homewood, Ill.: Dow Jones-Irwin, 1985), pp. 33-34.

that it is never invoked. A guarantee that is essentially risk free to the company will be of little or no value to your customers—and may be a joke to your employees.

Why a Service Guarantee Works

A guarantee is a powerful tool—both for marketing service quality and for achieving it—for five reasons.

First, it pushes the entire company to focus on customers' definition of good service—not on executives' assumptions. Second, it sets clear performance standards, which boost employee performance and morale. Third, it generates reliable data (through payouts) when performance is poor. Fourth, it forces an organization to examine its entire service-delivery system for possible failure points. Last, it builds customer loyalty, sales, and market share.

A guarantee forces you to focus on customers. Knowing what customers want is the sine qua non in offering a service guarantee. A company has to identify its target customers' expectations about the elements of the service and the importance they attach to each. Lacking this knowledge of customer needs, a company that wants to guarantee its service may very well guarantee the wrong things.

British Airways conducted a market study and found that its passengers judge its customer services on four dimensions:[1]

1. Care and concern (employees' friendliness, courtesy, and warmth).

2. Initiative (employees' ability and willingness to jockey the system on the customer's behalf).

3. Problem solving (figuring out solutions to customer problems, whether unusual or routine—like multiflight airline tickets).

4. Recovery (going the extra yard, when things go wrong, to handle a particular problem—which includes the simple but often overlooked step of delivering an apology).

British Airways managers confessed that they hadn't even thought about the second and fourth categories. Worse, they realized that if *they* hadn't understood these important dimensions of customer service, how much thought could their employees be giving to them?

A guarantee sets clear standards. A specific, unambiguous service guarantee sets standards for your organization. It tells employees what the company stands for. BBBK stands for pest elimination, not pest control; Federal Express stands for "absolutely, positively by 10:30 A.M.," not "sometime tomorrow, probably." And it forces the company to define each employee's role and responsibilities in delivering the service. Salespeople, for example, know precisely what their companies can deliver and can represent that accurately—the opposite of the common situation in which salespeople promise the moon and customers get only dirt.

This clarity and sense of identity have the added advantage of creating employee team spirit and pride. Mitchell Fromstein, president and CEO of Manpower, says, "At one point, we wondered what the marketing impact would be if we dropped our guarantee. We figured that our accounts were well aware of the guarantee and that it might not have much marketing power anymore. Our employees' reaction was fierce—and it had a lot less to do with marketing than with the pride they take in their work. They said, 'The guarantee is proof that we're a great company. We're willing to tell our customers that if they don't like our service for any reason, it's our fault, not

A service guarantee is valued when a customer's ego is on the line.

theirs, and we'll make it right.' I realized then that the guarantee is far more than a simple piece of paper that puts customers at ease. It really sets the tone, externally and, perhaps more important, internally, for our commitment to our customers and workers."

A payout that creates financial pain when errors occur is also a powerful statement, to employees and customers alike, that management demands customer satisfaction. A significant payout ensures that both middle and upper management will take the service guarantee seriously; it provides a strong incentive to take every step necessary to deliver. A manager who must bear the full cost of mistakes has ample incentive to figure out how to prevent them from happening.

A guarantee generates feedback. A guarantee creates the goal; it defines what you must do to satisfy your customers. Next, you need to know when you go wrong. A guarantee forces you to create a system for discovering errors–which the Japanese call "golden nuggets" because they're opportunities to learn.

Arguably the greatest ailment afflicting service companies is a lack of decent systems for generating and acting on customer data. Dissatisfied service customers have little incentive to complain on their own, far less so than unhappy product owners do. Many elements of a service are intangible, so consumers who receive poor service are often left with no evidence to support their complaints. (The customer believes the waiter was rude; perhaps the waiter will deny it.) Second, without the equivalent of a product warranty, customers don't know their rights. (Is 15 minutes too long to wait for a restaurant meal? 30 minutes?) Third, there is often no one to complain to–at least no one who looks capable of solving the problem. Often, complaining directly to the person who is rendering poor service will only make things worse.

Without a guarantee, customers won't complain. Or come back.

Customer comment cards have traditionally been the most common method of gathering customer feedback on a company's operations, but they, too, are inadequate for collecting valid, reliable error data. In the first place, they are an impersonal form of communication and are usually short (to maximize the response rate). Why bother, people think, to cram the details of a bad experience onto a printed survey form with a handful of "excellent–good–fair" check-off boxes? Few aggrieved customers believe that completing a comment card will resolve their problems. Therefore, only a few customers–usually the most satisfied and dissatisfied–provide feedback through such forms, and fewer still provide meaningful feedback. As a broad gauge of customer sentiment, cards and surveys are useful, but for specific information about customer problems and operational weaknesses, they simply don't fill the bill.

Service companies thus have a hard time collecting error data. Less information on mistakes means fewer opportunities to improve, ultimately resulting in more service errors and more customer dissatisfaction–a cycle that management is often unaware of. A guarantee attacks this malady by giving consumers an incentive and a vehicle for bringing their grievances to management's attention.

Manpower uses its guarantee to glean error data in addition to allaying customer worries about using an unknown quantity (the temporary worker). Every customer who employs a Manpower temporary worker is called the first day of a one-day assignment or the second day of a longer assignment to check on the worker's performance. A dissatisfied customer doesn't pay–period. (Manpower pays the worker, however; it assumes complete responsibility for the quality of its service.) The company uses its error data to improve both its work force and its proprietary skills-testing software and skills data base–major elements in its ability to match worker skills to customer requirements. The information Manpower obtains before and after hiring enables it to offer its guarantee with confidence.

A guarantee forces you to understand why you fail. In developing a guarantee, managers must ask questions like these: What failure points exist in the system? If failure points can be identified, can their origins be traced–and overcome? A company that wants to promise timely service delivery, for example, must first understand its operation's capability and the factors limiting that capability. Many service executives, lacking understanding of such basic issues as system throughput time, capacity, and process flow, tend to blame workers, customers, or anything *but* the service-delivery process.

Even if workers *are* a problem, managers can do several things to "fix" the organization so that it can support a guarantee–such as design better recruiting, hiring, and training processes. The pest-control industry has historically suffered from unmotivated personnel and high turnover. Al Burger overcame the status quo by offering higher than average pay (attracting a higher caliber of job candidate), using a vigorous screening program (making those hired feel like members of a select group), training all workers for six months, and keeping them motivated by giving them a great deal of autonomy and lots of recognition.

Some managers may be unwilling to pay for an internal service-delivery capability that is above the industry average. Fine. They will never have better than average organizations, either, and they will therefore never be able to develop the kind of competitive advantage that flows from a good service guarantee.

A guarantee uncovers errors—and opportunities to learn.

A guarantee builds marketing muscle. Perhaps the most obvious reason for offering a strong service guarantee is its ability to boost marketing: it encourages consumers to buy a service by reducing the risk of the purchase decision, and it generates more sales to existing customers by enhancing loyalty. In the last ten years, Manpower's revenues have mushroomed from $400 million to $4 billion. That's marketing impact.

Keeping most of your customers and getting positive word of mouth, though desirable in any business, are particularly important for service companies. The net present value of sales forgone from lost customers—in other words, the cost of customer dissatisfaction—is enormous. In this respect, it's fair to say that many service companies' biggest competitors are themselves. They frequently spend huge amounts of money to attract new customers without ever figuring out how to provide the consistent service they promise to their existing customers. If customers aren't satisfied, the marketing money has been poured down the drain and may even engender further ill will. (See the insert, "Maximizing Marketing Impact.")

A guarantee will only work, of course, if you start with commitment to the customer. If your aim is to minimize the guarantee's impact on your organization but to maximize its marketing punch, you won't succeed. In the long run, you will nullify the guarantee's potential impact on customers, and your marketing dollars will go down the drain.

Phil Bressler, owner of 18 Domino's Pizza franchises in the Baltimore, Maryland area, demonstrates the right commitment to customers. He got upset the time his company recorded its highest monthly earnings ever because, he correctly figured, the profits had come from money that should have been paid out on the Domino's guarantee of "delivery within 30 minutes or $3 off." Bressler's unit managers, who have bottom-line responsibility, had pumped up their short-term profits by failing to honor the guarantee consistently. Bressler is convinced that money spent on guarantees is an investment in customer satisfaction and loyalty. He also recognizes that the guarantee is the best way to identify weak operations, and that guarantees not acted on are data not collected.

Compare Bressler's attitude with that of an owner of several nationally franchised motels. *His* guarantee promises that the company will do "everything possible" to remedy a customer's problem; if the problem cannot be resolved, the customer stays for free. He brags that he's paid, on average, refunds for only two room guarantees per motel per year—a minuscule percentage of room sales. "If my managers are doing their jobs, I don't have to pay out for the guarantee," he says. "If I do have to pay out, my managers are not doing their jobs, and I get rid of them."

Clearly, more than two guests of *any* hotel are likely to be dissatisfied over the course of a year. By seeking to limit payouts rather than hear complaints, this owner is undoubtedly blowing countless opportunities to create loyal customers out of disgruntled ones. He is also losing rich information about which of his motels need improvement and why, information that can most easily be obtained from customer complaints. You have to wonder why he offers a guarantee at all, since he completely misses the point.

Why You May Need a Guarantee Even If You Don't Think So

Of course, guarantees may not be effective or practicable for all service firms. Four Seasons Hotels, for example, could probably not get much marketing or operational mileage from a guarantee. With its strong internal vision of absolute customer satisfaction, the company has developed an outstanding service-delivery system and a reputation to match. Thus it already has an implicit guarantee. To advertise the obvious would produce little gain and might actually be perceived as incongruent with the company's prestigious image.

A crucial element in Four Seasons's service strategy is instilling in all employees a mission of absolute customer satisfaction and empowering them to do whatever is necessary if customer problems do occur. For example, Four Seasons's Washington hotel was once asked by the State Department to make room for a foreign dignitary. Already booked to capacity, Four Seasons had to tell four other customers

Maximizing Marketing Impact

The odds of gaining powerful marketing impact from a service guarantee are in your favor when one or more of the following conditions exist:

The price of the service is high. A bad shoe shine? No big deal. A botched $1,000 car repair is a different story; a guarantee is more effective here.

The customer's ego is on the line. Who wants to be seen after getting a bad haircut?

The customer's expertise with the service is low. When in doubt about a service, a customer will choose one that's covered by a guarantee over those that are not.

The negative consequences of service failure are high. As consumers' expected aggravation, expense, and time lost due to service failure increase, a guarantee gains power. Your computer went down? A computer-repair service with guaranteed response and repair times would be the most logical company to call.

The industry has a bad image for service quality – like pest-control services, security guards, or home repair. A guard company that guarantees to have its posts filled by qualified people would automatically rank high on a list of prospective vendors.

The company depends on frequent customer repurchases. Can it exist on a never-ending stream of new triers (like small service businesses in large markets), or does it have to deal with a finite market? If the market is finite, how close is market saturation? The smaller the size of the potential market of new triers, the more attention management should pay to increasing the loyalty and repurchase rate of existing customers – objectives that a good service guarantee will serve.

The company's business is affected deeply by word of mouth (both positive and negative). Consultants, stockbrokers, restaurants, and resorts are all good examples of services where there are strong incentives to minimize the extent of customer dissatisfaction – and hence, negative word of mouth.

with reservations that they could not be accommodated. However, the hotel immediately found rooms for them at another first-class hotel, while assuring them they would remain registered at the Four Seasons (so that any messages they received would be taken and sent to the other hotel). When rooms became available, the customers were driven back to the Four Seasons by limousine. Four Seasons also paid for their rooms at the other hotel. It was the equivalent of a full money-back guarantee, and more.

Does this mean that every company that performs at the level of a Four Seasons need not offer a service guarantee? Could Federal Express, for example, drop its "absolutely, positively" assurance with little or no effect? Probably not. Its guarantee is such a part of its image that dropping the guarantee would hurt it.

In general, organizations that meet the following tests probably have little to gain by offering a service guarantee: the company is perceived by the market to be the quality leader in its industry; every employee is inculcated with the "absolute customer satisfaction" philosophy; employees are empowered to take whatever corrective action is necessary to handle complaints; errors are few; and a stated guarantee would be at odds with the company's image.

It is probably unnecessary to point out that few service companies meet these tests.

External Variables. Service guarantees may also be impractical where customer satisfaction is influenced strongly by external forces the service provider can't control. While everybody thinks their businesses are in this fix, most are wrong.

How many variables are truly beyond management's control? Not the work force. Not equipment problems. Not vendor quality. And even businesses subject to "acts of God" (like weather) can control a great deal of their service quality.

> An airline can't guarantee on-time flights – but it *can* promise courtesy.

BBBK is an example of how one company turned the situation around by analyzing the elements of the service-delivery process. By asking, "What obstacles stand in the way of our guaranteeing pest elimination?" Al Burger discovered that clients' poor cleaning and storage practices were one such obstacle. So the company requires customers to maintain sanitary practices and in some cases even make physical changes to their property (like putting in walls). By changing the process, the company could guarantee the outcome.

There may well be uncontrollable factors that create problems. As I noted earlier, such things as flight controllers, airport capacity, and weather limit the extent to which even the finest airline can consistently deliver on-time service. But how employees respond to such externally imposed problems strongly influences customer satisfaction, as British Airways executives learned from their market survey. When things go wrong, will employees go the extra yard to handle the problem? Why couldn't an airline that has refined its problem-handling skills to a science ensure absolute customer satisfaction—uncontrollable variables be damned? How many customers would invoke a guarantee if they understood that the reasons for a problem were completely out of the airline's control—if they were treated with warmth, compassion, and a sense of humor, and if the airline's staff communicated with them honestly?

Cheating. Fear of customer cheating is another big hurdle for most service managers considering offering guarantees. When asked why Lufthansa's guarantee required customers to present written proof of purchase, a manager at the airline's U.S. headquarters told me, "If we didn't ask for written proof, our customers would cheat us blind."

> A guarantee can generate breakthrough service and change an industry.

But experience teaches a different lesson. Sure, there will be cheats—the handful of customers who take advantage of a guarantee to get something for nothing. What they cost the company amounts to very little compared to the benefits derived from a strong guarantee. Says Michael Leven, a hotel industry executive, "Too often management spends its time worrying about the 1% of people who might cheat the company instead of the 99% who don't."

Phil Bressler of Domino's argues that customers cheat only when *they* feel cheated: "If we charge $8 for a pizza, our customers expect $8 worth of product and service. If we started giving them $7.50 worth of product and service, then they'd start looking for ways to get back that extra 50 cents. Companies create the incentive to cheat, in almost all cases, by cutting costs and not providing value."

Where the potential for false claims is high, a no-questions-asked guarantee may appear to be foolhardy. When Domino's first offered its "delivery within 30 minutes or the pizza is free" guarantee, some college students telephoned orders from hard-to-find locations. The result was free pizza for the students and lost revenue for Domino's. In this environment, the guarantee was problematic because some students perceived it as a game against Domino's. But Bressler takes the view that the revenue thus lost was an investment in the future. "They'll be Domino's customers for life, those kids," he says.

High Costs. Managers are likely to worry about the costs of a service-guarantee program, but for the wrong reasons. Quality "guru" Philip Crosby coined the phrase "quality is free" (in his 1979 book, *Quality Is Free*) to indicate *not* that quality-improvement efforts cost nothing but that the benefits of quality improvement—fewer errors, higher productivity, more repeat business—outweigh the costs over the long term.

Clearly, a company whose operations are slipshod (or out of control) should not consider offering an unconditional guarantee; the outcome would be either bankruptcy from staggering payouts or an employee revolt stemming from demands to meet standards that are beyond the organization's capability. If your company is like most, however, it's not in that shape; you will probably only need to buttress operations somewhat. To be sure, an investment of financial and human resources to shore up weak points in the delivery system will likely cause a quick, sharp rise in expenditures.

How sharp an increase depends on several factors: your company's weaknesses (how far does it have to go to become good?), the nature of the industry, and the strength of your competition, for example. A small restaurant might simply spend more on employee recruiting and training, and perhaps on sponsoring quality circles; a large utility company might need to restructure its entire organization to overcome years of bad habits if it is to deliver on a guarantee.

Even though a guarantee carries costs, bear in mind that, as Crosby asserts, a badly performed service also incurs costs—failure costs, which come in many forms, including lost business from disgruntled consumers. In a guarantee program, you shift from spending to mop up failures to spending on preventing failures. And many of those costs are incurred in most organizations anyway (like outlays for staff time spent in planning meetings). It's just that they're spent more productively.

Breakthrough Service

One great potential of a service guarantee is its ability to change an industry's rules of the game by changing the service-delivery process as competitors conceive it.

BBBK and Federal Express both redefined the meaning of service in their industries, performing at levels that other companies have so far been unable to match. (According to the owner of a competing pest-control company, BBBK "is number one. There is no number two.") By offering breakthrough service, these companies altered the basis of competition in their businesses and put their competitors at a severe disadvantage.

What are the possibilities for replicating their success in other service businesses? Skeptics might claim that BBBK's and Federal Express's success is not widely applicable because they target price-insensitive customers willing to pay for superior service–in short, that these companies are pursuing differentiation strategies.

It is true that BBBK's complex preparation, cleaning, and checkup procedures are much more time consuming than those of typical pest-control operators, that the company spends more on pesticides than competitors do, and that its employees are well compensated. And many restaurants and hotels are willing to pay BBBK's higher prices because to them it's ultimately cheaper: the cost of "errors" (guests' spotting roaches or ants) is higher than the cost of error prevention.

But, because of the "quality is free" dictum, breakthrough service does not mean you must become the high-cost producer. Manpower's procedures are not radically more expensive than its competitors'; they're simply better. The company's skills-testing methods and customer-needs diagnoses surely cost less in the long run than a sloppy system. A company that inadequately screens and trains temporary-worker recruits, establishes no detailed customer specifications, and fails to check worker performance loses customers.

Manpower spends heavily on ways to reduce errors further, seeing this spending as an investment that will (a) protect its market position; (b) reduce time-consuming service errors; and (c) reinforce the company's values to employees. Here is the "absolute customer satisfaction" philosophy at work, and whatever cost increase Manpower incurs it makes up in sales volume.

Organizations that figure out how to offer–and deliver–guaranteed, breakthrough service will have tapped into a powerful source of competitive advantage. Doing so is no mean feat, of course, which is precisely why the opportunity to build a competitive advantage exists. Though the task is difficult, it is clearly not impossible, and the service guarantee can play a fundamental role in the process.

Author's note: I thank Dan Maher for assistance in researching and writing this article.

Reprint 88405

"Actually, I don't want to make a deposit or a withdrawal I just wanted to make sure everything was, you know, fine."

IDEAS FOR ACTION

Exploit Your Product's Service Life Cycle

This cycle, lagging the product life cycle, needs sharp direction too.

by George W. Potts

"It is the capacity for maintenance which is the best test for the vigor and stamina of a society. Any society can be galvanized for a while to build something, but the will and the skill to keep things in good repair day in, day out are fairly rare."—Eric Hoffer in *Working and Thinking on the Waterfront* (1969).

By Eric Hoffer's measure, the United States is a vigorous culture. Repair services for electronic products alone are estimated to cost more than $60 billion annually and employ 400,000 people. The computer industry by itself generates more than $20 billion a year in maintenance service revenues. When including everything serviced in the private sector—elevators, construction machinery, typewriters, vending machines, autos, machine tools, cameras, airplanes, home appliances, industrial controls, turbines, trucks, and so on—the number grows to almost $200 billion, or about 6% of the GNP.

Service operations, however, do not always enjoy the same depth and quality of managerial controls found in the manufacturing environment. As a result, product management tools are often transferred unaltered to the service side. When a product is maturing in its life cycle, for instance, its service cycle is only beginning to generate steam. If a service manager uses this product life-cycle notion unthinkingly, the result can be an excessive spare parts inventory buildup, a self-defeating service pricing strategy, misallocation of field manpower resources, or a premature shutdown of product improvement programs.

> Some 70% of service income came as computer shipments were on the wane.

In this article I explore a way to look at maintenance control for products that have fairly long lives and require a good deal of service. This service life-cycle approach has been a fixture at Data General Corporation for several years.

The service life cycle covers the installed base of products needing maintenance. The installed base consists of the difference between total shipments and total "decay"—that is, the reduction in numbers still in use caused by product wear and discard, the customer's upgrading or switching to a substitute, or cannibalization of the product for spare parts.

Estimating the decay rate is very similar to calculating depreciation. Once a product is shipped to a customer there are measurable odds, in each year thereafter, that it will remain in the installed base. Data General found through experience that decay probabilities are reasonably stable by product class. By spreading the projected rate of decay of hardware shipped during the years of the product life cycle, Data General's forecasters could construct a good approximation of the total decay that would take place.

The difference between the cumulative shipments and this aggregated decay is in effect the service cycle. As the chart on timing shows, whereas the typical computer may reach its peak in shipments after only two or three years, the service cycle can easily last 15 years. An elevator may have a product cycle of only 10 years but a service cycle of 100 years!

At Data General, the service life cycle falls naturally into four phases:

1. Rapid growth—from the first shipment to the peak in the product cycle.

George W. Potts heads Occam Research Corporation, a microcomputer software development company in Wellesley, Massachusetts. For five years he was director of strategic planning for the service division of Data General Corporation.

2. Transition–from the peak in the product cycle to the peak in the service cycle.

3. Maturity–from the peak in the service cycle to the last shipment.

4. End of life–from the last shipment through the last unit in the installed base.

Almost 70% of service revenues for this product came in the last two phases. Four factors determined this phenomenon: distribution and installation delays, which combined to postpone service revenue flow well beyond that for products; the compounding effect of service price increases; product upgrade purchases, often producing more servicing opportunities and, therefore, more revenue; and certain service options (at premium prices) available later in the cycle.

For generation of service *profits* from installations, the last two phases were even more productive: more than 95% came during that period, which began two years after the product cycle had peaked. A main reason for this, of course, was the high revenue flow in those two phases. (See the chart contrasting the revenue and profits flows.)

Other factors were the front-end loading of many service costs, including repairer training, the product launch, and purchase of spare parts, and the sparse installation density of products (higher fixed costs per unit) in the early part of the service life cycle. In other words, about the time that manufacturing, development, and product marketing are leaving the scene, the service profit annuity is just beginning to kick in.

Often, however, there are forces working against this back-end loading of profitability. They include: (1) higher failure rates toward the end of a product's economic life, particularly for mechanical and electromechanical products; (2) the annual compounding effect of wage hikes for field repair personnel, particularly hikes not offset by service price increases; (3) mismanagement of spare parts acquisition, distribution, or repair; and (4) the loss, through neglect and field-force attrition, of repair skills.

In the following pages I take up the four phases of the service life cycle.

1. Rapid growth

At the outset, of course, expansion of the rate and extension of the length of the product sales surge are everybody's goals. There are many ways to gain an advantage through service at this time.

One way is by being very service-price aggressive against major competitors. The new product is perhaps being evaluated on a cost-of-ownership basis, so a trivial service price disadvantage can turn into a big sales headache. It is generally inadvisable to raise service prices during this phase.

A recently rediscovered wrinkle for many companies is the longer warranty, like Chrysler's seven years or 70,000 miles for its cars. These warranties appear to reduce service costs to zero during the period when discounting rates are the lowest in the cost-of-ownership analysis. (Obviously, the service cost is often buried in the product price anyway.) Such a ploy can also help the corporate image by carrying the implicit promise of high product quality.

During this period of product "infant mortality," ensure on-time distribution of enough spare parts to make prompt repairs. Vigorous stocking of field inventory can help build the reputation of the product and maintain the goodwill of "pioneering" customers.

Be ready to respond to complaints of product design or manufacturing process flaws. An effective early-warning system after the product launch will bring great rewards if it leads to engineering-out of the problems in later versions of the product. Moreover, when the buildup of spare parts reaches heavy proportions later, they will be of much higher quality. In this manner, Data General helped improve its product reliability at an annual compound rate of more than 10%.

The early-warning system may also call for upgrading and streamlining diagnostic procedures. Diagnostic methods for a new product that work well in the lab often do not in the field. A process whereby field input is quickly assimilated into diagnostics can pay huge dividends over the service life cycle.

Another aspect of response to customer complaints is training of field maintenance staff. It is better to err on the upside with expenditures on training (as well as on the high-

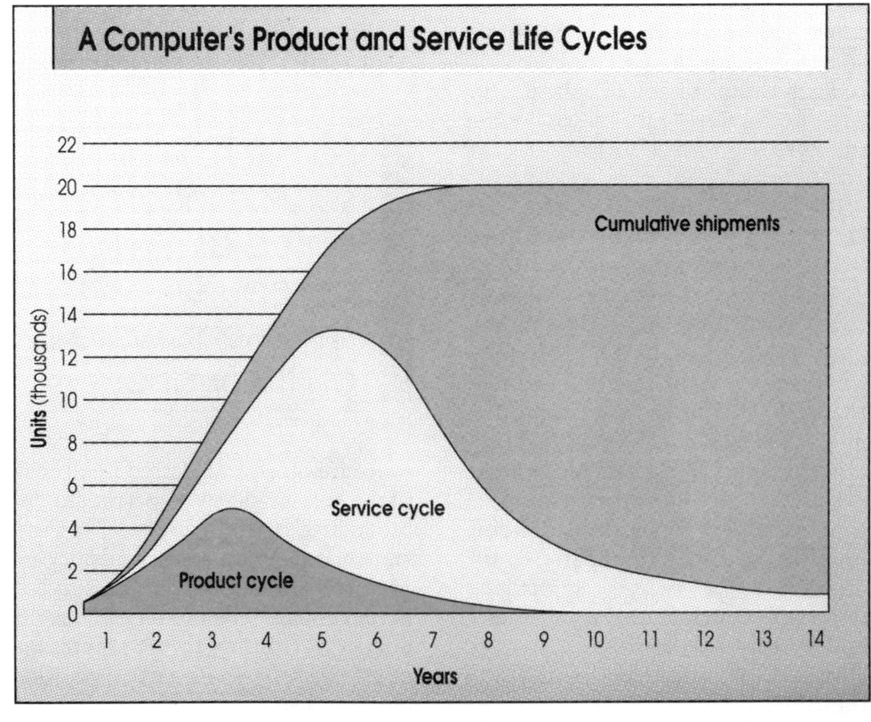

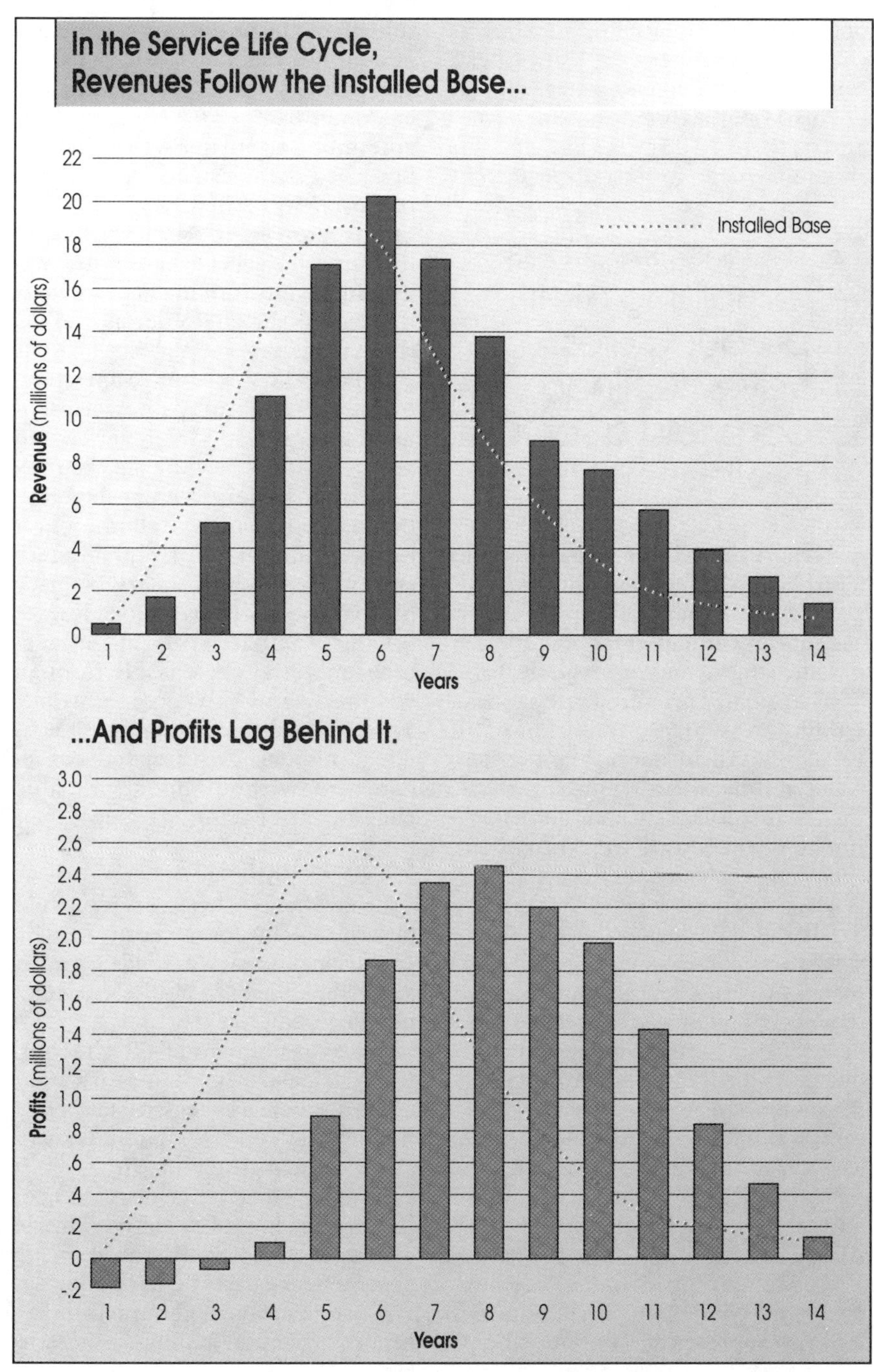

est quality tools and documentation) since continued growth in the residual installed base should easily absorb any apparent lavishness.

Early customers of a new product always appreciate aggressive technical activity of this kind. It alleviates fears of getting a lemon and substantiates their belief that they made the right choice. Satisfied customers may talk to friends and other customers, thus helping the vendor carry out one of the most effective and cheapest marketing techniques known – word of mouth.

2. Transition

During the interval between the time product shipments and service revenue have peaked, profit production from service is usually modest but growing. Whereas the theme of the first phase was "product growth at any cost," the theme of this stage is "controlling service resources." As revenues from the product decline and revenues from maintenance and service rise, management is faced with some critical issues.

One of them is whether to raise service prices. Usually these are not only justified – because the service buildup I described may make the service operation a money loser at this point – but also essential for continued effectiveness. A money-losing service operation is bound to get squeezed in the next budgeting session, which can lead to shortcuts in the initial stage of the next round of products. This, in turn, causes customer defections, which cause further budget cutbacks.

The solution lies in a fair price for service. A fair price often means annual price increases starting early in the transition phase and continuing through the service life cycle. The size of these increments should be tied to the product's failure rate and, to be fair, should seldom exceed the rate of inflation.

If failure rates are declining, it may be strategically smart to cut service prices for profitable products in the later stage of the service cycle. (Companies that don't offer service contracts – and therefore often don't differentiate service pricing by product – can still use the service cycle to set their spare parts pricing strategy.)

The acquisition of spare parts during this phase of the service cycle needs to be closely controlled. It's very easy to look down the road and extrapolate a promise of heavy material usage for a long time. But if the spare parts buildup continues after the growth rate of the service cycle starts to decelerate markedly, serious overstocking of spare parts will be the unhappy result. This will spoil the service profit potential. Therefore, a good fix on the rate of decay is important.

In 1985, field service logistics management at Data General set a policy of restricting purchases of repair material for any product not in phase 1 or 2 of its service cycle. In the three years since, service inventories have been reduced by as much as $30 million.

After the product cycle has peaked, some manufacturers unfortunately fail to maintain the reengineering activity they carried out in the period of fast sales growth. The service base is still growing, which presents opportunities to reduce product outages, material usage, or repair time. Phase 2 (and even phase 3) is not too late for installing engineering fixes that, though expensive to propagate in the field, still have many years of payback.

Data General has recently concentrated remedial reliability efforts on products no longer in the launch phase. In fiscal 1988 alone, this program is expected to save the service function upwards of $5 million.

Throughout this transition phase, the need for trained repair personnel continues to grow. Since by this time training should have become very efficient and effective, there is little point in being stingy with it now. Training more people than are currently needed may not be a bad idea so that enough maintenance experts will remain after attrition to handle the service requirements throughout the remainder of the product's service cycle.

3. Maturity

As with good wine or cigars, this is the time for the company to reap the rewards of patience. This is harvest time, bringing strong revenue and profit growth. Since all repair asset acquisitions should have been made by now, it will also be a time of very strong cash flow. Moreover, it is a period of the greatest equipment density, with the repair force being at its most proficient.

Unless there is unusually heavy competitive activity, the programmed service price increases should continue. If a product is attracting service competition because its service price is too high, pressure will remain on the manufacturer to make the product more reliable in order to reduce the cost of providing the service. The early part of the maturity phase is a good time to introduce premium service options – car dealers, for example, have a great deal more success selling service contracts on older cars than on new ones – or value-adding options, like the "disaster recovery" services some computer vendors offer.

This is not a time for spare parts aquisition. In fact, every effort should be made to start disposing of material through sale of it, through refurbishing old equipment for sale, through its demanufacture for components, or through scrapping.

> The installed base remaining after product sales have declined can yield a service profit annuity.

Some improvement programs can still be pursued for a product that has either a very high population or a very high failure rate. When these two circumstances occur together, the manufacturer still has an opportunity to recoup its investment in such an improvement effort.

4. End of life

While this term suggests that the product is ready for the glue factory, there is still plenty of life left for service revenue and profit generation. But since the item is no longer being manufactured, it may have vanished from headquarters' sight. Nevertheless, depending on the product cycle length and decay rate, as much as 50% of the equipment shipped may still be in use.

This remaining installed base not only yields a service profit annuity but also represents an opportunity for upgrading to newer products. If the manufacturer has prepared a migration path and has established a good service track record, customers may be quite ready to buy the next-generation product.

If service (or spare parts) price increases stopped in phase 3, a return of high failure rates at the end-of-life phase can justify a resumption, particularly for mechanical or electromechanical goods. (High failure rates at the front and back ends of the service cycle are often called the "bathtub effect.") Contract or spare parts price hikes made to offset poor service productivity, balance a defecting customer base, or support unprofitable manufacturing will backfire. But price rises designed to restore a reasonable return to a well-run maintenance function delivering high-quality services are not gouging. Such value pricing is in the best interest of the customer as well as the vendor.

If these hikes encourage upgrading to the manufacturer's newer products, then the service revenue and profit sacrifices become only temporary. If, however, product development has not established a clear migration choice for replacing an end-of-life product, a service price hike is obviously not a good idea.

Continued attrition of replacement material is advisable through scrapping and salvage operations. The only technical programs of benefit at this stage are those that cut repair time without any appreciable engineering or training expense.

Special challenges

Each phase of the service cycle poses problems for the entire service operation, but each extends its most severe challenge to a different business segment. In particular:

Phase 1 (and before) – The technical services unit must work very hard to ensure a successful launch of the product and the rapid remedy of any technical glitches in it.

Phase 2 – To avoid overstocking of inventory, logistics management must accurately call the turning point in spare parts demand.

Phase 3 – While generating premium and value-adding services to boost total revenue, the service marketing function has to assess the advisability of continued service price increases.

Phase 4 – Though the product may be passé in the minds of many at the company, field operations has to understand that it is not so in the eyes of customers. This function has to maintain a staff skilled with the product despite the attrition and relocation of personnel.

Reprint 88512

How to deal with this $7 billion to $10 billion problem–or opportunity

Gray Markets: Causes and Cures

by FRANK V. CESPEDES, E. RAYMOND COREY, and V. KASTURI RANGAN

An estimated $7 billion to $10 billion worth of products are sold every year in the United States outside manufacturers' authorized distribution channels. For these producers, controlling gray market distribution presents a serious problem. Or does it? Is it always a problem? When is it a symptom of more fundamental marketing issues? Can it also be an opportunity for a manufacturer?

Let's look at one situation. Some customers of a leading disk drive maker buy the computer component at volume discounts. But instead of "adding technical value to the products" (as the purchase agreement requires), the customers resell "raw" drives to major computer dealers, systems houses, OEMs, and end users. The manufacturer calls these customers "pseudo-OEMs" because they buy on OEM volume discount terms, operate on low gross margins, and undercut prices set by its authorized distributors.

In interviews, people at several levels in the company voiced concerns about the gray market, but often for different reasons. One person doing liaison work with distributors said, "When one of our distributors loses a sale to a pseudo-OEM, two things happen. First, the branch manager lets me know about it in seven different languages. Second, that distributor loses motivation to push our product."

A district manager expressed another viewpoint: "I get different stories from salespeople about pseudo-OEMs because some salespeople depend on them for a big portion of their quotas, and some do not. The result is tension in the office, often between people who share the same cubicle.

"Also, there's a vicious circle. In a business with short product life cycles, excess product can soon become a write-off if not sold. The result is that many salespeople feel pressure to sell to anybody, including

> When a distributor loses a sale to a gray marketer, the manufacturer hears about it in seven languages.

pseudo-OEMs, and this further erodes prices, fueling the whole thing all over again. I sometimes feel I'm being shafted by my own people, and I don't like it."

And this from a product manager: "Some of these gray marketers buy drives, stock them in a garage, and sell the lot to whoever they can find. But others are legitimate, important customers for our products who may be selling just 10% to 20% of their purchased drives without adding value. It's a tough situa-

The authors teach marketing at the Harvard Business School. For their forthcoming book on distribution-channel design and management, Going to Market: Distribution Systems for Industrial Products *(Harvard Business School Press), they did research at more than 60 companies, including IBM, GE, Becton-Dickinson, Control Data, and USX.*

tion. Short term, the gray market gives us good incremental business and it moves product. But longer term, we wind up competing with ourselves at a lower price."

The manager with P&L responsibility for these products, determined to "put the problem in perspective," said, "First our salespeople should emphasize to the customer that the gray marketer is not a reliable source of supply and that his units are not covered by our warranty. Salespeople can also emphasize that we sell the entire package the customer needs, whereas the pseudo-OEM cannot. Second, much of the gray activity is in products that major customers consider near-commodities. Capacity utilization is an important dimension of this business. Making money on drives requires high volume and these pseudo-OEMs often provide the incremental volume needed to cut our production costs significantly."

So the problem includes pricing policies, distributor relationships, sales force morale, customer service, and the measurements used to evaluate employee performance—which means that the various functional areas often look at the problem very differently. Once established, gray market sales can attract a constituency (as well as dedicated enemies) in the ranks of the manufacturer, making a coherent response hard to establish and sustain.

Whose Problem Is It?

As the responses at the disk drive maker show, there is no one answer to this question. For the manufacturer that uses distributors, a gray market usually poses several difficulties:

1. It upsets pricing stability among its distributors and can conflict with prices on direct sales, perhaps eroding them as well.

2. If prices and margins erode, the manufacturer usually finds it harder to maintain dealer support and point-of-sale services.

3. For many industrial goods, after-sale service is a prime source of revenue and earnings, often yielding a much higher margin than the sale itself. A gray market, however, tends to trigger unbundling of product sales from service income, causing an eventual drain on the product's revenue stream.

4. A gray market can create customer dissatisfaction. While caveat emptor might seem to be the right attitude toward buyers of gray market goods, many manufacturers find that product problems nonetheless are ultimately laid at their doorstep.

Recall, for example, the big gray market in IBM personal computers. The typical operator in this market provides no in-warranty repair service, so IBM's customer response center gets hundreds of telephone calls a day from owners of gray market PCs. IBM, unwilling to jeopardize its hard-earned and enviable reputation for attentive customer service, decided to direct these callers to company service shops that perform out-of-warranty as well as in-warranty repair. Unhappily for IBM, this posture naturally gives gray market sales an incentive by reducing the risks for end users. (Meanwhile, Big Blue's dealers clamor for it to "do something" about the "unfair" competition.)

> Gray marketers usually offer no extra service, so the manufacturer may bear the brunt of product complaints.

Even so, there may be benefits for a manufacturer in such a situation. For one thing, gray market outlets help keep products price competitive and widely available. Indeed, in the short term a gray market often appears to be exclusively the distributor's problem, as the producer enjoys a spurt in volume while its franchised resellers are left to lock horns with the under-the-counter price competition.

Secondly, as with disk drives, gray markets often consolidate around products with well-established price and performance criteria. These products, familiar to customers who may already have people trained in their use and repair, need less customer education or application development. So, from the manufacturer's viewpoint, gray market channels are an outlet for goods that have become price-sensitive "commodities" with little product differentiation.

Finally, the incremental sales volume can be very attractive in industries where scale economies and/or manufacturing throughput levels have a heavy impact on unit costs. For disk drives, the scale economies inherent in production oblige companies to work hard at driving costs down a steep learning curve. The volume represented by gray market channels often affects manufacturing plans and costs.

Considering the costs and perceived benefits, it is no wonder that our interviews at the disk drive manufacturer reflect ambivalence about the gray market. What some people in the field sales office see as a serious problem demanding immediate correction, many at headquarters see as less urgent and perhaps not entirely a problem.

Authorized distributors are usually less ambivalent; they see only lost sales. They are often paying for business development in the form of advertising, sales calls on potential customers, and demonstrations to showcase the product and its uses – only to find their accounts buying from a gray marketer who sells at a lower price but offers no services.

On the other hand, authorized distributors often supply gray marketers. Usually these distributors have taken advantage of the manufacturer's volume discount pricing schedules to order in quantities sufficient to qualify for the lower price. Then, having an oversupply, they sell some units to gray marketers outside their territories. In so doing, the distributors can continue to qualify for the volume discounts, thus lowering their cost of goods sold and inventory carrying costs, but create problems for other distributors in the manufacturer's network.

What Causes the Problem?

What factors allow unauthorized resellers to prosper? The answers are various, making generalizations from one industry to the next difficult. But certain patterns do emerge, and understanding these patterns is essential to crafting an appropriate response.

Supplier pricing policies are probably the most commonly cited factor. But for many manufacturers there are good reasons for pricing in favor of large orders. In disk drives, this policy partly reflects the scale and learning-curve economies inherent in large orders as well as the strategic importance of large customers for the company's cost structure, product development plans, and after-market replacement sales. Intense competition among drive vendors for big customers makes competitive pricing based on order size imperative, and the supplier that refuses to offer volume discounts will find itself left out in the cold.

In most industrial markets, negotiated or "bid" prices, lower than the manufacturer's book price, are common, especially for large orders. Bid customers often sell some of the merchandise to gray marketers, who in turn sell to other customers who would otherwise buy at the higher, book price. This is another way that price differentials, set for competitive reasons for different classes of accounts, help gray markets flourish.

International exchange rate fluctuations can cause price differentials and create arbitrage opportunities for gray marketers. In 1984 and 1985, when the dollar was strong and getting stronger against most other currencies, many products initially sold in one country found their way via agents to other countries as "parallel imports." For instance, into the United States gray marketers regularly imported Caterpillar excavators and loaders built in Scotland, Belgium, and Japan and priced to sell in local currencies. Even after shipping and insurance charges, these resellers won hosts of buyers among Caterpillar's U.S. dealers, who were paying 15% more for the same equipment made in Cat's domestic plants. At prices exceeding $200,000 for a single excavator, these price differentials sustained a thriving gray market.

Conversely in 1987 and 1988, with the dollar weak and the yen surging, a flourishing gray market formed in Japan based on some distributors' unauthorized reimportation of Japanese products from the United States and other countries, like Canon cameras and Panasonic cordless phones.

As more manufacturers adopt global product strategies, with uniform goods and even multilingual packaging for world markets, international gray markets in many goods may have a bright future. Batteries and other devices are a case in point.

Reseller cost differentials can be of two kinds: differences between the operating costs of full-line, full-service franchised resellers versus narrow-line, low-service discounters; and cost differences created by a product line's place in a reseller's strategy.

Franchised resellers usually offer important services like advertising, product demonstrations, and point-of-sale as well as postsale services. These functions cost the franchised reseller money, of course. Gray marketers enjoy a free ride on these services; many even honor manufacturers' discount coupons and coordinate their activities with manufacturers' promotions as a means of skimming the benefits generated by the regular channel's marketing efforts.

Ironically, a manufacturer's commitment to customer service sometimes aggravates the situation. In the early 1980s, IBM imposed stringent requirements on its authorized PC dealers; they had to allocate a certain amount of store space for product demonstrations, keep a certain number of store personnel trained in its equipment, and maintain stock parts sufficient to sustain an acceptable level of customer service. IBM's aim was to build a store of value in its product franchise and, through value-added services, encourage brand preference and win repeat business.

> Supplier pricing policies, especially discounts, often open the way to the graying of a market.

Situation in Flux

As this article went to press, developments had surfaced in Washington that could affect a manufacturer's ability to terminate authorized dealers for certain reasons. These developments, however, tug in opposite directions.

The Supreme Court ruled in May that a manufacturer that stops selling to a cut-price outlet, in response to complaints from competing, full-price stores, does not necessarily violate antitrust laws. This ruling seemingly introduces an important caveat to a 1911 ruling that since then has generally guided manufacturer-distributor relations in the United States. That ruling called resale price maintenance policies by a supplier "per se" (that is, automatically) illegal.

The 1988 ruling doesn't overturn the 1911 ruling and is limited to nonprice agreements between producers and distributors. But the majority opinion held that it is sometimes "legitimately and competitively useful" for manufacturers to curb competition among resellers when circumstances like free-rider effects inhibit the provision of necessary product services to full-price resellers.

Gray market operators are, of course, unauthorized distributors and so already stand outside the province of this decision. But it may affect manufacturers' ability to drop some authorized dealers in order to bolster their full-service dealers.

A bill in the U.S. Senate (a companion to the one already passed by the House) tugs the other way. It would make it easier for discounters to bring price-fixing cases against manufacturers and full-price retailers. The Justice Department announced its opposition, but the bill reportedly has substantial support in Congress.

At any rate, as this article argues, gray markets usually encompass factors other than pricing policies. While changes in the legal framework that govern channel relations are indirectly relevant, gray markets are likely to remain a real challenge for manufacturers of many kinds of industrial and consumer goods.

Retailers like 47th Street Photo in New York City, however, did not meet IBM's conditions, while other unsanctioned resellers of IBM products ran essentially cash-and-carry operations. Through their low-service/low-price selling strategy, they appropriated a big portion of the value IBM and its dealers had built, thus lowering the worth of the franchise for authorized distributors. As one dealer lamented, "It's tough to compete with someone whose major selling expense is a phone bill."

Differences in distributors' selling strategies can also sustain a gray market. A reseller that views a product as an incremental addition to its line may not allocate overhead in pricing the product, whereas a reseller that considers the product a staple of its line is likely to account for such costs in its pricing. Loss leaders are an extreme instance of this situation. Heavy advertising of a cut-rate price for a popular brand can be a big drawing card to get customers into the store. There the lure of regularly marked-up merchandise (often unbranded) awaits them. Loss-leader tactics to build traffic are common among gray marketers, if only because they often cannot count on frequent availability of the particular brand.

Supplier franchise practices can also foster gray markets. When demand is strong, suppliers often discourage intrabrand price competition among their accredited resellers. This creates a price umbrella likely to draw unfranchised dealers into the market.

Sometimes suppliers allow "block" franchising of their products, in which a franchisor in turn franchises all dealers in that chain. But the larger franchisees often want to buy direct from the manufacturer, which is obliged to honor the agreement with the parent and refuse them. To avoid the markup the parent generally takes in selling products to its dealers, the larger franchisees may buy on the gray market. IBM and other computer makers have encountered this situation in PCs.

Contract terms by which manufacturers rationalize production scheduling or smooth inventory levels can sustain gray markets. A common feature of industrial contracts is a returns penalty. In standard industry fashion, for example, the disk drive maker's contracts call for delivery of a given quantity of drives over a specified period (usually one to two years) and a charge of 40% of the order price for cancellation of an order less than 45 days before the scheduled shipment date, or 15% for cancellation 46 to 90 days before shipment.

In this business, lot size is important to production costs, and the company enforces these stiff stipulations to keep its scheduling efficient and its production costs competitive. But disk drives are a business in which demand fluctuates widely from quarter to quarter and new product introductions are frequent. So customers often find it hard to forecast precisely over a one- to two-year span. Therefore, some customers ship "excess" drives to gray marketers as a way to avoid cancellation charges.

In some industries, including disk drives, dynamic product performance improvements go hand in hand with downdrafts in prices caused by hot competition among suppliers. Falling prices make customers, as well as distributors, more price sensitive as they try to protect their cost structures against competition. So they willingly sign large-order contracts that qualify for the biggest discounts. At the same time, the fast pace of product introductions is increasing the risk of perceived product obsolescence over the one- or two-year lives of the purchase contracts. So customers try to find ways–perhaps through gray marketers–to escape the cancellation charges.

As for the manufacturer, this situation puts pressure on product management, operations staff, and especially the sales force to move the factory's output fast. Consequently, they may be inclined to condone sales to gray marketers, and the result can be a vicious circle. Note, however, that gray markets arise out of sound business practices and distribution strategy designed to respond to the manufacturers' constraints and opportunities: rationalization of production schedules, selective distribution to maintain the value and integrity of the sales network, block franchising to gain access to powerful distributors, and quantity discount schedules.

When the sparring between manufacturer and distributor becomes intense–the pages of trade publications often ring with accusations and counter-accusations–it is useful to recognize the irony of the situation. Even though good business practices can lead to a very undesirable outcome, they should not necessarily be abandoned when the manufacturer is evaluating the options for dealing with the problem.

What Are the Options?

In answer, manufacturers generally adopt one or more of the following responses. Each has its logic and its limitations.

Disenfranchisement of offenders is a stock (and emotionally satisfying) response. In an effort to identify suppliers to unauthorized dealers, Lotus Development Corporation recorded the bar-code numbers of its popular 1-2-3 software packages as they were shipped out. Meanwhile, Lotus operatives checked print ads to locate unauthorized dealers and occasionally had shoppers buy the company's products from mail-order houses and other gray outlets. Eventually Lotus eliminated from its list those distributors doing business with gray marketers and put a temporary freeze on agreements with new distributors.

Such moves send loud signals of commitment to distributors who abide by the terms of the franchise agreement. These signals often are a response to complaints from them. In the case of full-service dealers, the manufacturers will listen to those complaints, for they may need the distributors' market development help.

Tracking down offenders, however, costs money. Lotus spent more than $100,000 on the system to label the product and monitor its sales. Moreover, the manufacturer that selectively disenfranchises dealers runs the risk of being sued.

A one-price-for-all policy can eliminate an important source of arbitrage and allow the supplier to reassert a measure of channel control. Here is how one manager in the disk drive situation rationalized the policy: "Since it's different prices for different quantities that fuel the gray market, let's eliminate the differences. The distribution channel that's most efficient, and that can sell our product at the lowest realizable gross margin, should gain strength over time. And that's the channel we want to use to get our products to market."

But this policy often means sale of most of the output at lower prices to *all* customers, big or small, regardless of transaction costs. Furthermore, this strategy often forecloses valid price discrimination opportunities among classes of customers who are buying very different benefits in the same product. While price may be the main criterion for some customers, for others continuity of supply and aid in application development may be more important.

A meaningful one-price-for-all strategy must also include a way to reward the full-service dealers in the network. They usually have other supply options available. Most systems for direct payment to these dealers for the extra services they furnish are as financially and administratively cumbersome as procedures for tracking sales to unauthorized dealers.

Finally, as the disk drive managers' comments indicate, this strategy is a Darwinian "survival of the fittest" approach. While it may be the answer in the short term, in the long term it can limit the manufacturer's access to new and growing market segments and discourage distributors from supporting a manufacturer that refuses to recognize differences in distributors' market power. This strategy also may not eliminate arbitrage opportunities (since cost differentials and differing reseller strategies also give rise to gray markets) and may make it harder for the manufacturer to alter its distribution strategy as changing market conditions require.

Adding distributors (perhaps former gray market distributors) to the network can be a solution. By limiting circulation of a popular item to a few dealers, the supplier may inadvertently have created demand that can be satisfied only through transshipment to gray outlets. Or the supplier's dealer service criteria may be unnecessarily (or unrealistically) high, discouraging dealers that service price-sensitive market segments from joining the supplier's network. Franchising more distributors may give the supplier better control over the flow of its product to market.

The supplier must be careful, however, not to put itself in the middle of disputes among distributors over turf. Moreover, when customer bases overlap, the supplier's franchise loses value, and dealers lose incentive to provide service and sales support. Important dealers may switch to a competing line with less intensive distribution. Tinkering with relationships with channel mainstays by adding distributors can be a very dangerous business.

What Can You Do?

For the manufacturer, every option has costs and risks, but the status quo is also unacceptable. What, then, to do?

First, get accurate and timely *information*. In our research we found that managers were often woefully uninformed about the magnitude or channel dynamics of gray markets for their goods. As we have seen, the standard sources of market information, field salespeople and distributors, can be unreliable. Recall the district sales manager for the disk drive maker who reported that salespeople in the same branch office gave him different stories. And, as we have seen, distributors often have a foot on each side of the street.

Therefore, the supplier often must create, or bolster, alternative data sources. Product serial numbers, warranty cards, and factory rebate programs can help track the product's movement to unsanctioned resellers and generate information valuable in gauging the magnitude of these sales. As transaction volume rises, collection of such data on a timely basis can become costly. But the information is likely to be helpful to the company's other marketing programs, and the expense of gathering the information should be viewed in this light.

Another thing to do is reexamine the company's *distribution policies* and agreements. Unlike Gertrude Stein's unvarying rose, a distributor is not a distributor is not a distributor. The networks of most suppliers have distributors that perform various functions—which implies different operating costs for the distributor and different value-added opportunities for the particular product line.

Recognizing these differences, some manufacturers classify their distributors into "A," "B," and "C" categories, using criteria like level of sales performance, share of the local market, number of the supplier's product lines carried, services provided, and proportion of the reseller's total sales attributable to the supplier's product (a rough measure of the distributor's stake in providing needed support services).

In turn, the suppliers structure franchise agreements that extend higher levels of support to their full-service, broad-line distributors in product allocation, merchandising support, lead referrals from the supplier's salespeople, and discounts reflecting different levels of value added by the distributor. These suppliers look to full-service distributors to support product introductions and to service the high end of the market, while relying on low-service distributors for those market segments that are concerned mostly with price.

These manufacturers also generally avoid block franchising on the grounds that what they gain at first in lower selling expenses (usually for a new product line) they can soon lose in the form of gray market action and dilution of channel effectiveness. Square D, the supplier of electrical equipment, refuses to make block franchising agreements with big retail chains or industrial distributors. Instead, it franchises distributors on a location-by-location basis, even when working with large, multilocation distributors. Square D stresses big inventory commitments by a select number of channel elements and pull-through selling efforts by its own sales force aimed at generating end-user demand to be serviced by a particular distributor. This strategy is easier to carry out with one-outlet franchises.

The manufacturer should also reexamine the parts of its franchise agreements covering *reseller service support*. There are two related questions to be answered: What added operating costs does the reseller take on in furnishing the point-of-sale or postsale services called for in the agreement? What are the options, and what would be the costs, in shifting these services to other points in the channel? After analysis, the manufacturer may find that after-sale maintenance and repair service can be performed more efficiently at locations it owns or by third-party service providers—instead of at dealer locations—because these services demand large parts inventories and specially trained people.

Pricing is another area needing close attention. The objective should be to fashion quantity discount schedules that don't create incentives for customers to overorder and later sell on the gray market. This is easier said than done, but attention to quantity schedules can help. For example, manufacturers give gray marketers a welcome opening when the pricing brackets in a schedule are wide (that is, a single price holds for a wide range of order quantities).

The disk drive manufacturer–pricing mainly on the basis of production costs–sets the same unit price (about $500 each) on orders ranging from 1,000 to 2,500 units and contracts ranging from $525,000 to $1.3 million. The wide price breaks permit some customers to buy in quantity, use many of the drives for legitimate purposes, and still sell a large number on the gray market at prices higher than the purchase price but lower than authorized distributors' prices. In such a situation, narrower pricing brackets tying unit prices more closely to order volumes can mitigate the problem.

> One possible outcome of facing up to the problem: rethinking your marketing strategy.

Coordinated administration of bid and book pricing is also essential in preventing arbitrage opportunities. This requires accurate, timely information about competitors' pricing and resellers' market (not just list) prices, and the ability to handle price-exception requests efficiently. One major manufacturer of electrical equipment receives 30 to 40 price requests daily, usually for quotations on materials for large construction projects. Pricing in this highly competitive marketplace demands a fast response and, since most orders are filled through distributors, coordination between bid and list price. The company maintains a headquarters telemarketing group of specialists who, with the aid of computer programs, calculate job requirements, monitor prices in various markets, and send quotes to field salespeople or distributors bidding on projects.

Listen to the manager of this group: "We maintain current records on all pricing actions by trading area, whether we won or lost each order, and the price received (if we know it). We check to see who is the competition. We decide whether the price multiplier is out of line for that size of order. Finally, and this is especially important, we look at the product mix. If it includes items where we've got a low cost position and extra plant capacity, we're inclined to be aggressive. Also, when we respond to price-exception requests initiated through our distributors, we always quote the same price to two or more distributors bidding on the same project."

Through this procedure, the company coordinates bid and book prices, minimizes arbitrage opportunities for big customers or distributors, and monitors activity on big orders (those most vulnerable to gray market activity). The company can also tailor distributors' price-exception requests to the level of value-added support they are expected to supply, and thus protect its full-line, full-service distributors on large, price-sensitive orders.

Another thing management can do is reassess its *marketing priorities* in light of the gray market question. If the reassessment confirms, say, that increasing market share is a key objective, then the extent to which the gray market makes the product more available and augments volume becomes important in responding (or not) to distributors' complaints.

One company, intending to introduce several products through its normal channels, decided to place special weight on maintaining good dealer relations and so adjusted its pricing to dealers–despite the healthy volume represented by gray market sales.

It goes without saying that the manufacturer's *internal measurements* for evaluating employees' performance should promote pursuit of the organization's objectives. But when a gray market intrudes on the normal channels, the measurement system can sow internal discord. At the disk drive company, sales bonuses are based on achieving quotas. Depending on whether a particular salesperson sold to pseudo-OEMs, the gray market is a help or a hindrance in reaching quota. The same holds true for district sales managers, whose bonuses are based on total district volume. Manufacturing managers are measured on plant efficiency, and to them gray market sales often represent desirable incremental volume. Since manufacturing, marketing, and sales are all affected, all these functions should be represented in setting priorities and choosing a course of action.

What Are Customers Saying?

Because a gray market causes turmoil internally and in distribution channels, a manufacturer can lose sight of the ultimate arbitrator in this situation: the customer. When a substantial gray market develops, what are customers saying to the manufacturer about its product? The answer may force management to revise its marketing and distribution strategy.

A gray market often reflects the maturation of a product in its life cycle. As customers become familiar with a product category, they tend to place less value on the support programs offered by the manufacturer or its distributors. In their buying they become increasingly price sensitive. What they once purchased as a system they may unbundle into discrete purchases and then seek out channels that sell on price while furnishing little product support.[1] A gray market often signals the emergence of this group of customers. If authorized resellers require customers to buy a package of product and support features, the gray market gets added impetus.

Meanwhile, the manufacturer is trying to keep its distribution network intact. For the producers as well as distributors, exclusive or highly selective distribution arrangements have been advantageous, the former getting support service (often vital in a technical product like disk drives) and the latter enjoying limited competition. Small wonder that changes in distribution arrangements lag behind changes in customers and customer behavior.

Any move the manufacturer makes at this point is risky. If, say, it wants to boost direct sales to large, price-sensitive buyers or reach new market segments that purchase differently, it will run headlong into the interests of its existing channels. If the same distributors handle a manufacturer's product portfolio, action taken to deal with a gray market in one product line can affect the whole portfolio.

In this respect, gray markets often point to a larger issue: the limiting commitments at the heart of many distribution strategies. When a market is entered or a product introduced, elements of distribution strategy tend to cohere around the particular market circumstances and corporate objectives held at the time. As markets evolve, new distribution strategies are required. But each dimension of the existing arrangement tends to cement established patterns, making it difficult for the manufacturer to alter its channel strategy.

Yet inaction can be worse for the manufacturer–as the disk drive company was discovering at the time of our investigation. A fundamental alteration in distribution strategy is often necessary to attack the root causes of a gray market. Timely information about gray market activity, close attention to franchising and pricing policies, and coherent internal measurement systems can give an organization the managerial tools required to distinguish symptom from cause and stimulate efforts to make the hard choices implied by a gray market.

1. For an analysis of changing buyer behavior over the product life cycle, see F. Stewart DeBruicker and Gregory L. Summe, "Make Sure Your Customers Keep Coming Back," HBR January-February 1985, p. 92.

Reprint 88403

Getting the Product Right

SPECIAL REPORT

Customize Your Product Development

How to decide between a crash program and a perfect product.

by Edward G. Krubasik

In the typewriter business, as in many others, product life cycles have collapsed at an alarming rate. Mechanical typewriters had a 30-year life cycle; electromechanical ones had a life cycle of less than 10 years; and electronic machines have been quickly replaced by word processors and personal computers. When the competitive environment changes so rapidly, development time becomes critical. Companies have to respond quickly to each new product that enters the market. Getting the product to market fast is the name of the game.

But being fast to market is no advantage if you choose the wrong technology or create a design that customers don't want. In fact, when markets and technologies are uncertain, there is good reason to delay important choices as long as possible, gathering more information, testing everything in sight, and moving to product launch only when success is nearly guaranteed. This is especially true when development budgets are large in proportion to the company's resources, as in aircraft manufacture or computer-system design.

The opportunity cost of missing a fast-moving market window and the risk of entering a market with the wrong product pull managers in opposite directions. But in practice, the danger for managers lies not so much in their being whipsawed between these competing demands as in their tendency to act as if no such tension existed. Too often, managers respond with the same development strategy without considering the context in which they find themselves. In a relentless, pressure-cooker business environment, managers tend to fall back, by intuition or reflex, on a kind of generic "one size fits all" approach to new product development.

In product development, one size doesn't fit all.

But one size does *not* fit all. The best way to organize for successful innovation depends on the opportunity cost and entry risk in that instance. When market requirements are clear and competitors' plans are obvious, for example, development should have a markedly different focus than when user needs are in flux or when a core technology isn't working out or, for that matter, when competitors launch products sooner than expected.

Think of IBM's development of the personal computer. Demand was forecast to grow at 60% a year; companies like Apple and Tandy were controlling market developments and were beginning to cut into IBM's traditional office market; and there was the serious risk that if IBM were too slow, it might suffer an irrecoverable loss of share. Opportunity costs were high. At the same time, development costs, which were likely to run about $10 million, were quite low in proportion to IBM's equity value of some $18 billion. Development risk was also low: there was no real mystery about market requirements (the appeal of competitors' products told the tale), and the relevant technologies were available and easy to master or purchase.

Now, compare that with Boeing's development of the 767. With the market for a 727 replacement not yet crystallized but fairly predictable, there was still plenty of time to capture share and shape the market with product launch decisions–in other words, opportunity costs were low. By contrast, the enormous cost of R&D for the 767 relative to Boeing's equity value and the great uncertainty surrounding both technology and customer preferences added up to an immense entry risk.

Would it have made sense to manage the PC and the 767 identically? Of course not. To be sure, there are some general guidelines for managing development projects that are useful in any context. Shortening lead time and cutting expenses are

Edward G. Krubasik is a director in the Munich office of McKinsey & Company and is a leader of its technology practice.

always desirable goals in product development, especially for companies that depend on technology-driven products and that strive to cross technological discontinuities. Also, successful development programs suggest—and common sense confirms—that it is always helpful to:

- ☐ Set up separate, cross-functional business teams to conduct in-house development programs, especially when speed is important.
- ☐ Be sure all functions are represented in—and contributing to—all phases of the development process to ensure coordination among marketing, development, and manufacturing.
- ☐ Be selective in choosing project staff; do not just delegate the project to an existing department.
- ☐ Focus on early, tangible results, even when the results simply lead to a better understanding of where problems lie.
- ☐ Orient the efforts toward users, and keep in close touch with lead customers as the product is developed.

> When opportunity costs are high, a crash program makes sense.

In and of themselves, these goals and guidelines, however laudable, do not constitute a development strategy tailored to the particular mix of threats posed by opportunity cost and entry risk in a given situation. The simple but often forgotten truth is that *not all product development is alike*. Each situation has a different context, and these differences in context imply different managerial actions.

To make sense of the development strategies as well as the managerial skills and approaches best suited to any development effort, it is necessary first to understand the situation. One way to rationalize the process is to use a map of product development to show various contexts in which product development can occur (see accompanying map). Although the map may not cover all conceivable industry situations, it applies well to company-specific "new product" situations where entry risk and opportunity cost are the most important variables. Managers can better select the appropriate strategic choice by finding the place on the map that corresponds to the degree of entry risk and the opportunity costs the company faces for a given product.

The crash program

When entry risk is low but opportunity cost is high, it's important to manage the innovation process to get to market as quickly as possible. A *crash program* focusing on development speed rather than risk reduction is the best bet. In its development of the PC, for example, IBM cut down overall time to a level typical for "garage" companies—and to just one-third of the time IBM normally takes to develop its large systems products. What did IBM do differently?

With the PC, IBM concerned itself primarily with systems design. The company could have made the components in-house as it usually does. But because that would have taken longer than outsourcing them, IBM went with outside vendors instead. In fact, the only IBM components in the product were the keyboard and the main computer board. Even the microprocessor came from outside.

To make this approach work, IBM set tough standards for suppliers. For instance, Microsoft, which provided the operating system, had to deliver the system an unprecedented three months before the product was shipped. IBM established aggressive quality control routines for suppliers to follow and monitored them on site. It also supplied support systems and gave prototypes of the PC to software houses so they could write applications software quickly.

The PC was the first product IBM developed with only the domestic market in mind (it planned to redesign it later for international markets). Also, it offered only a 48K memory version and a basic kit of peripherals—in stark contrast to its usual practice of trying to cover the waterfront with every conceivable option. The point again was to cut development time to a minimum and get a foothold in the market.

One last feature of the PC development process was the "zero procedures" approach. IBM gave the development group complete freedom in product planning, kept corporate interference to a minimum, and allowed the use of streamlined, relatively informal management systems—as opposed to its usual eight-phase product-planning approach designed to reduce risk in the development of its large systems.

IBM's focus on systems design, core market segments, and simplified organization and control suited the PC situation. A different approach might have been appropriate in a smaller company where entering the market with the wrong product or a serious technology problem could devastate the business. But for IBM, development risk was low. Opportunity cost was the greater concern. That situation, represented by the top left corner of the product development map, called for a crash program. IBM framed its development effort in just that way and then approached product design, market segmentation, and organizational structure accordingly.

Getting it 100% right

Had Boeing tried to develop its 767 the same way IBM did its PC, the company might well have gone broke before it ever brought a plane to market. After all, when just one thing goes wrong in a crash program, everything can grind to a halt, causing massive—and irrecoverable—cost overruns. Given the high costs inherent in developing something as complex as an airplane, Boeing couldn't afford to make mistakes. If the product fell short in any way, it would mean financial disaster.

> IBM uses an eight-phase process for many products—but not for the PC.

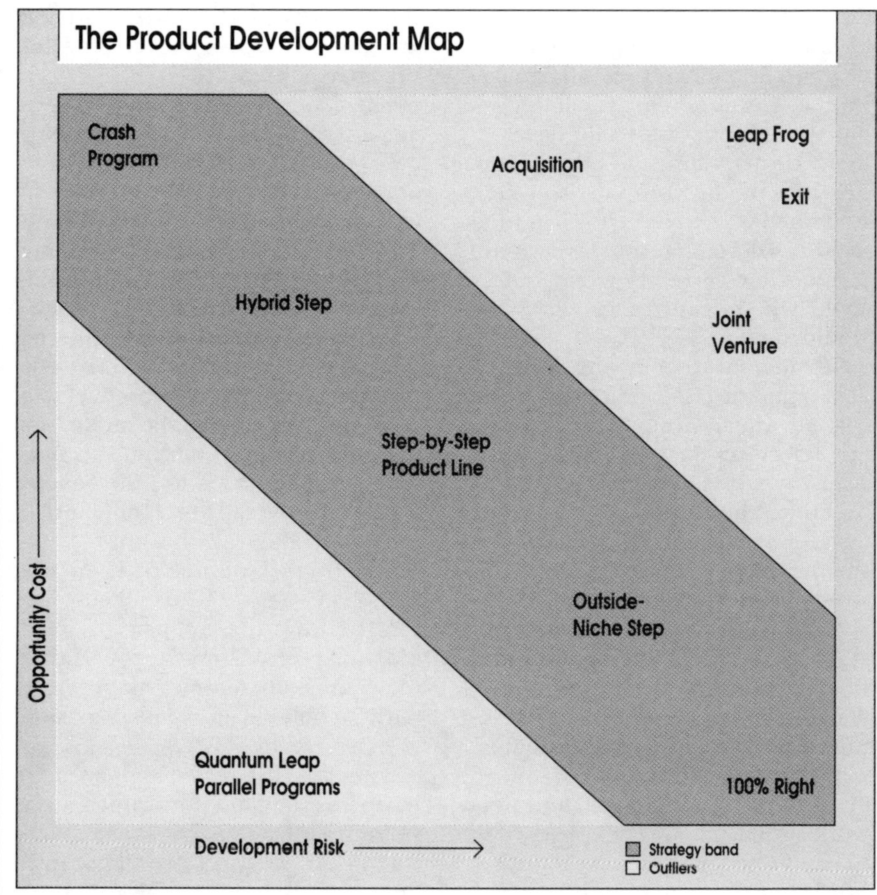

So unlike IBM, Boeing faced immense development risk. Also, unlike IBM, Boeing's opportunity costs were low. Although Boeing had missed the 300- to 350-seat market by underestimating the appeal of a new Airbus product, the 727 replacement market was thoroughly predictable, if not yet fully developed. Thus Boeing had to be able to get to the market quickly once it officially announced the new plane because Airbus would be close on its heels. But it could afford to move slowly during the upstream phase of development.

> For Boeing, getting it right was more important than doing it fast.

At the time Boeing began the long-term effort that led to the 767, its goal was to produce concepts and technology for a "next generation" plane. The idea was to combine a smaller size than the Airbus A300 with a longer range. But that was where the agreement ended. Should it be a 180-seater or a 200 or a 220? Should it have two engines or three? Should its cockpit be designed for two or three people? Everyone in Boeing and its customers had an opinion—all different.

Beyond design issues, there were also important unanswered questions about technology. To justify a new generation of aircraft, Boeing would have to improve operating costs significantly, and that meant advances in aerodynamics, digital avionics, engines, supercritical wing design, and both structural and surface materials. And it would have to design its new plane without knowing precisely where oil prices would be several years out and, thus, which operational performance targets were most important. Worse still, mounting so huge an effort across so many different leading-edge technologies would cost about $1.5 billion—more than the total value of the company's equity at the time!

Boeing's challenge—represented by a position at the lower right corner of the map—was not to keep from missing a fast-moving market window but to be certain that the product was *100% right* at market launch. What did Boeing do?

First, it completed the development of all new technologies in the early stages of the R&D process. When the 767 finally was specified, there was virtually nothing untested aboard. The supercritical wing, for example, had undergone 11,000 hours of wind-tunnel tests before program go-ahead, and 24,000 hours by 1983 as compared with some 10,000 hours that the Airbus wing had endured at that time. Digital avionics had been flown in testbeds—a 737 advanced cockpit and the Y14 NASA research plane.

Second, Boeing worked closely with customers, having them review nine different airplane concepts and even inviting their design teams on site to make sure that the basic design concept was right and that individual preferences were addressed.

And third, Boeing made extensive use of CAD/CAM to improve design quality, cut prototype development time, and hold down the cost of later design changes.

This extensive effort so early in the development of a next generation aircraft took guts. During the upstream phase, Boeing had roughly 400 engineers at work (boosted to 1,000 just before go-ahead), while Airbus had only 50 to 80. But the effort paid off. Although Boeing and Airbus announced new products within days of each other, the 767 got to market a full eight months ahead of the Airbus 310—a lead that translated into substantial sales.

The in-betweens

The IBM and Boeing examples are extreme cases for which the appropriate managerial response is fairly straightforward. In each, only one of the two key strategic variables matters. What happens, though, when *both* development risk and opportunity cost are significant? Just throwing resources at the effort will not work, nor will focusing attention solely on a stretched-out, upstream development process.

If customers demand, or competitors provoke, a new generation of product before the technology or market sorts itself out, neither a crash program nor an effort to get things 100% right is appropriate. One approach responds to opportunity cost, the other to development risk. Neither attempts to address both factors at once. What do you do then?

L.M. Ericsson preempted competitors with a switching device that was only partially digitized.

When Northern Telecom announced its "digital world" concept for central office switches, U.S. customers were so enthusiastic about the new technology that they stopped buying analog systems. This slump in sales made painfully clear the opportunity cost of not moving quickly to digital products. It even forced the company to push ahead its development of the DMS 100 switch by a whole year.

With AT&T/Western Electric dominating the market in analog systems, Northern Telecom saw a competitive advantage for its products by introducing digital technology and felt keenly the opportunity cost of further delaying its introduction. Long before its announcement of digital world had shifted customer preferences, the company's sales of analog switches had been dwindling and its main customer, Bell Canada, had signaled its readiness to go digital.

At the same time, there were big technical hurdles still to be crossed: the development of a family of local, transit, and international switches, of advanced semiconductor technology for access and filter-codec chips, of high-density packaging, and of a new, high-level software language, Protel. These technical challenges put a sizable price tag on the development effort—some $200 million, nearly half the company's equity. And moving onto such novel ground in switch design meant there was no comfortable certainty at the outset about which features the DMS 100 would include.

What should a company do when development risk and opportunity cost are equally important? Northern Telecom's answer was to adopt a *step-by-step* approach. The company broke the immensely complex development task into a series of smaller, more manageable steps. Instead of going for the local DMS 100 switch right away, the company started with the development of a PBX (private branch exchange), which gave it a base for understanding important new technologies, digitization techniques, advanced programming languages, and network design.

The next step was to produce a full-function transit switch using Protel and embodying the modular architecture essential to larger switches. The final step was to make the major technical leap to the DMS 100 itself, with its integrated filter-codec chips for each subscriber line. An important by-product of working toward the DMS 100 in this fashion was the cash flow the intermediate products generated along the way—an effective contribution to reducing opportunity cost.

Treating this effort as a step-by-step sequence of more limited challenges allowed Northern Telecom to contain its development risk and keep development costs from going through the roof. Many complex, big-jump efforts tend to get out of hand and start eating cash. By contrast, Northern Telecom held complexity in check by solving one set of problems at a time. Throughout the process, the company worked closely with its lead customer, Bell Canada, to make sure its performance goals matched customer requirements. That allowed the company to target its resources on what really mattered and not waste money developing unnecessary features.

There are, of course, many shades of gray in product development. Not every case falls neatly at one extreme or the other—or halfway in between. Other circumstances in which both cost and risk are present to varying degrees call for modification of the step-by-step approach.

When opportunity cost matters, but less so than entry risk, there is merit to testing the new product in a market niche outside the producer's normal range of activities. This *outside niche* approach has the benefit of reducing overall development risk without exposing the innovating company to troubles in its usual markets or among its usual customers. It allows the company to keep mature technology in profitable mass markets as long as possible without holding up experimentation with new technology.

Sony did this in the audio-studio business. Sony did not immediately go from a full 32-channel analog console to a 32-channel digital console. First it introduced a digital master console with 8 channels. This "proof of concept" machine was sold to the production studios that mixed digitally encoded sound tracks onto compact discs. There was no pressing need for it (analog would have done just as well here), but some musicians did not want their digitally recorded material touched by analog at all. Here, of course, was a chance to introduce a new technology with low risk and carry out a market test of digital signal processing.

When, on the other hand, entry risk matters, but less so than opportunity cost, there may be pressure to enter the main market directly with a *hybrid* product. Sweden's L.M. Ericsson, the telecom supplier, used this approach with its first AXE 10, a local switch that was only partially digitized. For European manufacturers of switching equipment, the home market was quite small and market share was spread over many national markets where purchase decisions were infrequent.

Ericsson therefore faced much greater opportunity cost than Northern Telecom did. If a competitor introduced its switch first, Ericsson would effectively be locked out of its markets for 20 years or so. This threat made it important to tie as many markets into Ericsson's new AXE system as early as possible. But while the company had to get to market promptly, it had little experience with digital switches.

To pass this test, Ericsson offered a new, full local switch that was at first only partially digitized. By slowing the move toward fully digitized switches, Ericsson cut development risk. But more important, Ericsson got the AXE to the market quickly, substantially reducing opportunity costs. Indeed, within four years some 32 countries opted for the AXE digital switch.

The outliers

When both opportunity cost and entry risk are extremely high, it may no longer make sense to attempt development work entirely in-house. In this case, *joint ventures* are the best way to go. If the risk of missing a market window is so high that even a joint venture cannot get to the market fast enough, then an *acquisition* may be necessary to provide a product immediately.

Covering present markets with the acquired product line can help focus in-house development work on the next-generation product. This *leapfrog* approach is precisely what one European company did after losing its lead in the first generation in the ultrasound business. It bought a U.S. company in order to stay in the game but directed its own R&D toward follow-on generation products. There is, of course, the further possibility that both risk and cost may be so overwhelming that the only reasonable course is to give up and *exit*, as Philips, the Dutch telecom supplier, did when it sold its public switching business to AT&T.

A happier possibility is that both risk and cost may prove so low that the innovating company has the luxury of commanding the rules of the game. At least in its engineering-oriented businesses, Hewlett-Packard, for example, is in the enviable position of being able to start up a multitude of *quantum leap parallel programs* with extremely high performance targets. This approach virtually guarantees market acceptance. It reduces the technical risk by running a number of small development efforts and weeding out those that are less attractive (in terms of potential sales) or that are technically infeasible.

Context matters

Despite the fact that contexts differ, managers, understandably, fall back on the same type of R&D organizations, the same supplier arrangements, the same kind of market research, and the same control mechanisms that have worked for them before. Such is human nature. A more effective approach is for managers to identify and act on the particular circumstances in which they find themselves. Even when a company has mastered a certain approach, say, the crash program, there can be no guarantee that the development effort will succeed if the setting doesn't call for that approach. IBM, remember, had to abandon its tested and immensely successful eight-stage approach to manage the huge opportunity cost represented by the PC market.

That said, it is occasionally true that because of their very structure and experience, some companies cannot realistically change their basic development approach. Designing and building a new aircraft is inherently so expensive that Boeing cannot really change the way it plays the development game without reducing the financial role involved by forming some kind of alliance or getting acquired by a company with enormously deep pockets. That may explain why Boeing did not try to catch up with a crash program when the Airbus 300 was introduced. It simply gave up 30% market share in that segment and focused on the battle between its 767 and the Airbus 310.

> Choose development strategies that fit each situation.

The proper choice of development strategy is, then, situation- and company-specific. It is not, however, industry-specific. Development work in some industries may fall in similar positions on the map – in consumer electronics, for example, extremely fast product life cycles make crash programs more common than for, say, large steam turbines. But competitors are unlikely to view their work on the same type of product in exactly the same way.

In their development work on nuclear magnetic resonance (NMR), for example, GE and Siemens were following quite different paths. GE was taking a 100%-right approach because it saw itself in a low opportunity cost, high entry risk situation: its computer tomography scanners at the time dominated the market. By contrast, Siemens, which had only 20% of the U.S. scanner market, saw its opportunity cost as much higher and therefore introduced innovation earlier by taking a step-by-step approach to NMR development.

Of course, sensible formulation of a development strategy can't guarantee faultless execution or a stable environment. In one of its development efforts, a leading copier company took the 100%-right approach and tried to develop the technology for microprocessor control upstream. But the new microprocessor control just would not work properly. So the company had to dust off some of its older technology, spruce it up a bit, and wedge it into development efforts that were already far downstream. The shift cost a year's delay and threw the whole program into a crash, catch-up mode.

The development map offers no easy recipes, but it does help managers understand the context in which individual development efforts occur so they can select the best strategies. New product development is not monochromatic. The map helps managers perceive its hues – and make the right strategic choices.

Reprint 88607

Design is a team effort, but how do marketing and engineering talk to each other?

The House of Quality

by JOHN R. HAUSER and DON CLAUSING

Digital Equipment, Hewlett-Packard, AT&T, and ITT are getting started with it. Ford and General Motors use it – at Ford alone there are more than 50 applications. The "house of quality," the basic design tool of the management approach known as quality function deployment (QFD), originated in 1972 at Mitsubishi's Kobe shipyard site. Toyota and its suppliers then developed it in numerous ways. The house of quality has been used successfully by Japanese manufacturers of consumer electronics, home appliances, clothing, integrated circuits, synthetic rubber, construction equipment, and agricultural engines. Japanese designers use it for services like swimming schools and retail outlets and even for planning apartment layouts.

A set of planning and communication routines, quality function deployment focuses and coordinates skills within an organization, first to design, then to manufacture and market goods that customers want to purchase and will continue to purchase. The foundation of the house of quality is the belief that products should be designed to reflect customers' desires and tastes – so marketing people, design engineers, and manufacturing staff must work closely together from the time a product is first conceived.

The house of quality is a kind of conceptual map that provides the means for interfunctional planning and communications. People with different prob-

John R. Hauser, at the Harvard Business School as a Marvin Bower fellow during the current academic year, is professor of management science at MIT's Sloan School of Management. He is the author, with Glen L. Urban, of Design & Marketing of New Products *(Prentice-Hall, 1980). Don Clausing is Bernard M. Gordon Adjunct Professor of Engineering Innovation and Practice at MIT. Previously he worked for Xerox Corporation. He introduced QFD to Ford and its supplier companies in 1984.*

lems and responsibilities can thrash out design priorities while referring to patterns of evidence on the house's grid.

What's So Hard About Design

David Garvin points out that there are many dimensions to what a consumer means by quality and that it is a major challenge to design products that satisfy all of these at once.[1] Strategic quality management means more than avoiding repairs for consumers. It means that companies learn from customer experience and reconcile what they want with what engineers can reasonably build.

Before the industrial revolution, producers were close to their customers. Marketing, engineering, and manufacturing were integrated – in the same individual. If a knight wanted armor, he talked directly to the armorer, who translated the knight's desires into a product. The two might discuss the material – plate rather than chain armor – and details like fluted surfaces for greater bending strength. Then the armorer would design the production process. For strength – who knows why? – he cooled the steel plates in the urine of a black goat. As for a production plan, he arose with the cock's crow to light the forge fire so that it would be hot enough by midday.

Today's fiefdoms are mainly inside corporations. Marketing people have their domain, engineers theirs. Customer surveys will find their way onto designers' desks, and R&D plans reach manufacturing engineers. But usually, managerial functions remain disconnected, producing a costly and demoralizing environment in which product quality and the quality of the production process itself suffer.

Top executives are learning that the use of interfunctional teams benefits design. But if top management *could* get marketing, designing, and manufacturing executives to sit down together, what should these people talk about? How could they get their meeting off the ground? This is where the house of quality comes in.

Consider the location of an emergency brake lever in one American sporty car. Placing it on the left between the seat and the door solved an engineering problem. But it also guaranteed that women in skirts could not get in and out gracefully. Even if the system were to last a lifetime, would it satisfy customers?

In contrast, Toyota improved its rust prevention record from one of the worst in the world to one of the best by coordinating design and production decisions to focus on this customer concern. Using the house of quality, designers broke down "body durability" into 53 items covering everything from climate to modes of operation. They obtained customer evaluations and ran experiments on nearly every detail of production, from pump operation to temperature control and coating composition. Decisions on sheet metal details, coating materials, and baking temperatures were all focused on those aspects of rust prevention most important to customers.

EXHIBIT I

Startup and preproduction costs at Toyota Auto Body before and after QFD

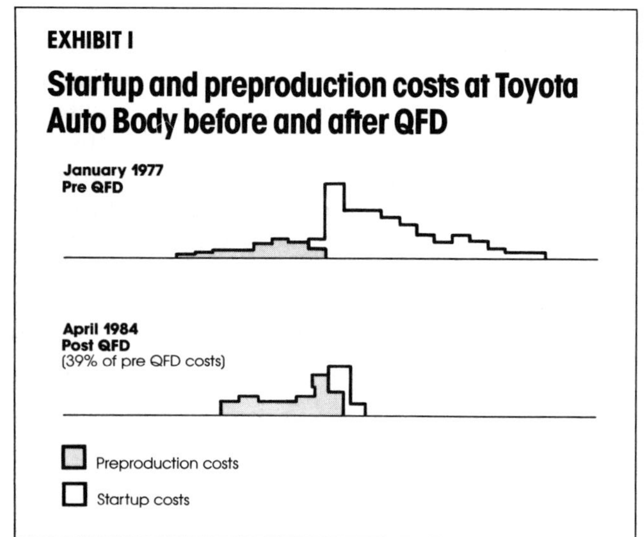

EXHIBIT II

Japanese automaker with QFD made fewer changes than U.S. company without QFD

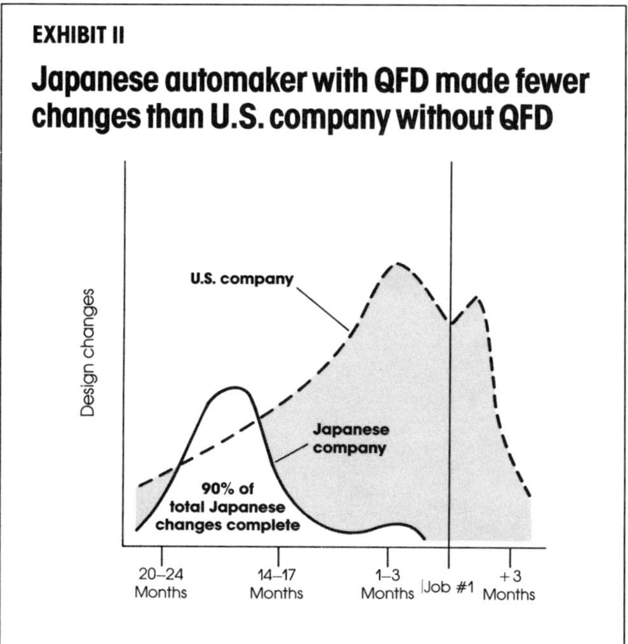

Source for Exhibits I and II: Lawrence P. Sullivan, "Quality Function Deployment," *Quality Progress,* June 1986, p. 39. © 1986 American Society for Quality Control. Reprinted by permission.

1. David A. Garvin, "Competing on the Eight Dimensions of Quality," HBR November-December 1987, p. 101.

Today, with marketing techniques so much more sophisticated than ever before, companies can measure, track, and compare customers' perceptions of products with remarkable accuracy; all companies have opportunities to compete on quality. And costs certainly justify an emphasis on quality design. By looking first at customer needs, then designing across corporate functions, manufacturers can reduce prelaunch time and after-launch tinkering.

Exhibit I compares startup and preproduction costs at Toyota Auto Body in 1977, before QFD, to those costs in 1984, when QFD was well under way. House of quality meetings early on reduced costs by more than 60%. *Exhibit II* reinforces this evidence by comparing the number of design changes at a Japanese auto manufacturer using QFD with changes at a U.S. automaker. The Japanese design was essentially frozen before the first car came off the assembly line, while the U.S. company was still revamping months later.

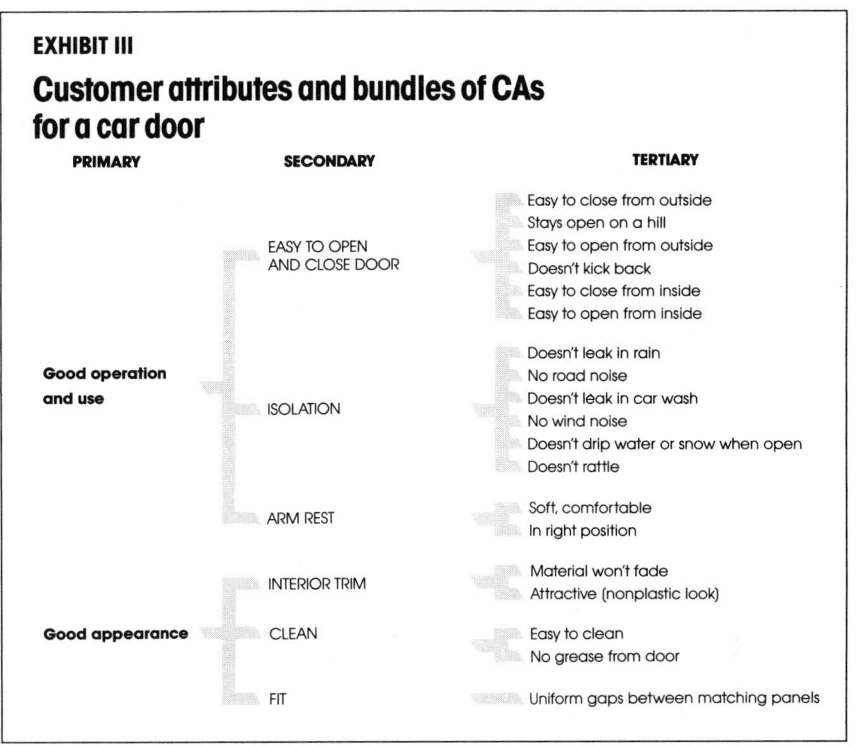

Building the House

There is nothing mysterious about the house of quality. There is nothing particularly difficult about it either, but it does require some effort to get used to its conventions. Eventually one's eye can bounce knowingly around the house as it would over a roadmap or a navigation chart. We have seen some applications that started with more than 100 customer requirements and more than 130 engineering considerations. A fraction of one subchart, in this case for the door of an automobile, illustrates the house's basic concept well. We've reproduced this subchart portion in the illustration "House of Quality," and we'll discuss each section step-by-step.

What do customers want? The house of quality begins with the customer, whose requirements are called customer attributes (CAs)–phrases customers use to describe products and product characteristics (see *Exhibit III*). We've listed a few here; a typical application would have 30 to 100 CAs. A car door is "easy to close" or "stays open on a hill"; "doesn't leak in rain" or allows "no (or little) road noise." Some Japanese companies simply place their products in public areas and encourage potential customers to examine them, while design team members listen and note what people say. Usually, however, more formal market research is called for, via focus groups, in-depth qualitative interviews, and other techniques.

CAs are often grouped into bundles of attributes that represent an overall customer concern, like "open-close" or "isolation." The Toyota rust-prevention study used eight levels of bundles to get from the total car down to the car body. Usually the project team groups CAs by consensus, but some companies are experimenting with state-of-the-art research techniques that derive groupings directly from customers' responses (and thus avoid arguments in team meetings).

CAs are generally reproduced in the customers' own words. Experienced users of the house of quality try to preserve customers' phrases and even clichés–knowing that they will be translated simultaneously by product planners, design engineers, manufacturing engineers, and salespeople. Of course, this raises the problem of interpretation: What does a customer really mean by "quiet" or "easy"? Still, designers' words and inferences may correspond even less to customers' actual views and can therefore mislead teams into tackling problems customers consider unimportant.

Not all customers are end users, by the way. CAs can include the demands of regulators ("safe in a side collision"), the needs of retailers ("easy to display"),

EXHIBIT IV

Relative-importance weights of customer attributes

BUNDLES	CUSTOMER ATTRIBUTES	RELATIVE IMPORTANCE
EASY TO OPEN AND CLOSE DOOR	Easy to close from outside	7
	Stays open on a hill	5
ISOLATION	Doesn't leak in rain	3
	No road noise	2
	A complete list totals	100%

the requirements of vendors ("satisfy assembly and service organizations"), and so forth.

Are all preferences equally important? Imagine a good door, one that is easy to close and has power windows that operate quickly. There is a problem, however. Rapid operation calls for a bigger motor, which makes the door heavier and, possibly, harder to close. Sometimes a creative solution can be found that satisfies all needs. Usually, however, designers have to trade off one benefit against another.

To bring the customer's voice to such deliberations, house of quality measures the relative importance to the customer of all CAs. Weightings are based on team members' direct experience with customers or on surveys. Some innovative businesses are using statistical techniques that allow customers to state their preferences with respect to existing and hypothetical products. Other companies use "revealed preference techniques," which judge consumer tastes by their actions as well as by their words–an approach that is more expensive and difficult to perform but yields more accurate answers. (Consumers say that avoiding sugar in cereals is important, but do their actions reflect their claims?)

Weightings are displayed in the house next to each CA–usually in terms of percentages, a complete list totaling 100% (see *Exhibit IV*).

Will delivering perceived needs yield a competitive advantage? Companies that want to match or exceed their competition must first know where they stand relative to it. So on the right side of the house, opposite the CAs, we list customer evaluations of competitive cars matched to "our own" (see *Exhibit V*).

Ideally, these evaluations are based on scientific surveys of customers. If various customer segments evaluate products differently–luxury vs. economy car buyers, for example–product-planning team members get assessments for each segment.

Comparison with the competition, of course, can identify opportunities for improvement. Take our car door, for example. With respect to "stays open on a hill," every car is weak, so we could gain an advantage here. But if we looked at "no road noise" for the same automobiles, we would see that we already have an advantage, which is important to maintain.

Marketing professionals will recognize the right-hand side of *Exhibit V* as a "perceptual map." Perceptual maps based on bundles of CAs are often used to identify strategic positioning of a product or product line. This section of the house of quality provides a natural link from product concept to a company's strategic vision.

How can we change the product? The marketing domain tells us what to do, the engineering domain tells us how to do it. Now we need to describe the product in the language of the engineer. Along the top of the house of quality, the design team lists those engineering characteristics (ECs) that are likely to affect one or more of the customer attributes (see *Exhibit VI*). The negative sign on "energy to close door" means engineers hope to reduce the energy required. If a standard engineering characteristic affects no CA, it may be redundant to the EC list on the house, or the team may have missed a customer attribute. A CA unaffected by any EC, on the other hand, presents opportunities to expand a car's physical properties.

Any EC may affect more than one CA. The resistance of the door seal affects three of the four customer attributes shown in *Exhibit VI*–and others shown later.

Engineering characteristics should describe the product in measurable terms and should directly affect customer perceptions. The weight of the door will be *felt* by the customer and is therefore a relevant EC. By contrast, the thickness of the sheet metal is a part characteristic that the customer is unlikely to perceive directly. It affects customers only by influencing the weight of the door and other engineering characteristics, like "resistance to deformation in a crash."

In many Japanese projects, the interfunctional team begins with the CAs and generates measurable characteristics for each, like foot-pounds of energy required to close the door. Teams should avoid ambiguity in interpretation of ECs or hasty justification of current quality control measurement practices. This is a time for systematic, patient analysis of each characteristic, for brainstorming. Vagueness will eventually yield indifference to things customers need. Characteristics that are trivial will make the team lose sight of the overall design and stifle creativity.

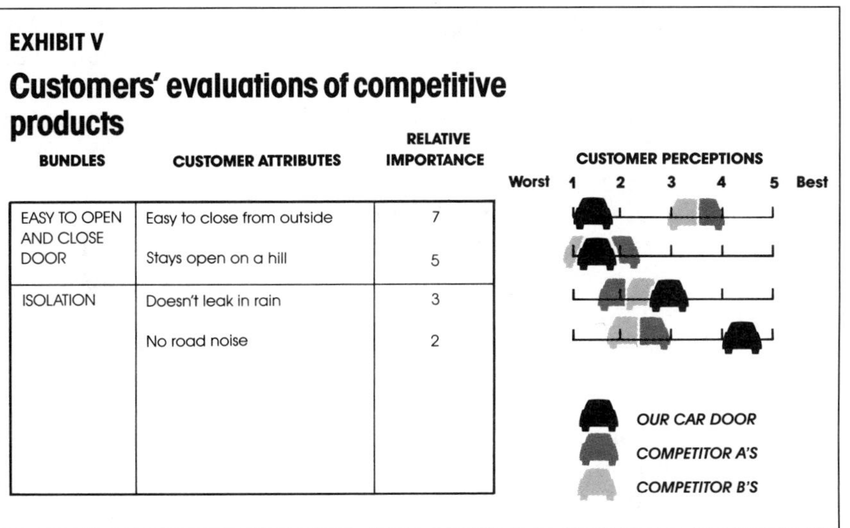

EXHIBIT V

Customers' evaluations of competitive products

BUNDLES	CUSTOMER ATTRIBUTES	RELATIVE IMPORTANCE
EASY TO OPEN AND CLOSE DOOR	Easy to close from outside	7
	Stays open on a hill	5
ISOLATION	Doesn't leak in rain	3
	No road noise	2

How much do engineers influence customer-perceived qualities? The interfunctional team now fills in the body of the house, the "relationship matrix," indicating how much each engineering characteristic affects each customer attribute. The team seeks consensus on these evaluations, basing them on expert engineering experience, customer responses, and tabulated data from statistical studies or controlled experiments.

The team uses numbers or symbols to establish the strength of these relationships (see *Exhibit VII*). Any symbols will do; the idea is to choose those that work best. Some teams use red symbols for relationships based on experiments and statistics and pencil marks for relationships based on judgment or intuition. Others use numbers from statistical studies. In our house, we use check marks for positive and crosses for negative relationships.

Once the team has identified the voice of the customer and linked it to engineering characteristics, it adds objective measures at the bottom of the house beneath the ECs to which they pertain (see *Exhibit VIII*). When objective measures are known, the team can eventually move to establish target values – ideal new measures for each EC in a redesigned product. If the team did its homework when it first identified the ECs, tests to measure benchmark values should be easy to complete. Engineers determine the relevant units of measurement – foot-pounds, decibels, etc.

Incidentally, if customer evaluations of CAs do not correspond to objective measures of related ECs – if, for example, the door requiring the least energy to open is perceived as "hardest to open" – then perhaps the measures are faulty or the car is suffering from an image problem that is skewing consumer perceptions.

How does one engineering change affect other characteristics? An engineer's change of the gear ratio on a car window may make the window motor smaller but the window go up more slowly. And if the engineer enlarges or strengthens the mechanism, the door probably will be heavier, harder to open, or may be less prone to remain open on a slope. Of course, there might be an entirely new mechanism that improves all relevant CAs. Engineering is creative solutions and a balancing of objectives.

The house of quality's distinctive roof matrix helps engineers specify the various engineering features that have to be improved collaterally (see *Exhibit IX*). To improve the window motor, you may have to improve the hinges, weather stripping, and a range of other ECs.

Sometimes one targeted feature impairs so many others that the team decides to leave it alone. The roof matrix also facilitates necessary engineering trade-offs. The foot-pounds of energy needed to close the door, for example, are shown in negative relation to "door seal resistance" and "road noise reduction." In many ways, the roof contains the most critical information for engineers because they use it to balance the trade-offs when addressing customer benefits.

Incidentally, we have been talking so far about the basics, but design teams often want to ruminate on other information. In other words, they custom-build their houses. To the column of CAs, teams may add other columns for histories of customer complaints. To the ECs, a team may add the costs of servicing these complaints. Some applications add data from the sales force to the CA list to represent strategic marketing decisions. Or engineers may add a row that indicates the degree of technical difficulty, showing in their own terms how hard or easy it is to make a change.

Some users of the house impute relative weights to the engineering characteristics. They'll establish that the energy needed to close the door is roughly twice as important to consider as, say, "check force on 10° slope." By comparing weighted characteristics to actual component costs, creative design teams set priorities for improving components. Such information is particularly important when cost cutting is a goal. (*Exhibit X* includes rows for technical difficulty, imputed importance of ECs, and estimated costs.)

There are no hard-and-fast rules. The symbols, lines, and configurations that work for the particular team are the ones it should use.

Using the House

How does the house lead to the bottom line? There is no cookbook procedure, but the house helps the team to set targets, which are, in fact, entered on the bottom line of the house. For engineers it is a way to summarize basic data in usable form. For marketing executives it represents the customer's voice. General managers use it to discover strategic opportunities. Indeed, the house encourages all of these groups to work together to understand one another's priorities and goals.

The house relieves no one of the responsibility of making tough decisions. It does provide the means for all participants to debate priorities.

Let's run through a couple of hypothetical situations to see how a design team uses the house.

■ Look at *Exhibit X*. Notice that our doors are much more difficult to close from the outside than those on competitors' cars. We decide to look further because our marketing data say this customer attribute is

EXHIBIT VI

Engineering characteristics tell how to change the product

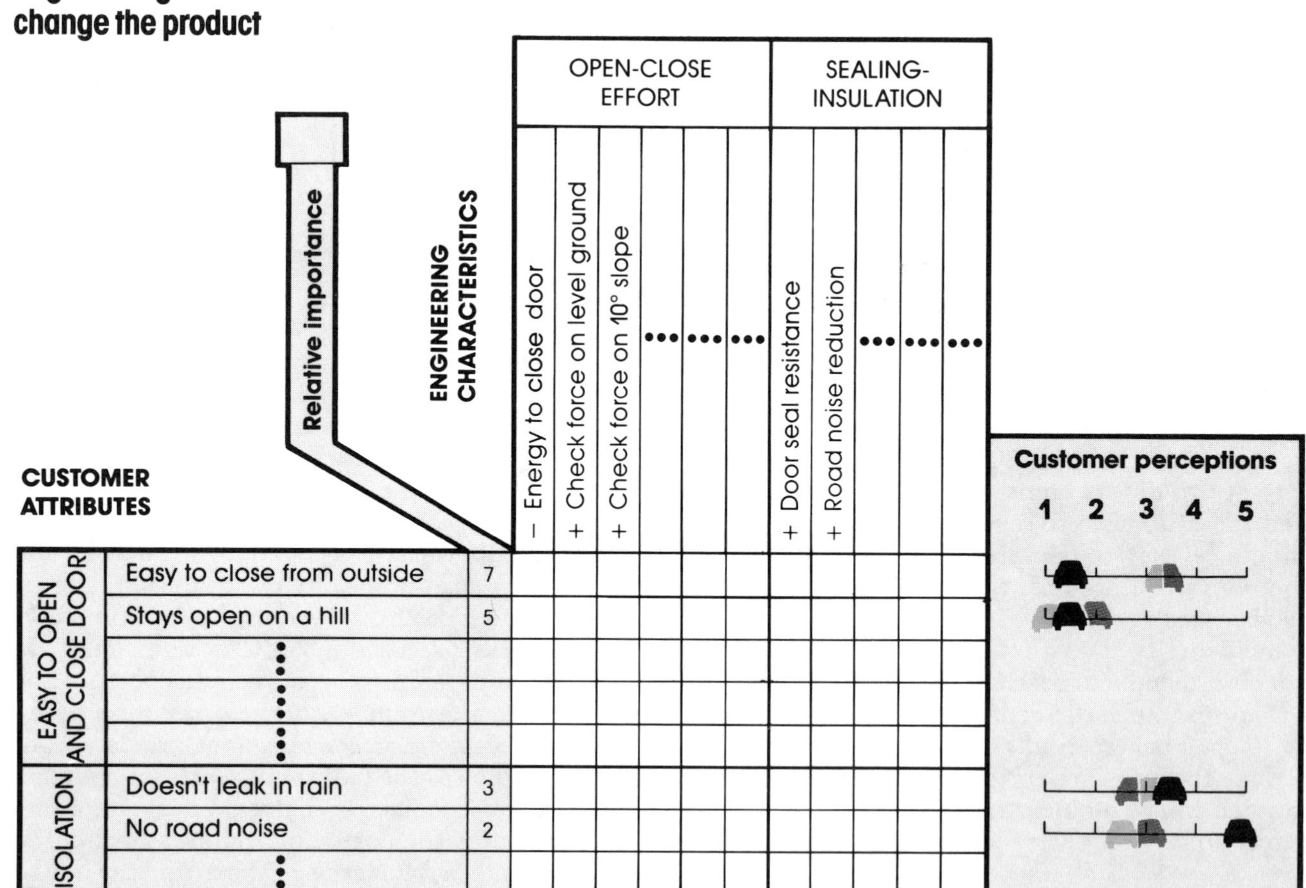

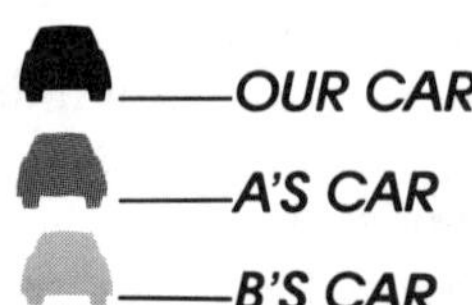

EXHIBIT VII

Relationship matrix shows how engineering decisions affect customer perceptions

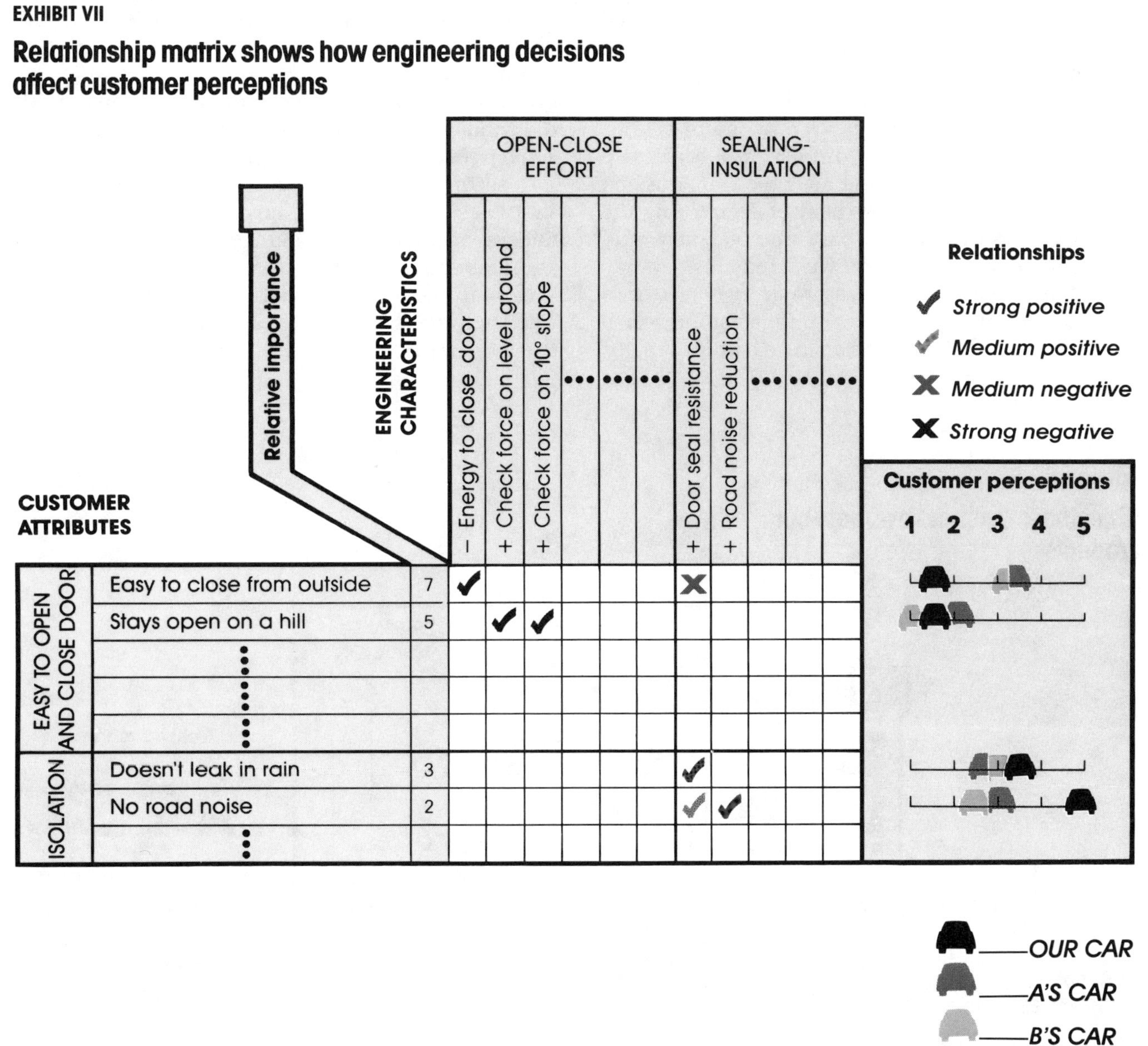

important. From the central matrix, the body of the house, we identify the ECs that affect this customer attribute: energy to close door, peak closing force, and door seal resistance. Our engineers judge the energy to close the door and the peak closing force as good candidates for improvement together because they are strongly, positively related to the consumer's desire to close the door easily. They determine to consider all the engineering ramifications of door closing.

Next, in the roof of the house, we identify which other ECs might be affected by changing the door closing energy. Door opening energy and peak closing force are positively related, but other ECs (check force on level ground, door seals, window acoustic transmission, road noise reduction) are bound to be changed in the process and are negatively related. It is not an easy decision. But with objective measures of competitors' doors, customer perceptions, and considering information on cost and technical difficulty, we – marketing people, engineers, and top managers – decide that the benefits outweigh the costs. A new door closing target is set for our door – 7.5 foot-pounds of energy. This target, noted on the very bottom of the house directly below the relevant EC, establishes the goal to have the door "easiest to close."

■ Look now at the customer attribute "no road noise" and its relationship to the acoustic transmission of the window. The "road noise" CA is only mildly important to customers, and its relationship to the specifications of the window is not strong. Window design will help only so much to keep things quiet. Decreasing the acoustic transmission usually makes the window heavier. Examining the roof of the house, we see that more weight would have a negative impact on ECs (open-close energy, check forces, etc.) that, in turn, are strongly related to CAs that are more important to the customer than quiet ("easy to close," "stays open on a hill"). Finally, marketing data show that we already do well on road noise; customers perceive our car as better than competitors'.

In this case, the team decides not to tamper with the window's transmission of sound. Our target stays equal to our current acoustic values.

In setting targets, it is worth noting that the team should emphasize customer-satisfaction values and not emphasize tolerances. Do not specify "between 6 and 8 foot-pounds," but rather say, "7.5 foot-pounds." This may seem a small matter, but it is important. The rhetoric of tolerances encourages drift toward the least costly end of the specification limit and

EXHIBIT VIII

Objective measures evaluate competitive products

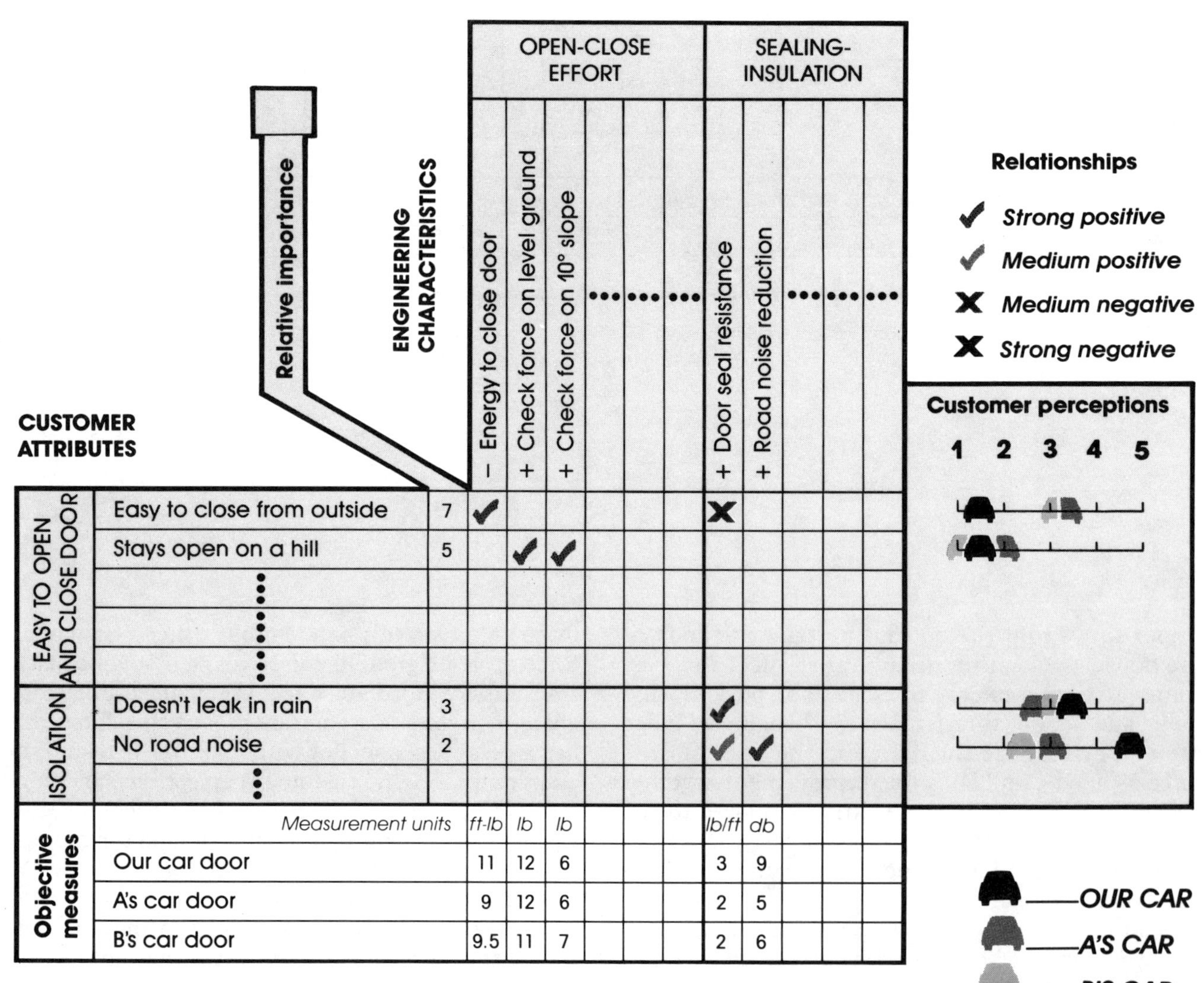

Objective measures	ft-lb	lb	lb			lb/ft	db			
Measurement units	ft-lb	lb	lb			lb/ft	db			
Our car door	11	12	6			3	9			
A's car door	9	12	6			2	5			
B's car door	9.5	11	7			2	6			

EXHIBIT IX

Roof matrix facilitates engineering creativity

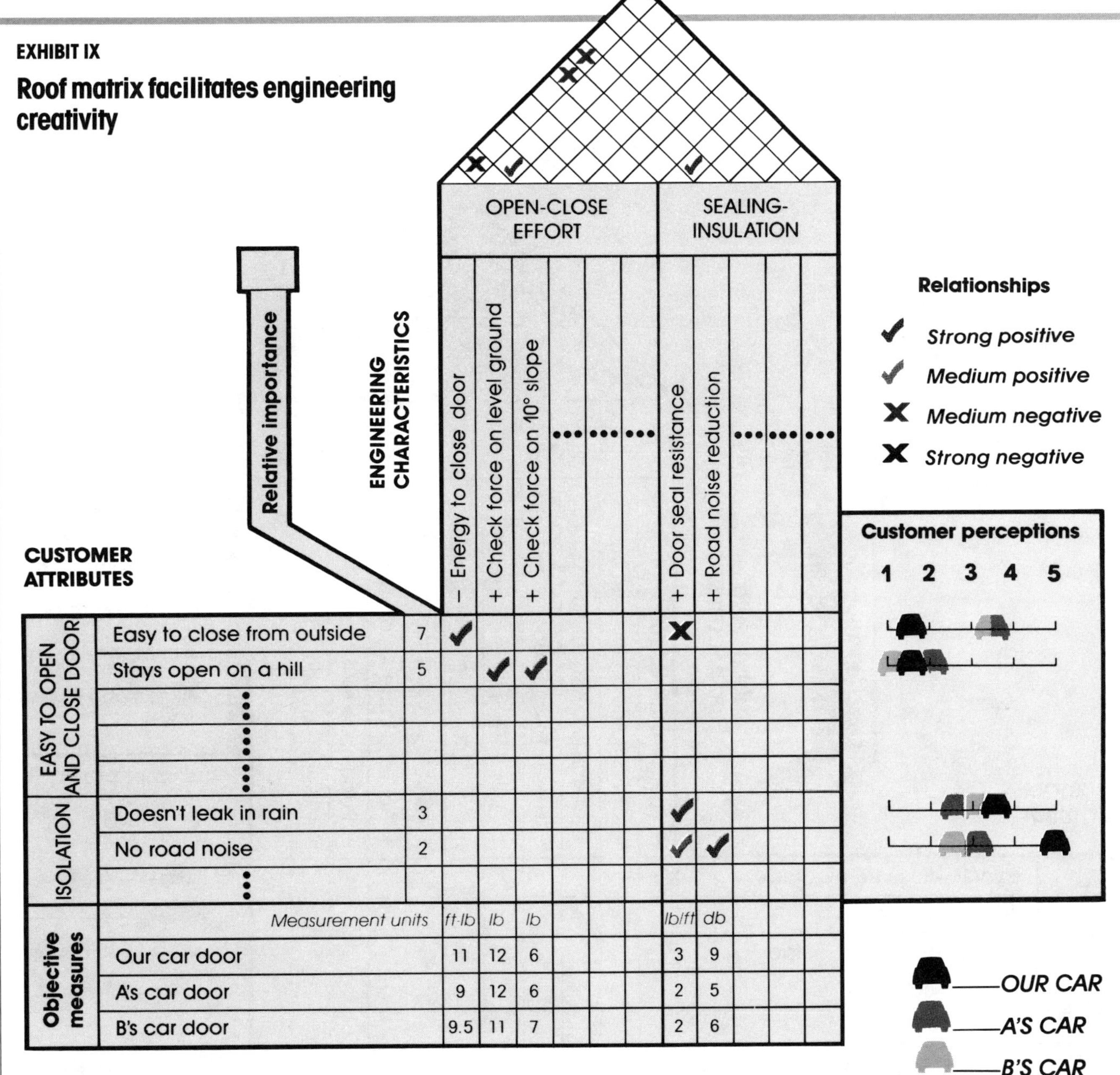

does not reward designs and components whose engineering values closely attain a specific customer-satisfaction target.

The Houses Beyond

The principles underlying the house of quality apply to any effort to establish clear relations between manufacturing functions and customer satisfaction that are not easy to visualize. Suppose that our team decides that doors closing easily is a critical attribute and that a relevant engineering characteristic is closing energy. Setting a target value for closing energy gives us a goal, but it does not give us a door. To get a door, we need the right parts (frame, sheet metal, weather stripping, hinges, etc.), the right processes to manufacture the parts and assemble the product, and the right production plan to get it built.

If our team is truly interfunctional, we can eventually take the "hows" from our house of quality and make them the "whats" of another house, one mainly concerned with detailed product design. En-

EXHIBIT X

House of quality

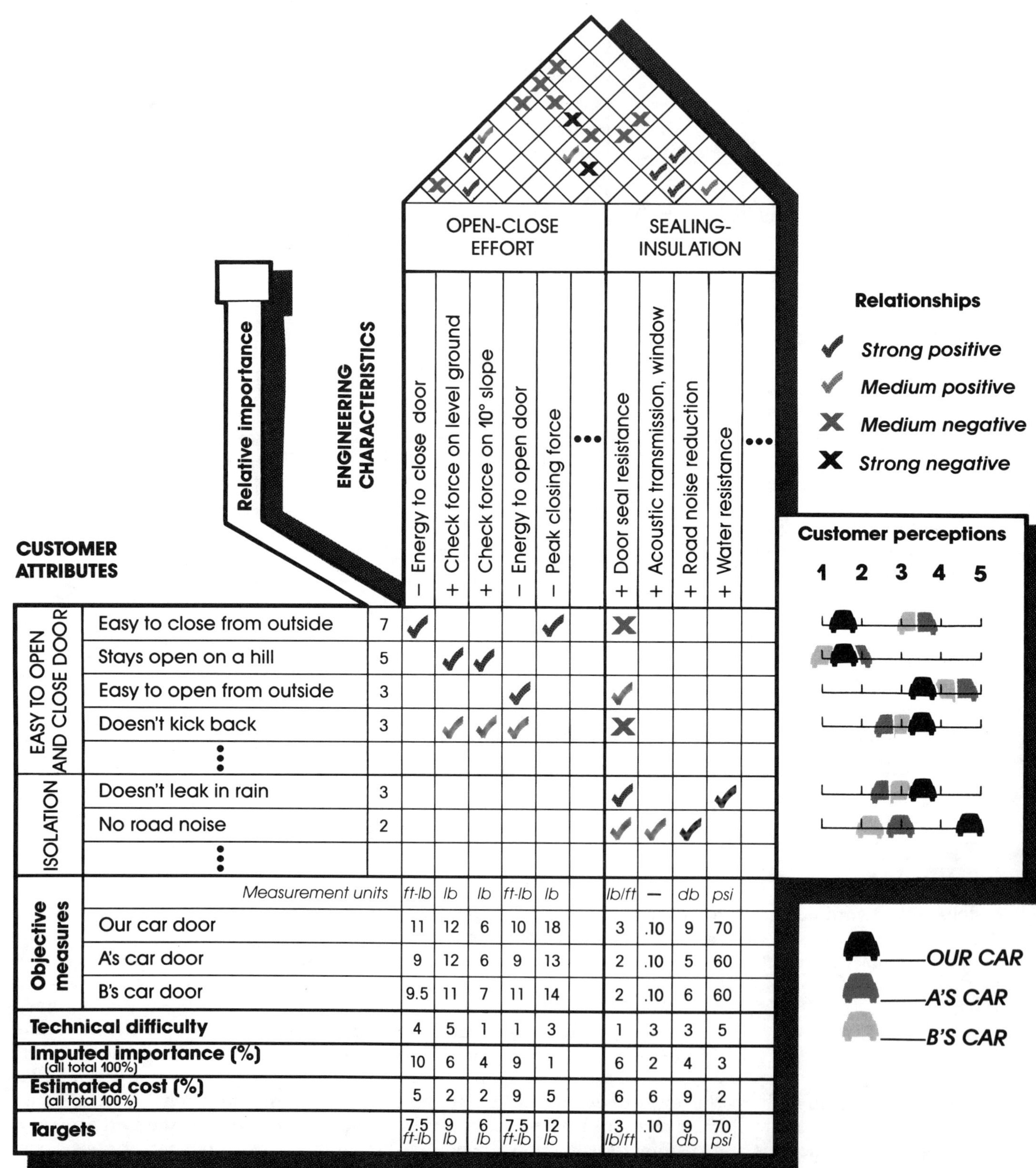

EXHIBIT XI

Linked houses convey the customer's voice through to manufacturing

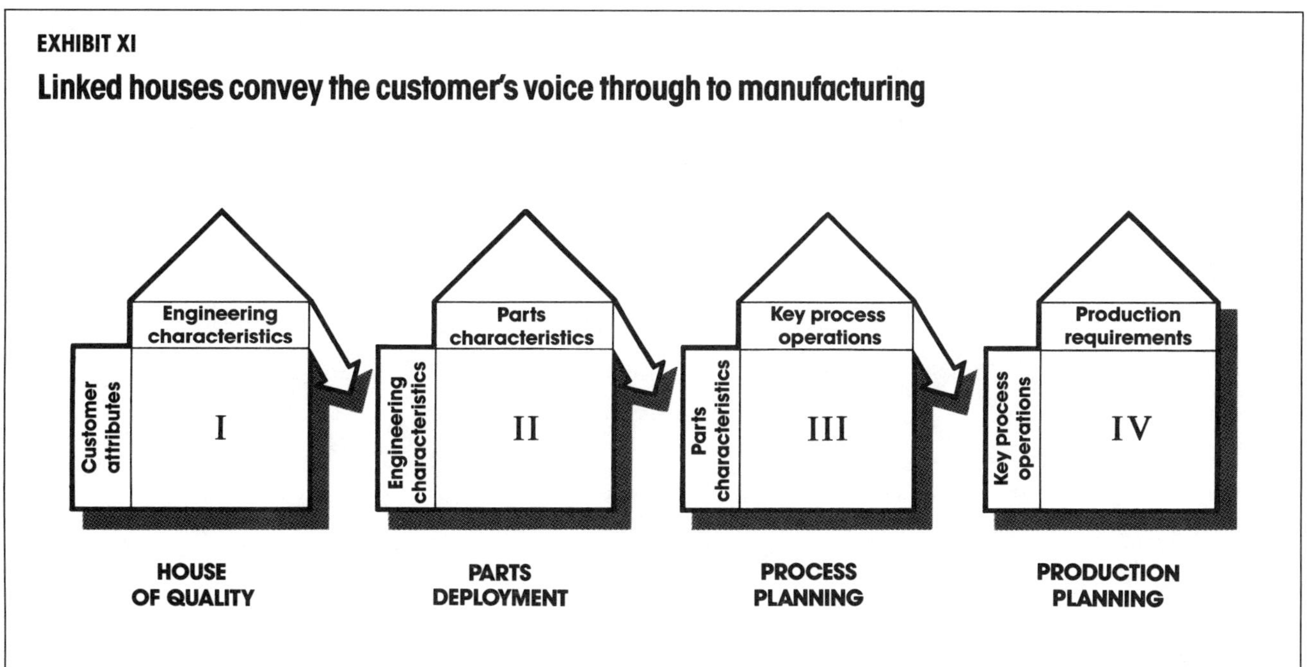

Source: Modified from a figure supplied by the American Supplier Institute, Inc., Dearborn, Michigan.

gineering characteristics like foot-pounds of closing energy can become the rows in a parts deployment house, while parts characteristics–like hinge properties or the thickness of the weather stripping–become the columns (see *Exhibit XI*).

This process continues to a third and fourth phase as the "hows" of one stage become the "whats" of the next. Weather-stripping thickness–a "how" in the parts house–becomes a "what" in a process planning house. Important process operations, like "rpm of the extruder producing the weather stripping" become the "hows." In the last phase, production planning, the key process operations, like "rpm of the extruder," become the "whats," and production requirements–knob controls, operator training, maintenance–become the "hows."

These four linked houses implicitly convey the voice of the customer through to manufacturing. A control knob setting of 3.6 gives an extruder speed of 100 rpm; this helps give a reproducible diameter for the weather-stripping bulb, which gives good sealing without excessive door-closing force. This feature aims to satisfy the customer's need for a dry, quiet car with an easy-to-close door.

None of this is simple. An elegant idea ultimately decays into process, and processes will be confounding as long as human beings are involved. But that is no excuse to hold back. If a technique like house of quality can help break down functional barriers and encourage teamwork, serious efforts to implement it will be many times rewarded.

What is also not simple is developing an organization capable of absorbing elegant ideas. The principal benefit of the house of quality is quality in-house. It gets people thinking in the right directions and thinking together. For most U.S. companies, this alone amounts to a quiet revolution.

Reprint 88307

To stay competitive, stay home.

Manufacturing Offshore Is Bad Business

by Constantinos C. Markides and Norman Berg

July 1985: AT&T decides to transfer production of residential telephones from its only U.S. telephone manufacturing plant, in Shreveport, Louisiana, to Singapore.

February 1986: United Technologies announces it will close its diesel-engine parts plant in Springfield, Massachusetts and transfer operations to a nonunion plant in South Carolina and two plants in Europe.

February 1987: General Motors plans to phase out the production of A-body cars in the United States and move it to its Ramos Arizpe, Coahuila plant in Mexico.

For decades, foreign direct investment has been a common practice among American companies, so investments like these don't seem particularly noteworthy. But they are. In the past, U.S. companies went abroad primarily to secure a foreign market or to obtain raw materials. Now they go overseas to buy or make products and components to ship back to the United States. The new investments are not complementing domestic production; they are replacing it.

Constantinos C. Markides is a doctoral candidate studying business policy at the Harvard Business School. His research centers on U.S. competitiveness in the world economy. Norman Berg is professor of business administration at the Harvard Business School, where he teaches in the Program for Management Development. His longtime interest is in conglomerate management, a subject on which he has frequently written.

Manufacturers defend sourcing from overseas as the only way to compete with inexpensive, high-quality imports. They say that moving to cheap-labor countries like Mexico, Taiwan, and Malaysia for export back to the United States is allowing U.S. industry to regain its world standing. Economists generally approve. They consider the migration to low-wage areas an adjustment caused by changes in international comparative advantage.

Companies should face manufacturing at home – like Kodak and Black & Decker.

Others are less enchanted by the trend. Labor unions claim that it deindustrializes the country and destroys American jobs. Some observers have argued that it "hollows" the nation's industrial base and threatens the standard of living.

In the debate over whether offshore manufacturing is good for the nation, it is always assumed that it is good for an individual company. But we challenge that notion. The mere fact that a lot of companies are doing it doesn't make it smart. Going overseas is hardly the panacea many people think it is. At best, it is just another quick fix. In their rush to save money, managers often lose sight of the high penalties of moving abroad. And by continually shifting manufacturing to the areas with the lowest labor costs, they are merely postponing the inevitable day of reckoning when they must confront the parts of the business that really need reform.

It's Not the Only Option

American manufacturers claim that going offshore is their only alternative if they are to stay competitive against foreign rivals. It's either offshore manufacturing or no manufacturing at all. As powerful as this argument may seem, it doesn't hold up well in light of several facts.

First, an increasing number of U.S. companies are responding to the import threat by improving their competitive position at home. They are convinced that creating long-term competitive advantage requires a commitment to a new way of doing business—not just a shortsighted attack on labor costs.

Take Eastman Kodak. After a disappointing 1985, in which earnings dropped 31% from the year before (excluding the $563 million Kodak lost when it withdrew from instant photography), the company decided to drastically change its strategy. While still relying on some offshore manufacturing, Kodak also embarked on an aggressive and multifaceted program to restore its competitive position at home. It made an all-out attempt to create long-term competitive advantage by addressing the business as a whole, not just isolated parts of it.

Consider some of the steps Kodak has taken or plans to take: reduce overhead by trimming employment, especially in middle management; revise the wage dividend plan; cut operating and expense budgets; eliminate inefficient operations and marginal product lines; reorganize internally; increase R&D expenditures; move into new technologies; introduce new products; and improve quality and cost efficiency. The effect of these changes was immediate: in 1986, sales grew by 9% to $11.5 billion, while earnings from operations climbed 24% to $724 million. Earnings per share were $3.52 in 1987, versus only $1.10 in 1986.

Black & Decker is another case in point. It reduced its work force by 40%, consolidated operations to achieve economies of scale, eliminated hundreds of administrative positions at corporate headquarters, modernized plants, introduced new manufacturing methods, standardized models, expanded and upgraded marketing and engineering capabilities, and moved aggressively into the low end of the professional power-tool market. The results: for fiscal year 1986 the company reported net earnings of $6.3 million—that compares with a net loss of $158.4 million the previous year. EPS went from 49¢ to 95¢ between 1986 and 1987.

Litton Industries is making similar changes in its operations to fight foreign competition in microwave ovens. The company has redesigned its product line, improved the quality of its products, cut down on labor costs, and introduced new models.

Some companies have embraced automation to stay competitive. In 1985, GM had more than 4,000 programmable robots in operation; it expects to have 10,000 in place by the end of 1988. Xerox has spent more than $100 million to automate manufacturing and materials handling, and Fairchild Semiconductor moved its assembly operations back to the United States after automating the welding of semiconductor chips and the inventory tracking system.

Second, more Japanese companies are building manufacturing plants in the United States at precisely the time when many American companies are claiming it is impossible for them to stay home and be competitive. Every major Japanese automaker has an assembly plant in the States. By one count, there are more than 600 Japanese plants operating on American soil. Honda's plant in Marysville, Ohio, Nissan's plant in Smyrna, Tennessee, and Mazda's plant in Flat Rock, Michigan are but a few. Japanese electronics companies are also operating in the United States. Fujitsu, Hitachi, Mitsubishi, NEC, Toshiba—all have assembly or manufacturing facilities in America.

> If the Japanese can manufacture in the United States, so can Americans.

The Japanese are investing in the United States for four reasons: to increase their political clout and prevent further trade restrictions by creating jobs for Americans; to ensure access to the American market in case exports to the United States are restricted further; to get a better feel for their most important export market so they can be more responsive to it; and to hedge against fluctuations in the value of the dollar.

To be sure, the Japanese in the United States enjoy some advantages over existing U.S. plants. Because of a younger work force, they have low pension expenses and low insurance costs. They also have newer facilities. But these benefits are not the chief reason Japanese factories are competitive. The plants are successful because of their manufacturing techniques. Studies have shown that the main reason the

The Race to Manufacture Offshore

It's a fact that the electronics, textile, machine tool, subcompact auto, and other industries are moving their manufacturing operations abroad. The evidence is all around us. Although no one set of statistics accounts for all the forms of offshore manufacturing–be it setting up plants abroad, purchasing from a foreign subsidiary or joint venture, subcontracting from a foreign company, or buying from foreign companies through market transactions–the available data are persuasive.

The best information on products manufactured or assembled abroad is a set of numbers from the U.S. International Trade Commission on imports entering under tariff items 806.30 and 807.00. These provisions permit the portion of the product made of U.S. components to enter the United States duty free. A quick glance at the 806 and 807 statistics shows a dramatic rise in the value of offshore-manufactured imports (the accompanying table of selected years illustrates the trend).

Offshore imports rose continually from $953 million in 1966 to $36.5 billion in 1986, despite fluctuations in the dollar. Their share of U.S.-manufactured imports nearly doubled in the same period.

Most of these imports are in three price-sensitive industries: autos (59% of the total in 1985), electronics (15%), and textiles (3%). Most of the auto industry's investments have been in Europe, Japan, Canada, and Mexico. The electronics industry has invested mostly in East Asia, while the textile investments are concentrated in Latin America and the Caribbean.

These figures grossly underestimate the true extent of the phenomenon. They exclude, for example, products of a U.S. company manufactured abroad containing only foreign components. Such items are considered ordinary imports and don't fall under the 806 and 807 provisions. Similarly, products of a foreign company under contract with a U.S. business enter as ordinary imports. And much of what a U.S. affiliate abroad ships to its domestic parent does not appear in the 806 and 807 statistics. (Note that at least 35% of U.S. imports and exports from 1977 to 1980 were intracompany.*)

Obviously, U.S. companies are augmenting their overseas facilities: capital expenditures by majority-owned foreign affiliates of U.S. manufacturing companies climbed from $12 billion in 1978 to $17 billion in 1986. Meanwhile, U.S. manufacturing capacity utilization fell from 84.2% to 78.8%.

*Jane Sneddon Little, "Intrafirm Trade and U.S. Protectionism: Thoughts Based on a Small Survey," *New England Economic Review*, January-February 1986, p.42.

Aggregate statistics aside, evidence abounds. In 1974, some 70,000 workers were employed in 450 plants along the Mexican border under the in-bond, or *maquiladora*, program. By 1986, the figures had grown to 300,000 workers and 1,100 factories. The value added by these plants grew from $300 million to more than $1.3 billion in those 12 years. American businesses, operating 865 of these factories, account for most of the production.

In 1985, U.S. companies like RCA, Motorola, and Texas Instruments employed more than half the 73,000 people working for the electronics industry in Malaysia and sent back to America more than $300 million worth of semiconductors. In Mexico, the three U.S. automakers accounted for more than 55% of Mexico's total car production in 1986, and all three were planning to expand there. U.S. companies' imports from South Korea, Taiwan, Mexico, and Brazil are estimated to rise from 100,000 units in 1984 to 500,000 in 1988.

The Growth of 806 and 807 Imports

Year	*Total Value of 806 and 807 Imports (in millions of dollars)*	*Percentage of Total U.S. Imports*	*Percentage of U.S.-Manufactured Imports*
1966	$ 953.0	3.7%	6.4%
1967	1,035.1	3.8	6.5
1969	1,838.8	5.1	8.0
1970	2,208.2	5.5	8.5
1973	4,247.1	6.0	9.4
1975	5,162.4	5.3	10.1
1978	9,735.3	5.5	9.1
1982	18,275.5	7.4	12.1
1983	21,845.7	8.1	12.8
1985	30,535.1	9.0	12.3
1986	36,469.9	9.9	12.4
1987	39,820.1†	10.0	12.9

Sources: U.S. Tariff Commission, *Economic Factors Affecting the Use of Items 807.00 and 806.30 of the Tariff Schedules of the United States*, Publication 339 (Washington, D.C.: USTC, September 1970); U.S. International Trade Commission, *Imports Under Items 806.30 and 807.00 of the Tariff Schedules of the United States, 1982-85*, Publication 1920, and *The Use and Economic Impact of TSUS Items 806.30 and 807.00*, Publication 2053 (Washington, D.C.: USITC, December 1986 and January 1988); and U.S. Department of Commerce, *Survey of Current Business*, various issues.

†Projected figure.

Japanese were able to dominate the market for small cars over the last decade was not because of higher capital investment rates or more advanced technology but because of management philosophy and excellence in manufacturing.[1] By emphasizing superior product designs, high quality, minimum inventories, waste elimination, and worker participation, the Japanese emerged as the cost and quality leaders in the industry. Now, using the same techniques, the Japanese are outperforming domestic rivals on their home turf.

The ability of the Japanese to manufacture in the United States raises serious questions about the rationale American companies use for going offshore. In particular, if the Japanese can manufacture in the United States and still be competitive, why do U.S. companies have to go offshore to stay alive? More important, if U.S. companies have the option of becoming more competitive by improving manufacturing at home, why do they choose the quick fix of manufacturing offshore?

Third and last, Japanese companies have managed to stay competitive over the years without resorting to offshore manufacturing. Overseas production of the Japanese semiconductor industry, for instance, has amounted to less than 4% of total production.[2] Even when the yen got strong, the Japanese found it unnecessary to search for low-cost labor. They stayed world-class competitors by investing in automatic wire-bonding machines and by using flexible manufacturing.

In consumer electronics, the Japanese didn't go offshore but instead used intelligent product design and simple automation to stay competitive. In the early 1970s, while U.S. color TV manufacturers like RCA, GE, and Zenith were rushing to the Far East, Japanese manufacturers switched to 100% solid-state chassis, automated insertion and testing, and reduced component counts through extensive use of integrated circuits, early use of in-line tubes, and single-circuit board designs.

> Lowering wages helps a little – but labor is only 15% of total costs.

The few Japanese companies that chose to go offshore did so either to supply their export markets or, more commonly, to get around trade restrictions. Japanese textile companies went to Asia in the 1970s, for example, to avoid OMAs (orderly marketing agreements) imposed on exports of apparel to the United States and Europe. Similarly, Sanyo, Sony, and Hitachi have been moving manufacturing and assembly operations to Mexico to circumvent U.S. trade laws and to preempt American protectionism.

In the period 1985 to 1987, when the yen gained by more than 60% against the dollar, 53% of the 214 Japanese manufacturers responding to a Keidanren survey stated that they would cope with the strong yen by shifting their emphasis to domestic markets. They planned to do so by upgrading their products, incorporating greater value added, and minimizing costs. More important, 73% of the companies surveyed reported that they will not resort to more outside contracting, and 77% reported that they do not plan to cut wages. The 29% that planned to shift some production overseas were doing so to supply export markets, not the Japanese market. Nearly three-fourths of the companies expected to replace or had already replaced outside subcontracting with internal production. This behavior is in sharp contrast to that of American companies in the early 1980s when the dollar was strong.

The Bush Is Full of Thorns

Offshore manufacturing is not, then, the only option available to companies under competitive siege. It is, in fact, a poor option for many organizations. Managers should know that offshore manufacturing is not all roses and labor savings. Before they make the move, they should have a fuller picture of where they're headed. They should know that there are some powerful reasons *not* to go offshore.

The savings can cost a lot. Granted, companies can often save money on labor and materials by purchasing or manufacturing overseas, but other costs – some not so obvious – may well offset the gains. Offshore sourcing usually involves larger inventories, for example, and higher administrative costs. Parts made overseas are less likely to meet specifications, so quality costs may be higher. Factor in higher transportation expenses and tariffs, and don't forget the cost of training foreign workers.

It takes longer to get supplies from an offshore location, so companies operating abroad are slower to respond to changing market demands. That too has its price. In 1984, some big U.S. retailers were stuck with huge inventories of imported goods they had

1. See, for example, William J. Abernathy, Kim B. Clark, and Alan M. Kantrow, "The New Industrial Competition," HBR September-October 1981, p. 68.

2. Dennis J. Encarnation, "Cross-Investment: A Second Front of Economic Rivalry," *California Management Review*, Winter 1987, p. 38.

3. Kenichi Ohmae, *Triad Power* (New York: Free Press, 1985), p. 5.

ordered the year before—when a slowdown in consumer spending was nowhere in sight!

These costs may seem obvious, but companies rarely take them into account when making the offshore manufacturing decision. According to a survey commissioned by the National Tooling and Machining Association, American tool and die makers routinely ignore these "hidden" costs of offshore manufacturing. Yet according to the survey, these costs typically add 5% to 15% to the foreign vendors' bid price for shipping, 3% for additional paperwork and communications, 5% to 10% for added inventory, and up to 35% for unanticipated design changes.

Other costs are less direct. Shifting some production operations overseas may prevent the company from exploiting economies of scale at home as well as abroad. The implications can be especially grave during a recession. Going offshore can also cause underutilization of existing manufacturing capacity and, ultimately, plant closings and layoffs.

Finally, companies that move outside the United States may lose valuable customers, who may switch to other U.S.-based suppliers. Italian chip maker Dynamit Nobel Silicon is among the foreign companies that opened a factory in the United States to be closer to its American customers. The managing director explained the decision by saying that "the distance between Italy and California is such that [customers] do not want to get any more than 10% of their needs from us."

You don't really save much on labor. On the surface, looking for low-wage sites for manufacturing is a logical way to reduce total production costs. But workers in less developed countries tend to be less productive than Americans, so a straight comparison of wages gives an inaccurate reading of the potential savings. Worse, in most businesses, direct labor is no longer a significant portion of total costs.

A survey of manufacturers by the National Association of Accountants found that on average labor represents only 15% of the cost of making a product. For most electronic items, labor is only 5% to 10% of the total cost. The wage savings are therefore unlikely to have a big impact overall. In some cases, they are offset by higher transportation costs alone. According to one expert, the typical cost of transporting a color TV set from Southeast Asia to the West Coast is 13% of its value at the time of shipping; making the set in Asia saves just 10%.[3]

Managers' preoccupation with labor costs deflects attention from the other 85% of the cost structure. Opportunities to save money in administration, inventory control, marketing, R&D, and distribution far exceed those relating to labor alone, but they are often overlooked.

You'll hollow the corporation. The semiconductor industry has split into two market segments: commodity and semicustom. Advocates of offshore manufacturing claim it doesn't matter if the commodity side of the business goes offshore in search of lower wages. As long as the design and R&D talent remains in the United States, so will the value added. Other industries have adopted this argument as well: as long as the company focuses on innovation, advanced technology, and excellent service, it doesn't really matter if it manufactures products abroad.

But a business cannot design in a vacuum. It cannot exploit new technologies if it has no chance to apply them. And it needs the profits from commodity production to fund R&D. The fact is, design and manufacturing are linked. A company that subcontracts its manufacturing to foreigners will soon lose the expertise to design and the ability to innovate, because it won't get the feedback it needs. Moving engineering offshore along with manufacturing is not a solution; it just accelerates the process. When companies do that, they give potential competitors not

"Looks like the gods are angry."

only finances and managerial expertise but also engineering skills.

The TV industry's inability to design and develop the new generation of TV products – the videocassette recorders and camcorders – is the perfect example. The U.S. television industry began assembling black and white sets overseas in the late 1960s. Assembly of color TVs soon followed black and white, and manufacturing followed assembly. By 1987, not one U.S. company was producing black and white TVs domestically, and only two – Zenith and Curtis Mathes – were making color TVs. Many people contend that the move offshore dispossessed U.S. manufacturers of manufacturing and design technologies needed to innovate or even compete with the innovators.

The semiconductor industry has fallen into the same trap. Americans have all but given up on the production of high-volume semiconductors such as 64K RAM chips. But memory chips are the cornerstone of semiconductor technology. Because they are a high-volume product, they serve as a testing ground for engineers trying to produce new technologies for other applications and for manufacturers trying to perfect delicate processes. In addition, they generate earnings for further research. By abandoning the commodity memory products, electronics companies put their design capabilities and technological leadership at risk.

Even normal product development suffers. As a senior executive of a large corporation explained: "I don't think people realize when they make the offshore decision that it is really a commitment to freeze the product. There is no way to make rapid design changes and product updates at a remote location."

Meanwhile, collaborators become competitors. The same senior executive continued: "To survive, the offshore manufacturer must build his own design or technology capability, and very quickly the game is over. He has the capability and the market." Consider Taiwan's Sunrise Plywood and Furniture. For years the company acted as an export platform for California's Mission Furniture. It relied on Mission's designs and blueprints to manufacture furniture suitable to American tastes. Now the Taiwanese company is one of Mission's competitors, exporting directly to the United States through its own marketing subsidiary.

The pattern is widespread. Hitachi, which has made microprocessors under license from Motorola, is now introducing its own 32-bit microprocessor. Toshiba, which acted as a supplier of copying machines to 3M, is now promoting its own brand name. Singatronics, which for years produced electronic games and pocket calculators for multinationals, is now pushing its own proprietary line of electronic medical instruments. And Daewoo, while still a subcontractor to U.S. companies, now sells its own personal computer.

The danger that collaboration will give way to competition is immediate and real. As the newly industrializing countries of Asia lose their advantage as low-wage producers to places like China and Thailand, they are increasingly anxious to develop their own technology-intensive industries and marketing capabilities. One executive of a large multinational told us, "Many Americans are naive about how insistent other nations have become on developing a full capability. Even in aerospace, it is hard to satisfy a coproduction requirement anymore by just letting the foreign plant rivet an aluminum assembly. The host country wants the whole technology, and it is not long before a competitor has been developed."

Many offer U.S. manufacturers incentives to bring their technology with them. Taiwan offers R&D facilities plus attractive loan packages. Malaysia has stepped up its efforts to get companies to invest in research, and Ireland has been encouraging foreign businesses to boost their product development efforts there.

U.S. companies that transfer technology across national borders don't have the same protection against piracy they enjoy at home. Indonesia, for example, has no patent protection at all. Korea denies copyright protection to software, semiconductors, or foreign works. Other countries require an importer of technology to license local companies to use that same technology for modest fees.

> First you build an offshore plant, then you give away your technology – then you're out of business.

The advantage doesn't last. Offshore manufacturing is most promising when three conditions hold: the dollar is strong, foreign wages are low, and trade barriers are absent. None of these factors is within a company's control. Most of the offshore investments between 1982 and 1985 were motivated by the strong dollar. Now that the dollar is considerably weaker, running those operations is more expensive. U.S. companies that purchase or produce abroad are not as price competitive as they were three years ago; the price of their products has gone up, along with those of all the other imports. There is no simple solution to their dilemma. Deere & Company, for example, makes its small tractors for the U.S. market in Japan and its midsize models in Germany. As the dollar declines, Deere will have to either raise prices or lower profit margins. Indeed, the aggregate figures for Deere's return on sales show a marked drop between 1984 and 1986: from 2.3% to −6.3%.

Reducing offshore activities when the dollar weakens is not a realistic option. Most of the offshore investments are irreversible capital expenditures, and they are hard to liquidate. But even purchasing arrangements are hard to change overnight. And it's unwise to sever a sound relationship with a foreign supplier when you know that the dollar may strengthen in a year or two.

Moreover, foreign wages inevitably rise. As workers learn and become more productive, they command higher pay. And as foreign countries grow economically, workers want a bigger piece of the pie. In Mexico, the minimum wage was increased three times in 1986–in January, June, and October. In Taiwan, average monthly earnings in manufacturing quadrupled in a ten-year period, from 2,929 Taiwanese dollars in 1974 to 12,844 Taiwanese dollars in 1984. In Korea, employee compensation doubled from 1979 to 1984. U.S. companies could run themselves ragged chasing low wages from one country to another.

Remember too that the threat of protectionism always looms. Importers are always risking a toughening of import restrictions. When a country's trade surplus with the United States swells, protectionism pressures intensify. Taiwan's $15.7 billion surplus in 1986, for instance, heightened pressures in the United States to impose trade restrictions on Taiwanese products–even though most of these products are exported to America by U.S. companies, including GE (Taiwan's biggest exporter), IBM, Hewlett-Packard, and Mattel. Such trade restrictions could have wiped out any cost savings from subcontracting or operating in Taiwan. To avoid rough treatment from the U.S. administration, Taiwan eventually increased the value of its currency, a move that made offshore imports originating in Taiwan more expensive.

U.S. companies could become gypsies, moving from one location to another as the cost of protectionism rises. U.S. retailers and clothing importers, for example, have embarked on systematic island-hopping, moving from one island to another to bypass limits on clothing imports. As soon as a new source of merchandise is found, the U.S. government moves in and imposes quotas, forcing the American importers to move on to other islands. This could be an acceptable short-term strategy, but sooner or later you run out of islands.

You may get trapped. Once a company moves its manufacturing operations to a developing country, the host government may begin to pressure management to transfer more advanced technologies or to support local spin-off industries. In many instances, the host countries insist on domestic content, technology transfer, and domestic equity positions that eventually lead to independent production capabilities. The company is often trapped: if it wants to stay in that country, it has no choice but to accede.

Overseas cost advantages are fleeting: wages rise, and the dollar weakens.

Mexico is a case in point. In early 1985, it rejected IBM's plan to build a plant there to produce microcomputers. But when IBM agreed to increase its plant investment from $6.1 million to $91 million, to buy parts built in Mexico, and to export 92% of its production, the government reversed itself. In the auto industry, Mexico has a 60% domestic content requirement for cars produced for the domestic market and a 30% domestic content requirement for cars destined for export. In addition, foreign businesses are limited to 40% ownership of joint ventures in auto parts.

Consider also India. In 1973, India passed a new law, the Foreign Exchange Regulation Act, under which foreign companies operating in India had to dilute their equity positions. When in 1977 the government asked IBM to dilute its equity to 74% and Coca-Cola to 40%, both companies decided to leave India rather than comply. Coca-Cola didn't want to disclose its syrup formula, and IBM didn't want to lose control of its marketing operations. India didn't miss the two companies: Burroughs and ICL are now doing IBM's work, and an Indian soft drink company called "77" has taken over Coke's market. But IBM and Coke no doubt miss India.

You'll lose valuable friends at home. When companies move operations overseas, life at home changes. Labor unions, resenting the loss of domestic jobs, are less likely to cooperate on other fronts. Their dissatisfaction is particularly important because U.S. companies need their help if they are to become more competitive. As UAW President Owen Bieber put it in a 1986 speech, "If we can't get support from the main players in the industry on our public policy agenda, the question might be asked why we should continue to work with them on the productivity side."

Labor dissatisfaction can also be expensive. In November 1986, the UAW struck GM's Delco Electronics plant in Kokomo, Indiana over a plan to boost outsourcing from Mexico. After a seven-day strike, GM canceled the plans. The National Association of Machinists and Aerospace Workers has proposed a "Rebuilding America" program that would force companies to contribute 1% of after-tax profits to a fund used to create new industries to replace those that leave the country. Similarly, the Teamsters union has proposed a plan that would require U.S. companies making products abroad for import back to the States to pay their foreign workers at least the going U.S. wage or forfeit the privilege of access to the U.S. marketplace. American companies paying less than the prevailing U.S. hourly compensation would have to put the difference into a fund for retraining U.S. workers.

Clothing importers have been island-hopping across Asia – forced to move each time wages rise.

Pressure can come from society as a whole. As more companies go offshore, more jobs are lost and the trade deficit worsens. Growing unhappiness over these conditions can create pressure on the government to intervene and force companies to assume part of the social costs they are generating. The government might, for instance, pass legislation forcing companies to give their workers "early" notification of plant closings or to assume responsibility for the training of their laid-off workers.

Offshore manufacturing has another effect of political significance: companies that may have lobbied collectively five years ago may become divided on issues of protectionism. That is, those who import most of their products and components have different concerns from their industry counterparts that manufacture in the United States. The whole industry loses clout. The semiconductor industry experienced such a split. In June 1985, Micron Technology Inc. of Idaho filed an antidumping petition against seven Japanese producers of 64K DRAM chips. The Semiconductor Industry Association, however, did not support the move because some of its members – like Motorola and Texas Instruments – produce in Japan. The association's official policy is to improve member access to the Japanese market.

The auto industry is another divided industry. GM, the industry's leader in forging international alliances, has vigorously opposed protectionism. Ford and Chrysler, on the other hand, have repeatedly asked for surcharges on Japanese imports. Similarly, in the textile industry, apparel manufacturers and big retail stores have paid no attention to the "Crafted with Pride in U.S.A." campaign that the textile industry and labor unions are promoting. Why should they, when 20% of their brand-name products are imported?

Of course, offshore manufacturing isn't wrong in every case. Indeed, there are legitimate reasons to locate overseas – to take advantage of certain natural resources, to expand export markets, or to be more responsive to local markets. But managers should question the assumption that it is always right. Chances are, in their eagerness to save money on labor, many companies are giving up more than they bargained for, not the least of which is their future competitive position.

Companies must recognize that offshore manufacturing does not constitute a long-term strategy. At best, it is merely a short-term tactical move that buys time for companies to restore their competitive health at home. Unless they break away from old traditions and look at their business as a total package, American companies cannot expect to become world competitors.

Reprint 88510

Keeping Informed

Product liability: you're more exposed than you think

Marisa Manley

Though the product liability crisis has fallen off the front pages, the problem has not gone away. Lower insurance rates, anticipated by liability law reforms, have seldom materialized. Liability insurance premiums remain a tremendous burden for businesses in many industries. Legislation aimed at limiting liability, enacted just last year, has been declared unconstitutional. Moreover, some U.S. courts are moving toward standards that will actually increase liability, even for businesses not at fault under the traditional legal doctrines.

Among these uncertainties there is one unhappy certainty: in this litigious society, companies cannot escape being sued. A business is always vulnerable to a lawsuit.

Recently I surveyed a wide range of cases to get answers to crucial liability questions confronting corporations: Just what are we liable for? What product design standards must we meet? How rigorously do we have to test our products? What are the risks of packaging? What is the effect of product service on liability? What defenses are available in a liability suit? No infallible defenses emerge, but there are ways to reduce the likelihood of facing a product liability lawsuit, and especially of losing one.

Handling the product

Your company can't be held liable unless there's a defect in your product or service. Of course, zero defects, and therefore zero liability, are almost impossible to achieve. But striving to reach that goal is the key to steering clear of ruinous claims.

Target and eliminate those defects that can cause injuries. Have your investigation range wide. Defendants in litigation are often surprised by the product characteristics courts identify as defects and hold them responsible for, even if these defects pop up somewhere else in the distribution chain.

The first step in limiting risk is to examine the design of the product and think of what could go wrong when someone uses it. Keep in mind that courts have the privilege of 20/20 hindsight. They're allowed to tell you how your product should have been designed.

General Motors faced this situation in San Francisco. While riding in a city bus, Florence Campbell was thrown from her seat, across the bus, and into the aisle when the bus made a sharp right turn from Market Street to Eighth Street. She reached out to steady herself, but there was no rail or strap. Hospitalized for 18 days, she had medical problems for years afterward. She sued GM, claiming the bus design was faulty. Mrs. Campbell lost at trial, but the California Supreme Court decided that all she had to prove was that if there had been a handrail within reach, she probably wouldn't have been seriously hurt. GM then had to prove that the design wasn't at fault.

Design defect litigation can be most expensive and troubling for businesses because it delves unabashedly into the gray realm of what should have been done and what would have happened if.... Almost every court acknowledges that a design defect, as opposed to a manufacturing defect – in which case a product is clearly not what it was intended to be – is difficult to identify. One thing is clear from case history: even if your product is as safe as anyone else's in your industry and does what customers expect it to do, if a feasible design alternative could have prevented an accident, your product is at fault. In any design decision that may affect the safety of your product, it's important to compare the benefits of that design solution – like cost savings or speed or ease of manufacturing – with the risk of harm to customers your decision may entail.

You may never achieve zero defects. But if you want to avoid lawsuits, try to reach that goal.

As you evaluate the design of the product, determine how well it will do what people may use it for. Don't limit your evaluation to how you *intend* people to use your product, as Ford and Goodyear did. Ford's 1976 Mercury Cougar came equipped with a 425-

Marisa Manley has written on legal matters for the Wall Street Journal, Barron's, *and* Inc. *She served IBM as an attorney for four years and is now with the Ginsberg Organization, a New York City real estate brokerage and consulting firm.*

horsepower engine and Goodyear radial tires. When Shelby Leleux pushed his Cougar to more than 100 miles an hour, a tire exploded, triggering an accident. Leleux was killed. His friend Floyd Dugas was seriously injured.

Leleux' mother and Dugas sued Ford and Goodyear for selling a defective product. According to testimony, Goodyear's tires had a maximum safe speed of 85 miles an hour. The companies claimed they weren't responsible because Leleux hadn't used the car as they intended. A Louisiana judge ruled that since the Cougar could go as fast as 105 miles an hour, Goodyear and Ford should have expected that some people might drive that fast and should have equipped the Cougar with tires able to handle that speed. It was insufficient for Ford's driver's manual to warn against going faster than 90 miles an hour. The companies were liable. As a manufacturer, you have to design your product to be safe in all the ways people are likely to use it.

Furthermore, product design can extend beyond what you think of as the product–packaging, for instance. Center Chemical Company made a drain cleaner that was almost pure sulfuric acid. Archie Parzini tried to open a bottle of cleaner at the restaurant where he worked. But the top was stuck. A coworker couldn't get it loose either. They worked at it with a pair of pliers. Suddenly the top came off, and Center's pliable plastic bottle gushed, sending drain cleaner into Parzini's eyes. It blinded him. He sued Center, claiming the product was defective. The court agreed, not because sulfuric acid is dangerous but because customers buy a product and package as a single unit. The package must be as carefully designed as the product.

You probably won't be liable, however, if people tamper with your product and put it in a dangerous condition. Warren Silverstein sued Walsh Press & Die Company for damages after losing several fingers when a Walsh-built punch press malfunctioned. He argued that Walsh hadn't built adequate safeguards into its machine and had never warned people about the potential hazards.

Walsh, however, demonstrated that the punch press had been modified by others in the 34 years since it had left the factory. The motor, pedal assembly, flywheel guard, and cam switch differed from those Walsh had installed. Somebody had removed the original safety devices. A manufacturer can't be held liable for injuries, the court decided, when a product is radically altered.

Absence of a proper warning may be as dangerous as a defect in design.

And if people use your safe product in combination with others, you may not be held responsible for any harm. Take the case of Spider Staging Sales Company, which made staging equipment for building construction and maintenance. Howard Antcliffe and James Hathcock were using Spider's ST-18, an aluminum platform raised and lowered by a powered winch, when sandblasting the State Employees Credit Union building in Lansing, Michigan. The two men hung the platform from wooden outriggers projecting over the roof and weighted on the other end by sandbags. When an outrigger broke, the ST-18 plunged to the ground, disabling Antcliffe. His wife sued Spider, claiming the company should have supplied metal outriggers.

The court ruled in favor of Spider. Metal outriggers weren't part of the product Spider sold, and the company was not responsible for accessories people might use with it. Platforms like the ST-18 can be rigged any number of ways, and Spider itself sold nine types of rigging devices. Moreover, professionals like Antcliffe often prefer their own methods. The platform Spider sold was safe, and just because Antcliffe rigged it in an unsafe way didn't make the company liable. A manufacturer, the court explained, need not find out everything about its customers' jobs and tell them how to proceed.

Adequate warning

Courts asked to decide on the soundness of a product often have ruled that the absence of a proper warning may be as dangerous as defects in design or fabrication. Norwich Pharmacal Company makes Furadantin, a prescription drug for urinary tract infections. Norwich advised physicians to monitor their patients. Dr. Elizabeth Wilbur gave Ellen McCue an open-ended prescription for Furadantin. Two years later, McCue contracted pulmonary fibrosis, a degenerative lung disease. The culprit: Furadantin. In the resulting litigation, Norwich blamed Dr. Wilbur for not monitoring her patient properly. Norwich knew that long-term use of Furadantin could cause pulmonary fibrosis, the judge noted, yet the company had provided no warning. He held Norwich liable.

The warning has to be specific. General warnings won't do, as executives of James B. Day & Company learned. It manufactured Kut-Koat, a furniture stripper used by Phil Sampson Interiors of Minneapolis. While a Sampson employee was using Kut-Koat, a nearby water heater ignited vapors from the liquids. The blaze burned the Sampson store, as well as neighbors Vic's Barber Shop, Chicken Pete, and Anderson Hardware.

The three businesses sued Sampson and the Hardenbergh Company, which sold Kut-Koat to Sampson, and Sampson in turn sued Day and Hardenbergh. Sampson was found to be partly liable because of its carelessness. While the label on the Kut-Koat can said the product could catch fire, it didn't specify that Kut-Koat *vapors* were also a fire hazard. Day and Hardenbergh were liable even though the label complied with federal and local regulations. (Government standards on labeling, testing, manufacturing, even product configuration and composition are minimums, of course.)

Even with full disclosure, you may be liable if your warning fails to reach the right people. The Heil Company built a hydraulic hoist that

Beno Truck Equipment installed on a dump truck belonging to the Thomas Heard Construction Company. While Heard employee Milton Marshall was beneath the raised truck bed, repairing its differential gear, he brushed against an exposed cable. This triggered the release of the hydraulic lift, and the truck bed collapsed on him, crushing his spine and shoulder muscles.

During the litigation that followed, Heil pointed out that its instruction manual cautioned users to block the dump truck's body before anyone worked beneath it. This wasn't good enough, the Louisiana judge ruled. There was no evidence that Marshall had ever read the manual. He didn't need to since his work had nothing to do with the hydraulic system. Heil was liable. According to the judge, the company should have anticipated that a mechanic who was not a hydraulic expert could be endangered by the system it had designed. The best place for a warning is probably on the product itself.

Who are the ultimate customers you should warn about your product's dangers? Everyone you can reasonably expect will come into contact with it during normal use.

But you needn't disclose risks that are considered obvious. Charles Posey was moving boxes of furnaces into high stacks with a forklift made by the Clark Equipment Company. Because the forklift was designed for use in low spaces, it had no overhead safety guards. The forks caught the edge of an adjacent stack of boxes, and a carton fell, seriously injuring Posey. In his suit against Clark, Posey insisted that the company should have posted a notice on the forklift telling people to use safety guards when working around high stacks. The Indiana judge rejected Posey's claim without a trial. His reasoning: it's obvious that if you're working around high stacks, something can fall and hurt you.

But you must take care in determining what's obvious. What may be apparent to you, an expert, may not be so to someone who buys your product. Virginia Burke sued Almaden Vineyards when a plastic cork launched itself, unaided, from a champagne bottle, shattering her eyeglass lens and hurting her eye. Almaden argued that popping corks and champagne bottles go together; the danger is clear. Hence it didn't have to warn customers. But a California judge disagreed. Most people, he ruled, don't know that a plastic cork can eject at speeds up to 49 miles an hour. When in doubt, warn.

Like warnings, adequate instructions on safe product use are important. Make sure your label is specific and easy to understand. Many states have laws prescribing the content of certain product labels. If your failure to heed a statute deprives consumers of information that could have kept them safe, you'll be a fair target for a product liability claim.

In distribution channels

You cannot determine who will ultimately use your product, but you can protect yourself by advising those who distribute it to try to limit purchases to consumers you're aiming at. If you know your distributors are selling your product to people who shouldn't have it and you do nothing about it, you'll probably be liable in any litigation. Warn unwanted users that your product isn't intended for them.

This step saved Helene Curtis Industries from a civil penalty. Curtis's New Blue bleach and Cosmair's L'Oreal Creme developer were sold only to beauty parlors and marked clearly "for professional use only." But Ms. Hendren, an amateur, bought some of each at a Terrell, Oklahoma beauty shop to bleach Marjorie Ann Pruitt's hair. Ignoring the directions on the New Blue package, she mixed incompatible solutions. While she then enjoyed an iced tea, the solutions burned Pruitt's scalp. Pruitt sued Helene Curtis and Cosmair, claiming the products were defective. She lost because both companies had clearly made an effort to limit distribution to professionals. Hendren had no training as a beautician and had failed to take the precautions a beautician normally would.

Other members of the distribution chain, your suppliers, for instance, are also potential sources of liability. But you can minimize the risk. American Radiator & Standard Sanitary Corporation could not escape. One

Your suppliers can be a source of liability.

of its water heaters blew up, hospitalizing Myrtle Rauch for more than a year. Though the culprit was a safety valve made by another company, an Iowa court found American liable and upheld the state's largest verdict in a personal injury case to date (1960), $90,000. The court's reasoning: a catalog American distributed to its dealers listed this safety valve as the correct replacement part for its heaters. The valve was sold under American Radiator's aegis, hence the company was liable for any malfunctioning.

The best way to minimize risk is to test components you get from suppliers or have them furnish you with enough data about tests they perform to make you feel comfortable about the components. Consider incorporating into your contracts with suppliers provisions that will allow you access to their test data or that will give you enough time to test what they deliver before you have to accept their goods.

Businesses that supply components to someone else can also be liable for defects in the final product. California oil derrick man Edward Edison plunged 90 feet to his death, the victim of a faulty safety belt. As you might expect, his widow sued the Lewis Manufacturing Company, which had assembled the belt, and the North & Judd Manufacturing Company, which had made the flawed component, a D-ring anchoring Edison's belt to the derrick. North & Judd advertised its D-rings as "tested safety hardware," and although the company had indeed conducted tests, it hadn't tested how well the D-

Limit liability via a subsidiary?

Shifting a high-risk venture into a subsidiary or affiliated corporation seems a logical way to limit the prospect of product or service liability lawsuits. But the new corporation has to be carefully structured. The key question is whether the subsidiary is actually a distinct corporation empowered to act on its own initiative.

Consider the case of Mr. Wind, owner of One-Hour Dura Cleaning, which served his six Dura Clean dry-cleaning stores in the Buffalo, New York area. Wind set up each outlet as a separate corporation. Antoni Geletucha, who worked at one of them, died after breathing too much perchloroethylene, a cleaning solvent. His widow sued both the store and the parent company. Wind convinced a lower court to throw out the case on the grounds that since One-Hour Dura and the store were separate entities, the management company was not liable.

But all his companies had the same officers, directors, and stockholders. Every store was identified with a similar sign and was listed under "One-Hour Dura Cleaning" in the Buffalo phone book. Every store gave customers "Dura" receipts and protected their clothing in plastic wrapping marked "Dura." The parent company kept the books and filed income tax returns for the six corporations; handled all repairs, office supervision, and clerical work; and ordered all supplies, including perchloroethylene. An appellate court reversed Wind's early victory, ruling that since Dura apparently controlled the six corporations, it was up to a jury to decide whether One-Hour Dura itself should be liable for its mistakes—and Geletucha's death.

A key element of distance between the parent and the subsidiary is a measure of financial independence. The parent must endow the unit with enough capital to carry on business; it isn't enough to provide the sometimes nominal "consideration" required for many contracts. The subsidiary (or affiliate) must be able to handle its liabilities.

A case in point is Taylor Oak Flooring, a timber-processing company in Warren, Arkansas that went bankrupt. Lumber wholesaler George Henderson and other creditors were asked to settle their unpaid invoices for 20 cents on the dollar. Instead, Henderson sued Rounds & Porter Lumber Company, which owned half of Taylor.

Although Rounds didn't have a clear majority interest, it was responsible for Taylor's financial position. From the day Taylor had been formed, a contract required it to sell lumber to Rounds at 50% below market price. Taylor's costs of handling and finishing the flooring always amounted to more than it charged Rounds—which Rounds's management knew. Taylor quickly depleted its initial capital of $60,000. Rounds took over the management when Taylor's cofounder resigned and, in a couple of months, by continuing to buy at below-market prices, Rounds had stripped Taylor of its liquid assets. Because Taylor had always been financially dependent on Rounds, the judge ruled that Rounds was liable for Taylor's debts.

But if you endow a new corporation with a reasonable amount of money to carry on its business, give it the authority to act in its own best interests, and follow the formal procedures that identify it as a separate company, courts will generally respect that corporation as a real legal entity—making it a shield for other parts of your business, no matter what your motivation was in creating it.

Geletucha v. 222 Delaware Corp. et al., 182 N.Y.S.2d 893 (S. Ct., App. Div., 4th Department, 1959).

Henderson et al. v. Rounds & Porter Lumber Co., 99 F. Supp. 376 (U.S. District Court, W.D. Arkansas, 1951).

ring could withstand sudden strain like the weight of a man falling. North & Judd was held liable for Edison's death.

In testing, simulate the toughest conditions your product is likely to encounter. Courts say that a trouble-free history doesn't entitle you to assume your product is defect free.

If you sell a component of another product, it's up to you to make sure your item is suited for its end use. In a product liability action, you will have to account for what you actually know about how another manufacturer uses your product and most likely for what you should have known. Information that your sales representatives and executives pick up from customers can be valuable to the people who design and test your products.

Retailers too can be held responsible for selling defective goods. Macrose Lumber & Trim Company sold Paul Schwartz a box of masonry nails that proved too brittle: the very first one he hammered shattered, sending splinters into his right eye. A New York State court sided with the plaintiff. Schwartz collected from Macrose, and it was the retailer's problem to collect what it could from the wholesaler and manufacturer.

Since the retailer is the last link in a distribution chain that encourages a customer to buy, courts say they're justified in holding retailers liable for defects in the products they sell. Before you put any product on your shelf, make sure it's at least reasonably suitable for the ways a customer would ordinarily use it. As a retailer, you alone have the responsibility for flaws you can discover through inspection.

Those in the leasing business can also get embroiled in lawsuits through faulty service. Consider the case of Hawk Aviation, which leased airplanes at the Farmington, New Mexico municipal airport. One of its airplanes crashed a few minutes after takeoff, killing the pilot, Dr. Stanley Rudisaile. Investigation showed that Hawk's maintenance man had drained the airplane's oil but hadn't replaced it. Although a routine preflight check would have revealed to Dr. Rudisaile that he had no oil, Hawk was found liable. The product (the airplane) was more dangerous than a customer would ordinarily expect. Here, as in many other liability cases, the customer's carelessness was no defense.

Hertz learned a similar lesson. On a vacation, the Knapp family crashed a Hertz station wagon into a concrete wall at a Pennsylvania toll plaza. Even if Mrs. Knapp had contributed to the accident by driving with the hand brake partially applied, the court held, Hertz was liable on three counts: the hydraulic brake system didn't work properly, she shouldn't have been able to drive with the hand brake partially applied, and the hand brake didn't work when the foot brake system failed. Better maintenance would have prevented the Knapps' accident and avoided 15 years of litigation.

For the defense

How can you defend yourself if a defective product slips through your most rigorous quality controls? By design, defenses to strict product liability claims are few. Like it or not, the intention is to shift risk away from customers and to those in the chain of distribution who, theoretically at least, can better handle the risk.

Some 46 states have mandated that manufacturers are strictly liable for product defects. (Strict liability means that you can be held liable even if you're not at fault in the traditional sense.) These laws differ on many points, including the time a plaintiff has to bring a lawsuit, how much a plaintiff has to prove, and the defenses available to manufacturers. For instance, a California manufacturer may be faced with evidence of subsequent changes as proof that its product was at one time defective; in Louisiana, such evidence is prohibited in strict liability actions.

State laws not only differ from one another but are also a moving target. This past year, at least 19 states modified laws affecting a manufacturer's liability. The effect of those changes is still largely untested.

Still, most states accept certain defenses. If a customer knows your product and its dangers, you may be absolved of liability, but only if you can show that the injured person was aware of specific risks. Think of the plight of Emerson Electric Company, which produced a power chain saw professionals used to cut pulpwood. One of these saws caused Howard Thompson's death. Apparently (no one saw the accident) the saw hit something it couldn't cut through and jumped back and struck Thompson, severing his jugular vein. He died before the ambulance arrived.

In testing, simulate the toughest conditions your product is likely to encounter.

In its defense, Emerson argued that as a woodcutter, Thompson must have known the risks in using a chain saw. Moreover, the instruction manual explained that chain saws can kick back. But a Louisiana judge faulted Emerson's disclosure: it should have warned that kickback can't be avoided and that serious, even fatal accidents can result. Thompson was using the chain saw properly, the judge reasoned, and there was no proof he knew how dangerous kickback could be. Thompson's widow and daughter were awarded over a quarter of a million dollars.

Contrast this case with that of Wysong & Miles Company, which sold a Model 150 press brake – 9 feet high, 12 feet wide, weighing more than 20,000 pounds – to Metal Fabricators of Jacksonville, Florida, where riggers James Alderman, Phil Harbison, and Butch Carter were to install it. As they moved it into place, it toppled onto Alderman. He later died from his injuries.

Alderman's widow sued Wysong, arguing that the company's press brakes were poorly designed; they were so top-heavy that they tended to topple over. Wysong acknowledged this but pointed out that all press brakes are top-heavy, and professional riggers know it. That press brakes are top-heavy doesn't make them defective. In his testimony, Harbison confirmed that he, Alderman, and Carter knew that press brakes are top-heavy. Because they were experienced, none of them had read Wysong's manual for installing the Model 150. The court ruled that Alderman had assumed the risk of working with the product.

Finally, even if you did produce or sell a defective product, you can be held responsible only if the defects caused the plaintiff's injuries. When Mildred Stammer's new Chevrolet rolled into the path of a train, she sued General Motors. She claimed the automatic choke was defective, causing the car to stall. But whether your car's engine is running or not, the judge ruled, if you take your foot off the brake pedal and don't use the hand brake, your car will roll down a slope. The accident couldn't be blamed on the choke, and General Motors wasn't responsible for Mrs. Stammer's accident.

From General Motors on down, anybody in business may have to contend with a lawsuit. Zero defects are seldom possible. But by understanding the range of product defects that can lead to liability and by targeting resources to eliminate those most likely to cause injury, you can sharply reduce the risk of losing a product liability lawsuit.

Cases listed in order of mention

Campbell v. General Motors Corp., 649 P.2d 224 (Cal. S. Ct., 1982).

Duhon v. Goodyear Tire & Rubber Co. et al.; Dugas v. Goodyear Tire & Rubber Co. et al., 451 F. Supp. 253 (USDC, La. 1978).

A.A. Parzini v. Center Chemical Co., 214 S.E.2d 700 (Ga. Ct. of Appeals, 1975); 234 S.E.2d 580 (Ga. S. Ct., 1975); 221 S.E.2d 475 (Ga. Ct. of Appeals, 1975).

Silverstein v. Walsh Press & Die Co., 501 N.Y.S. 2d 97 (1986).

Antcliffe v. State Employees Credit Union & Spider Staging Sales Company, Inc. et al., 290 N.W. 2d 420 (Mich. Ct. of Appeals, 1980); 327 N.W.2d 814 (Mich. S. Ct., 1982).

McCue v. Norwich Pharmacal Co., 453 F.2d 1033 (1st. Cir. 1972).

Blasing v. P.R.L. Hardenbergh Company; Sampson Interiors Inc. v. Hardenbergh Company, 226 N.W.2d 110 (Minn. S. Ct., 1975).

Marshall v. Beno Truck Equipment, Inc. et al., 481 So.2d 1022 (La. Ct. of Appeals, 1986).

Posey v. Clark Equipment Co., 409 F.2d 560 (7th Cir. 1969).

Burke v. Almaden Vineyards, Inc. et al., 86 Cal. 3rd 419 (Cal. Ct. of Appeals, 1978).

Pruitt v. Helene Curtis Industries Inc. & Cosmair Inc., 385 F.2d 841 (5th Cir. 1967).

Rauch v. American Radiator & Standard Sanitary Corp., 104 N.W.2d 607 (Iowa S. Ct., 1960).

Edison v. Lewis Mfg. Co. & North and Judd Mfg. Co., 336 P.2d 286 (Cal.App. Div., 1959).

Schwartz v. Macrose Lumber & Trim Co., 270 N.Y.S.2d 875 (1966).

Rudisaile v. Hawk Aviation Inc., 592 P.2d 175 (New Mexico S. Ct., 1979).

Knapp v. Hertz Corp., 375 N.E.2d 1349 (Ill. App. Ct., 1978).

Thompson v. Tuggle et al., 486 So.2d 144 (La. Ct. of Appeals, 1986).

Alderman v. Wysong & Miles Co., 486 So.2d 673 (Fla. Ct. of Appeals, 1986).

Stammer v. General Motors Corp., 259 N.E.2d 352 (Ill. App. Ct., 1970).

Building Brands

Walter J. Salmon and Karen A. Cmar

Private labels are back in fashion

Combat between manufacturer and private brands in the same product categories is as much a feature of modern marketing as combat among manufacturer brands. Now the battle between manufacturer and private brands has taken a new turn. Strong brand names and private labels, originally confined mainly to packaged-goods businesses, have become immensely important in the fashion industry. The reactions of retailers and manufacturers have implications that transcend the boundaries of the soft-goods trade.

Ralph Lauren, Benetton, and Liz Claiborne are now brands as well as fashions. Brands once associated only with function like Jockey underwear and Sperry Top-Siders also have introduced style and color into their products and now stand for fashion as well as function.

Private labels will grow. National brands will dominate.

The ascension of manufacturer brands in the fashion world has stimulated other important developments. Ralph Lauren and Coach, and a number of European retailers including Burberry, Benetton, and Laura Ashley, have opened their own or franchised stores that sell only merchandise of their own labels.

Confronted suddenly by manufacturers that as a result of the acceptance or cachet of their brand names possess "consumer power," traditional retailers have reacted decisively:

☐ Macy's has boosted its private-label sales from 6% of volume in 1980 to more than 20% in 1986 and currently has more than 50 in-house labels. In some categories, private-label merchandise represents as much as 50% of sales.

☐ The Limited, one of the fastest growing fashion specialty chains, has made private-label merchandise a cornerstone of its strategy. Such goods represent 70% of its sales. The Limited's private brand Forenza and Outback Red combined are the third largest in sales of women's apparel in the country.

☐ Sears Roebuck and J.C. Penney, in contrast, are adding national brands to what were assortments of almost entirely private-label merchandise. Safeway and Kroger, the nation's two largest food chains, are also reemphasizing national brands at the expense of private labeling.

The explanation of these apparently contradictory developments is complex. It involves:

Changing consumer shopping habits.

The impact of sophisticated management information systems on the technology and scale of retailing.

New relationships between retailers and manufacturers.

Shifting consumer merchandise tastes.

Waning dedication of several chains to private labels.

1 **Changing consumer habits.** One impediment to private-label programs in fashion retailing has been the belief that stores have to carry a broad selection of styles to satisfy diverse consumer interests. Because it demands so much design and procurement skill, a broad selection in a private-label program has

Walter Salmon is the Stanley Roth, Sr. Professor of Retailing at the Harvard Business School. He is the author of several books and articles on retailing and a director of several companies, including Carter Hawley Hale Corporation, the Quaker Oats Company, and Zayre, Inc.

Karen Cmar is an associate in the New York City office of the consulting firm of McKinsey & Company, where she specializes in assisting consumer products and retailing companies.

been difficult for a retailer to create. In this age of heterogeneous life-styles, however, many customers prefer to shop in convenient, mall-oriented specialty stores carrying limited selections of items targeted to their needs. Since they concentrate on fulfilling the interests of narrow market segments, specialty retailers are especially well suited to developing targeted private-label merchandise. They can focus their buying, design, and procurement functions on a limited range of styles. They can thoroughly research their customers' needs. Because they concentrate their purchases in a few product categories, they build buying power that – along with steadfast relationships with vendors and raw-materials producers – leads to better purchasing terms.

Better and faster information cuts the risk of private-label programs.

Specialty retailers can also use private labels to create cohesiveness between their merchandise and its retail presentation, which becomes an important competitive edge. Creating a product design in concert with a point-of-sale presentation concept enables the retailer to make a clear fashion statement and generate excitement about the product. The result is salespeople who are enthusiastic and customers who understand how the new designs coincide with their life-styles. Stores like The Limited, The Gap, Benetton, and Laura Ashley are particularly skillful in creating this synergy.

2 **Information technology.** One of the obstacles to a private-label program in the field of fashion used to be that it represented a high level of risk. Retailers had to make fashion commitments far in advance of the selling season. They could neither return private-label merchandise nor get markdown allowances from vendors. The availability of better information, however, has sharply reduced this risk. Point-of-sale information systems that send feedback on sales instantly to the buying function help cut lead times and pare inventory. The result is lower carrying costs, fewer markdowns, faster execution of design changes, and quicker response to in-season reorders.

At Macy's, for example, private-label merchandise is coded to generate point-of-sale data permitting the corporate buying office to track the sales of each style, color, and size on a daily basis. Retailers thereby get a much better handle than manufacturers on customers' reactions to new styles.

(Some retailers share such information with their suppliers. But these cooperative programs have their drawbacks: retailers' and suppliers' economic objectives may differ, disputes may arise over the division of the derived benefits, and uncertainty inevitably endangers the continuity of the relationship. Of course, the retailers may also fear leaks of information to competitors.)

An information system supporting a private-label program also enables retailers to test new products, interpret the test results, and react quickly. A retailer with stores in most states can test summer clothes in Florida in the winter and use the results in time to have goods made for sale nationally in the ensuing spring and summer.

These circumstances may make test marketing an advisable option in many fashion product categories. Test marketing reduces the need for "gut feel" merchandising and can make marketers of private-label goods more confident in committing big inventory dollars to definite fashion statements.

At The Limited, for example, when the store division designers send a test design to the procurement division, they can have samples in the stores for testing within a week. The procurement division speeds the work by dealing with the factories in the Far East via facsimile. If the test results are positive, stock quantities can usually be delivered within two months.

Increasingly sophisticated and affordable information systems have been particularly helpful to specialty chains. Not long ago, the great distance between these chains' central buying organizations and their widely scattered stores meant that the central buyers lacked timely and accurate details on what was and was not selling. So the chains maintained conservative fashion postures, and their private-label mer-

chandise was conservative in style too, or in fashion lingo, "dumb." The combination of advanced information systems, narrow market focus, and strong central procurement organizations, however, has enabled specialty store chains to create more fashionable private-label merchandise.

These information systems also facilitate overseas procurement of private-label merchandise. Import programs require long lead times and severely complicate communication. Software systems not only expedite the consolidation and interpretation of sales and stock status data from stores but also speed order quantity revisions to overseas suppliers. A good information system is essential for supporting a private-label program oriented to foreign factories.

Factory automation has also augmented the benefits of integrating manufacturing with retailing functions. The recent development of flexible, automated equipment for making fashion goods has created great economies of scale. Scale economies often lead to integration as manufacturers try to protect their capital investment by controlling their distribution channels and as retailers try to win a cost advantage by guaranteeing volume-sensitive manufacturers a steady quantity of production. Benetton's expanding network of franchised stores is an example of a chain that has, in effect, integrated forward to ensure volume for its increasingly capital-intensive knitting and dyeing facilities.

3 **New relationships.** Changing relationships between retailers and manufacturers have also contributed to the prominence of private-label goods in fashion retailing. In recent years, as designer names and national advertising have grown in importance, most retailers have felt compelled to feature the offerings of fewer large vendors. Furthermore, young, inexperienced department store buyers often tend to purchase "safe" merchandise from established sources. As a consequence, retailers have seen their assortments become disturbingly similar to the competition's and differentiation more difficult to achieve. Retailers have also noted that their major vendors were earning high returns on investment and often manufacturing overseas.

Meanwhile, some vendors have become competitors. Manufacturers from abroad, including Laura Ashley, Benetton, and Burberry, have opened their own stores. Ralph Lauren, a noted U.S. designer who licenses the use of his name on home furnishings and a wide range of men's and women's apparel, now has Lauren-franchised as well as two Lauren-owned stores. The stores sell only Lauren-brand products and compete directly with existing customers. Some of these suppliers argue that their own stores have helped their arm's-length customers by expanding recognition of their brand names, displaying all their merchandise attractively and cohesively, and acting as test sites for new merchandise and display concepts. But retailers have remained suspicious of their suppliers' ultimate intentions.

Retailers have also been under sales and profit pressures as a result of excess capacity. In square feet per capita, the United States has, in comparison with other Western countries, far more retail space than it needs.

The response to the pressures has been bigger markups on merchandise and attempts to extract concessions from vendors like more markdown allowances, more liberal merchandise return privileges, higher advertising allowances, and easier credit terms. Because big retailers have immense buying power, even major vendors have found these demands hard to resist.

The next development to affect manufacturer-retailer relationships has been off-price retailing, which grew from sales of $3 billion in 1979 to more than $8 billion in 1986. It now represents about 7% of total apparel sales. This innovation has been particularly threatening to traditional retailers because, unlike discount department stores, off-price retailers offer consumers department-store quality apparel at savings of 20% or more. Furthermore, consumer awareness of designer and brand names has made this merchandise easy to recognize as the equivalent of what traditional retailers offer.

The behavior of the traditional retailers themselves, of course, has given off-price retailing a boost. Their higher initial markups established an umbrella that made the price tags of apparel in off-price stores appear attractive. Moreover, the markdown allowances and other concessions that traditional retailers were extracting from vendors made the terms off-price retailers offered to the vendors appealing. While off-price retailers demanded lower purchase prices than the competition, they paid up promptly and sought no extra concessions.[1]

For traditional stores, the threat of off-price retailing crystallized the need for and the advantages of private-label merchandise. Here was an answer to the differentiation problem. Here was at least a partial shield from price competition and margin erosion. By procuring private-label goods overseas directly, a chain could also bypass the designer and name-brand sources and perhaps capture some of the high ROI their vendors were enjoying.

4 **Changing consumer tastes.** The aging of the baby-boom generation has produced shifts in apparel demand. The fad orientation of the 1960s and early 1970s gave way to the "preppie look" in the late 1970s. This look has evolved into a new approach to dressing consisting of classically styled pieces in updated colors and traditional items combined in innovative ways. The "layered look" and "investment dressing" are terms fashion-conscious people use to describe these classically styled items.

Retailers with strong private-label programs and manufacturers with their own outlets tend to favor these classics. Benetton brings new fashion to its classic sweaters, for example, through exciting color selection, creative layering, and eye-catching display. Benetton calls this look "industrial fashion," meaning simple styling that fits well, is comfortable to wear, and most important, lends itself to efficient production. In a more obvious attempt to create fashion excitement, The Limited offers private-label goods in basic silhouettes and updates them through colors, textures, minor detailing, layering, and accessories. In higher price ranges, many manufacturers owning or franchising retail outlets offer more classic merchandise. Through classic styling, Burberry, Laura Ashley, Gucci, Ralph Lauren, Louis Vuitton, and Charles Jourdan reduce the risk of inventory obsolescence and make demand more predictable.

Sears and Penney are doing something about their "dumb" merchandise.

The way the industry tells consumers about the latest look has also shifted. Advertising, particularly by designers and manufacturers, has become more prominent. Point-of-sale displays, music, video, and, in specialty stores, well-trained sales help have taken on greater importance in educating customers and promoting new styles. The excitement of fashionable classics comes less from the design room and the factory than from the way the product is advertised, promoted, displayed, and sold. These merchandising devices have reduced the risk of product obsolescence and thus eased the integration of the retailing and manufacturing functions.

5 **The big chains' reaction.** While department and specialty stores have been stressing private labels in clothing, Sears Roebuck and J.C. Penney as well as Safeway and Kroger in food retailing have been downplaying their own brands.

In contrast to specialty stores, Sears and Penney cater to a wide spectrum of consumers. The Sears slogan, "Where America shops," is testimony to that. As a result of efforts to appeal to everybody, much of their private-label merchandise has turned out to be "dumb," if not bland, in style. Moreover, in contrast with the specialty chains, authority for merchandise assortments at both Sears and Penney had always been shared by the headquarters and field organizations. This division of responsibility, with the inevitable compromises to satisfy diverse needs, probably contributes to making their private-label merchandise dull.

1 See Jack G. Kaikati, "Don't Discount Off-Price Retailers," HBR May-June 1985, p. 85.

In an era of increasingly heterogeneous life-styles, such an assortment appealed to a declining portion of the American public. Moreover, while the private labels of Sears and Penney once offered excellent value, the advent of promotional department stores like Mervyn's, upscale discounters such as Target (both owned by Dayton Hudson), and the off-price retailers have eroded this advantage.

Sears and Penney have acted to repair the damage. By taking advantage of the data-gathering potential of their information systems, they have vested more responsibility for merchandise assortments at headquarters. They have added national brands to their assortments. Using the output of design talent – external like Halston in the instance of Penney and internal like the Cheryl Tiegs collection in the instance of Sears – they have endeavored to create more fashionable private-label merchandise and to give it a certain élan. The changing posture of Sears and Penney toward private labels is not actually a contradiction of the underlying factors we have cited but a departure from what had become a religious and possibly irrational dedication to this type of branding.

There are two quite different explanations for the retreat from private brands at certain large food chains, particularly Safeway and Kroger. Although they hardly sell fashion products, their experience is relevant to fashion retailers.

For a number of years, these chains minimized their national brand assortments, the quantity and quality of shelf space afforded these brands, and the role they played in promotional programs. Only when customers began to desert them for retailers with more balanced assortments did these chains question their devotion to private labels. Fashion retailers should remember that consumers also want good selection, and good selection means national brands – unless the retailer is large enough and serving a market niche narrow enough to permit the development of expertise equal to that of brand-name manufacturers.

To boost their margins, many food chains acquired facilities to produce private-label merchandise. But failure to keep up with technology and difficulty in attracting top-flight manufacturing talent to these essentially nonmanufacturing businesses diminished their competitiveness. The consequence for the private-label items was either higher prices at the checkout station or lower gross margins. Either way, Safeway and Kroger lost much of their enthusiasm for manufacturing their own brands. This experience suggests that integration by retailers, including those in the fashion industries, all the way back into manufacturing is difficult and risky.

Yet another lesson for fashion retailers from the food industry has to do with measuring product profitability. Gross margin, or the difference between sale price and purchase price stated as a percentage of the sale price, has long been the general measure of product profitability. A new standard, however, is gaining acceptance in the food industry: "direct product profit," which measures the contribution to fixed cost and profit per unit of selling space. In addition to gross margin, it takes account of differences in sales volume, inventory turnover, handling costs, and sales promotion support and credit terms from suppliers. Because national food brands often have higher volume, faster turnover, and higher prices than private-label food items, national brands often yield greater direct product profit. The emergence of this standard has stimulated Safeway and Kroger, among other food chains, to reconsider their unswerving support for private label. They have shifted assortments to put more emphasis on national brands and less on their own brands.

The next round

What will be the outcome of this round in the battle between national brands and private labels in the fashion business? We believe that private-brand sales will continue to grow but that national brands will maintain their dominance of most product categories in most distribution channels.

The exception will be specialty chains. Excluding those that sell high-price, high-fashion goods, such stores will carry mainly private-label merchandise. Benetton, The Gap, and The Limited, with their narrow focus, mid-price points, fashionable non-leading-edge orientation, and excellent information systems, exemplify such chains. These features give them an advantage over manufacturers in developing products for their specific markets.

Department stores, chain stores, and other retailers serving a broad spectrum of consumers will continue to rely heavily on national brands. Building an adequate assortment of attractive private-label merchandise for a target market with such varied tastes is impracticable. If most consumers continue to shop in these stores (and we think they will), national brands will maintain a solid distribution channel. The goal of most department stores has therefore become to raise private-label sales to 20% to 25% of volume.

In high-fashion, high-price goods, demand is dizzyingly fickle.

The disposition toward private labels varies not only by channel but also by product category. In some categories, private brands will improve their penetration. One of these is moderate-priced apparel for 15- to 35-year-old women, the largest segment of the fashion apparel business. A large market enables a chain to spread both the costs of manufacturing and a centralized design and procurement operation over larger lot sizes and more styles. This market is also well suited for import programs because its design demands can often be satisfied with "fashionable classics," which is the type of moderate-risk merchandise most appropriate for private branding and for overseas procurement with its longer lead times.

Classic, expensive clothes for men as well as for women are other product categories in which national brands as traditionally defined will continue to lose luster. Wholly or partly vertically integrated manufacturer-retailers like Brooks Brothers, Coach, and Burberry are strong and growing stronger in this market. Most of them produce goods that vary little from year to year. Because most had been manufacturers before entering retailing, they already had established brand names. They broke into retailing not so much to build profits as to control or enhance their brand images and to create laboratories for new products. These companies will grow in retailing because stores give them a valuable communication channel with customers and, contrary to expectations, have turned out to be highly profitable. While opening more of their own outlets, these companies will continue to sell through higher priced specialty and department stores.

In some product categories and types of stores, designer names and manufacturer brands will still prevail. One of these is high-fashion, high-price goods, where demand is uncertain, the volume potential of each style small, and the risk of inventory obsolescence very high. Moreover, talented designers of this merchandise are in short supply and expensive. For reasons of money and ego, they are loath to substitute store names for their own names on products they create. Taken together, these factors suggest that private labels are unlikely to encroach much on high-fashion, high-price merchandise or on the stores that sell it.

Clouds on the horizon

While the future of the private label in the apparel industry looks bright, several caveats deserve mention. One factor powering private branding's gains is consumer interest in fashionable classics. Should this interest fade and merchandise with a greater fad element win consumers' favor, the retailer would take on more risk by emphasizing private-label items. Since the retailer and the manufacturer of a national brand share the risk of fashion obsolescence, retailers may decide to protect themselves by partly shifting their focus back to national brands.

A second cloud on the private-label horizon is the prospect of acceptance in fashion retailing of the concept of direct product profit. Indisputably, general merchandise retailers' enthusiasm for private labels stems partly from its higher gross margin. Under the direct product profit concept, private labels would not fare well in comparison with national brands. This possibility would mean, of course, not elimination of private labels—only the containment of excess enthusiasm for it.

Naturally, the forces with a stake in national brands will not stand on the sidelines and let private labels grow uncontested. The national brands can be expected to respond with more branded boutiques within large stores, more cooperative advertising, more point-of-sale material, and more information sharing (both electronically and informally). Fashion manufacturers will act more like cosmetics companies that market through, not to, retail channels. Marginal brands, which lack the clout to develop such relationships, will likely lose further share to the stronger brands and to private brands.

The growth of these cooperative relationships may change the face of the fashion industry. It will become harder for smaller apparel producers to break into the large stores. Only in the high-fashion segment will small brands remain important.

Another obstacle to a private-label program is the difficulty of execution. Most retail institutions lack the skills to excel at developing fashion products. Even when they hire talented design and merchandising professionals, retailers must still loosen their enduring bonds with national-brand manufacturers and accept higher inventory risk. Establishing information, logistics, and production systems to support a large private-label program is also a formidable task. An international network of manufacturing affiliations, for example, may take years to develop.

Private-label programs also require a minimum scale in a given product line. A particular style must generate enough volume to allow production of an economic lot size, and overall volume must be large enough to engender clout with suppliers. Therefore, only large, sophisticated retailers are likely to be winners in the private-label game.

But merchandising remains the key to success in the fashion business. Integrating information systems and cooperative problem solving can help improve the odds for the retailer trying to develop the right merchandise at the right time, but there will always be an element of art. As Leslie Wexner, president of The Limited, once told us about this company's phenomenal success in private-label products, "You are really talking about the ability to buy great products. It's a merchandising skill. If you don't have the merchandising skills, it won't work. Private-label skills are buying skills, the execution of fundamental buying skills. Then you get to marketing the products, and one plus one can equal three."

For the business that can develop these skills and build a structure that will allow retailing and the relationship with private-label suppliers to function separately but harmoniously, there is great potential. The risks are high but so are the opportunities. Private labels are back. They are important and here to stay, and they represent a serious competitive threat to fashion retailers that ignore them.

Consequences for manufacturers

The success of private labels in the fashion business has implications for apparel manufacturers as well as producers of other merchandise. They face four issues: whether to become private-label suppliers, how to defend their own brands from encroachment by private labels, whether to integrate vertically, and what distribution opportunities will emerge out of shifting emphasis onto private-label products.

Becoming a private-label supplier often produces higher immediate profits, but they are not always sustainable. Although enlightened retailers recognize that their suppliers must be profitable, part of the reason for going into private label is to capture manufacturing profits in excess of the cost of capital. So from a manufacturer's point of view, big profits for the supplier of private-label goods are unlikely, and even sustained profitability at a level equal to the cost of capital may demand exceptional production efficiency and superior service to customers.

Manufacturers that opt out of the private-label supply business have to devise a plan for defending their own brands against attack. They must:

1 Be sure that the fashion, features, quality, retail price, and overall appeal of their own brands represent at least fair value for the consumer compared with private labels.

2 If this value is in doubt, accept some immediate profit sacrifice for restoration of a favorable value comparison.

3 Encourage retailers to use a fair yardstick for comparing private-label with national-brand profitability. Direct product profit, rather than initial markup or gross margin, is such a yardstick. When it is used, the purported profit advantage of private-label merchandise often declines or even disappears.

4 Develop relationships with store executives that simulate the information sharing that occurs between retailers and their private-label suppliers.

For some manufacturers, the best defense (as well as a powerful marketing strategy) may be to integrate vertically in addition to or in lieu of selling through the usual channels. This course of action is wise, however, only if the product line is important enough to the target market to warrant the effort consumers must make to shop in a specialty store; if the ambience, service, and selection the manufacturer can offer fit the target market's interests better than what is available elsewhere; and if the manufacturer is prepared to sacrifice support or even distribution through existing channels.

The most difficult element of this assessment is the selection of a fair price for transferring merchandise from production to retailing. The transfer price should represent the same amount at which the goods are sold to arm's-length channels, plus or minus any costs or savings in dealing with owned or franchised outlets. By these criteria, few manufacturers facing private-label competition will find distribution through owned or franchised stores attractive.

The final issue for manufacturers in the shift toward private label is the impact on their distribution strategy. Many manufacturers of fashion goods, for example, have been reluctant to take advantage of the emerging interest of J.C. Penney and Sears Roebuck in selling branded merchandise. They have feared retaliation from traditional department and specialty stores. Given the growing infatuation of such stores with private-label merchandise, however, manufacturers of certain branded fashion items may find good reasons for exploring new alliances with national chains.

The consequences of the new penchant for private labels in fashion portend changes in the marketing of all consumer goods. Today, wearing apparel is not the only fashion category. Industries as diverse as food, electronics, and financial services are seeing themselves as purveyors of fashion products. Manufacturers of all consumer products must begin to think more broadly about branding and the role it plays in their relationship with consumers and with retail channels. Manufacturers and retailers need to assess whether these changes call for strategies of defense or offer an opportunity for aggressive marketing.

Reprint 87312

"Mr. Chairman, make him stop bragging about how much money he's losing being in public service."

In only a few years they have grabbed a sizable share of sales in soft goods, accessories, and footwear – and the share is still growing

Don't discount off-price retailers

Jack G. Kaikati

The face of retailing is continually being changed by somebody who gets a "bright new idea," as one sage of the industry put it long ago. The latest alteration comes in this decade from the phenomenal expansion of the off-price retailers, whose promotion of nationally known brand names at low prices has earned them a niche in the industry, especially in apparel, accessories, and footwear. Some of the traditional retailers have decided to fight; more frequent sales promotions are one weapon. Others have chosen to join the enemy with off-price operations of their own. While it is still too early to tell whether this development is a temporary wrinkle or a permanent crease in the face of retailing, the industry remains very unsettled.

Mr. Kaikati is professor of marketing at Southern Illinois University at Edwardsville. He has written a number of articles concerning strategic marketing management and international marketing in various business journals. This is his third contribution to HBR, the last being "Marketing Without Exchange of Money" in the November-December 1982 issue.

In the current decade, off-price retailing is being widely heralded as a phenomenon that is altering the face of the industry. Occupying the gray area between full-service stores and discounters, off-price retailers carry nationally recognized brand names (mostly in soft goods) in no-frills, pipe-rack style stores. Indications of the strength of this group include the following:

☐ According to industry analysts, some 10,000 stores nationwide sell off-price clothing, accessories, and footwear, and ring up about 5% of all sales in these categories. By 1990, their volume will amount to about $16.8 billion, or 9.2% of total apparel and footwear sales, according to one authority.[1]

☐ Annual sales per square foot, the industry's productivity standard, are an estimated $200 for OP retailers – about twice that of conventional retailers. In addition, off-price inventory is turning over 9 times a year, compared with 3.3 times for an average department store.

☐ Several of the most successful retail operations have decided to co-opt the competition by going into off-price merchandising themselves. Associated Dry Goods, owner of Lord & Taylor, acquired Loehmann's, the grandmama of off-price retailers. K mart has opened 29 OP outlets called Designer Depot.

☐ Some of the independent off-price retailers – such as the Dress Barn, Burlington Coat Factory Warehouse, and Syms – became public corporations in 1983, often at prices more than 30 times earnings. Burlington Coat, a chain of 31 better quality apparel outlets, sold 1.5 million shares and the family of

1 Daniel J. Sweeney, "Manufacturers and the New Environment," in *Off-Price Retailing: Current Issues and Trends in Marketing of Branded Merchandise,* ed. Linda Nagel (New York: New York University and Retail Research Society, 1983), p. 18.

Chairman Monroe Milstein another 2.5 million at $28 per share. (To be sure, the market price has dropped considerably since.) Early this year the company was listed on the New York Stock Exchange.

□ The heightened interest in the concept has led to the inception of a monthly newsletter devoted exclusively to topics in the outlet/off-price field. Its name is *Value Retail News.*

What makes the trend

OP retailers often buy goods at below-wholesale prices (even below those paid by discounters). Unlike department stores, they rarely ask for such perks as promotional allowances, markdown money, return privileges, and extended payment terms. As a result, they have had little difficulty obtaining merchandise.

Capitalizing on other merchants' mistakes is another way for off-pricers to buy goods at below-normal wholesale prices. A department store may have overstocked a certain dress and returned a large share of its order to the manufacturer. Rather than let the inventory pile up, the manufacturer sells it to an off-price operator at cost or even less. Off-pricers also absorb goods from bankrupt stores and from manufacturers with irregular merchandise, production overruns, or unsold end-of-season output. Nevertheless, industry analysts categorize 85% of OP retailers' goods overall as being of first quality, and 60% as current goods.[2]

There are at least three types of off-pricers: factory outlet stores or direct manufacturer's outlets, independents, and club or members-only operations.

Factory outlets are owned and operated by manufacturers. They normally carry one line of merchandise—usually their own closeouts, discontinued items, irregulars, and cancelled orders. Through them, manufacturers can regulate where their surplus is sold and avoid the lower profit margin realized by disposal of the goods through independent distributors (jobbers). These stores usually feature pipe-rack fixtures, wooden tables, linoleum flooring, and an austere decor, and their assortments may lack continuity. For years manufacturers like Carter's, Levi Strauss, and Ship 'n Shore have operated retail shops in out-of-the-way (but not always rural) locations to dispose of surplus goods.

Independent OP retailers are owned and run by entrepreneurs or are full-scale divisions of traditional retail operations. They normally carry a broader array of merchandise than the factory outlets, consisting of branded and designer-labeled merchandise that includes manufacturer's overruns, closeouts, or damaged goods. The independents buy merchandise at steep discounts and sell it 20% to 60% below department stores' markups. A bare-bones shopping environment, distinguished by an abundance of inelegant, functional displays and a dearth of sales help and service, reduces their operating costs.

Members-only outlets were common in the 1950s and 1960s. Sol Price put the off-price members-only concept on a systematic basis when he formed the Price Company in 1976 in San Diego. The company's success has been startling; the Price Clubs, as they are called, had grown to 20 outlets by the end of 1984, and the company had plans for 9 more in 1985.

The Price Company began as a cut-rate wholesaler to small retailers and other businesses, charging a $25 annual admission fee. Later the company broadened membership to individuals on a group basis, including government employees and members of selected credit unions and financial institutions. These members pay no membership fee but are charged 5% over the marked wholesale price of merchandise. This membership policy reduces the incidence of bad checks and shrinkage, thereby keeping costs down. Other contributors to the low-expense structure are small advertising budgets and out-of-the-way store sites.

The Price Clubs sell a limited selection of brand-name appliances, household items, and groceries in warehouse outlets on a cash-and-carry basis. Merchandise is generally offered in bulk quantity, displayed and stacked in packing cartons on pallets and steel racks. Traditional retail store amenities such as paper bags and restrooms are unavailable. Price bypasses the need for a central warehouse by purchasing almost all its goods from the manufacturers, who ship directly to each outlet.

Price's success has inspired imitators. Sam Walton, chairman of Wal-Mart Stores, had opened 11 Sam's Wholesale Clubs in the Midwest and Southwest at this writing and had laid plans for 11 more by the end of this year. The Zayre Corporation has launched three BJ's Wholesale Club membership warehouses, two in the Northeast and one in Miami. In 1984 the Seattle-based Pay 'n Save Corporation opened four buying clubs in three cities.

Other newcomers represent companies founded by entrepreneurs seeking to capitalize on this trend, in some cases managed by persons formerly employed by Price Company or with a background in retailing. These include wholesale clubs in Seattle, Denver, and Chicago. By the end of 1984 the eight largest club companies operated a total of 64 outlets. One

2 Pat Sloan, "Gloves Off in Off-Price Battle," *Advertising Age*, October 17, 1983, p. 3.

Exhibit **The wheel of retailing**

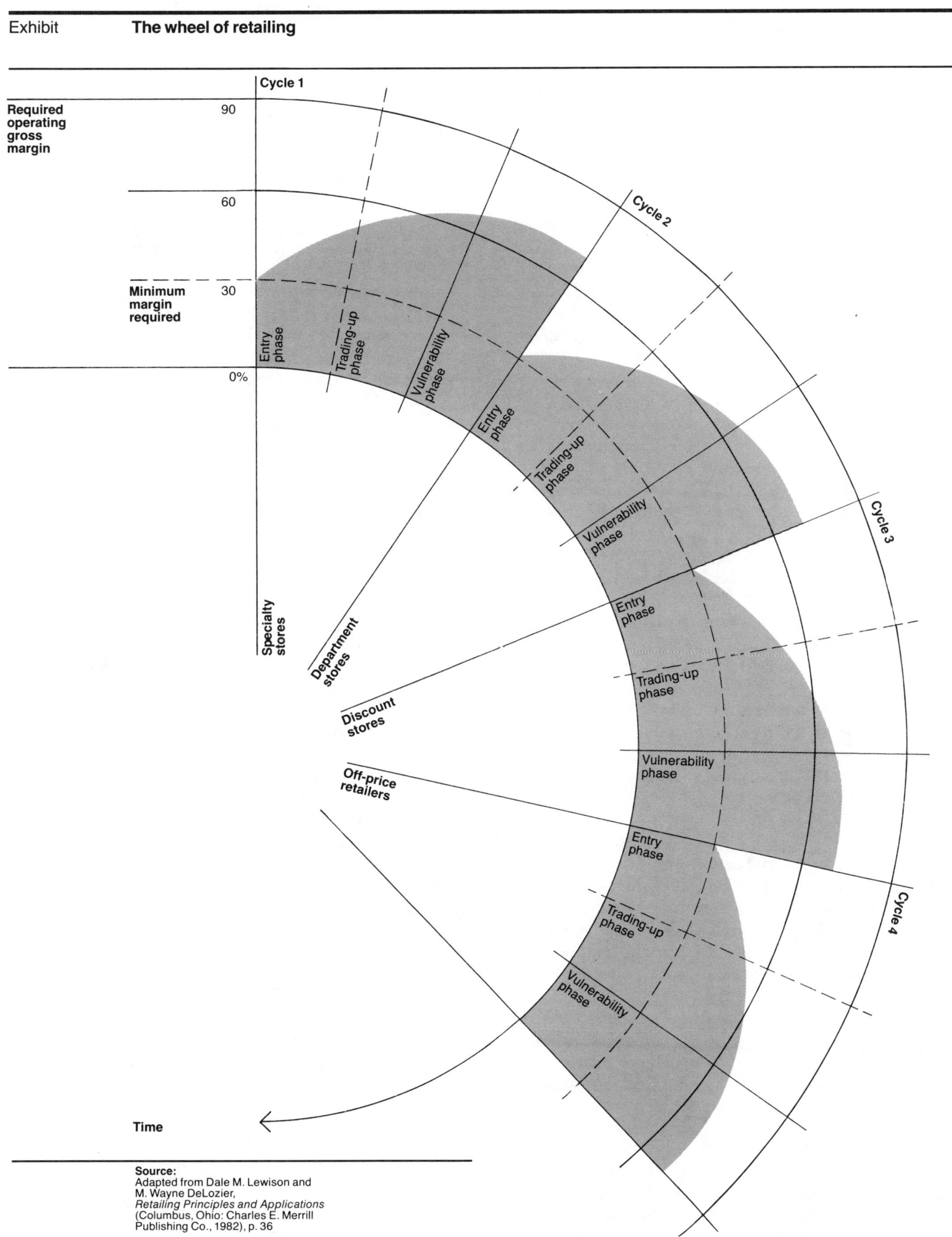

Source:
Adapted from Dale M. Lewison and M. Wayne DeLozier, *Retailing Principles and Applications* (Columbus, Ohio: Charles E. Merrill Publishing Co., 1982), p. 36

estimate predicted there would be 111 outlets by the end of 1985 with a sales volume of $4 billion.[3]

Favorable factors

Although off-price outlets have existed on the fringe of retailing for nearly three generations, they represented a negligible force in the industry until a few years ago. The impetus for their recent phenomenal growth came from the demise of fair-trade laws, adverse economic conditions, strong demand for widely recognized brands, and continuing consumer disenchantment with traditional retailers.

Demise of fair-trade laws. The decline and then repeal of resale price maintenance laws–commonly known as fair-trade laws–facilitated the growth of the OP phenomenon. From 1931 till the 1960s, a series of state and federal laws permitted manufacturers to determine the minimum retail prices at which their products could be sold to consumers. Stores selling the designated products below the specified minimum price were subject to prosecution and fines. The intent of the legislation was twofold: to protect the right of manufacturers to maintain the prestige of their brands against retailers' price cutting, and to protect small retailers from being overwhelmed by lower prices set by larger retailers, especially chain stores. Over the years, fair-trade laws declined in importance as price competition became a more important marketing strategy. Their ultimate demise came in March 1976 with the passage by Congress of an act abolishing the use of fair-trade pricing in interstate commerce.

Economic conditions. As the economic vise has tightened on both manufacturers and consumers, OP chains have grown. Consumers, looking for value for their shrinking dollar, have turned to retailers who can offer brand-name goods and the quality they imply at lower prices. Shrewd off-price operators have capitalized on the squeeze applied to manufacturers by higher costs coupled with consumers' search for value. The original off-pricers, such as Loehmann's and Marshalls, profited by buying manufacturers' closeouts, overruns or irregular goods, and retailers' leftovers, then slashing prices to consumers.

When the recession of 1982 left many producers with idle capacity and big inventories, off-pricers urged the manufacturers to sell them in-season, first-quality goods. At that time the manufacturers, hampered by traditional retailers' increasingly troublesome late-ordering and late-paying habits, were eager to reduce inventories that they had to maintain at crushingly high interest rates. Selling to off-pricers helped ease the burdens of excess goods on hand and underused capacity.

While the economy has improved greatly since 1982, the off-pricers continue to take advantage of manufacturers' cost problems and consumers' willingness to look hard for bargains in goods with recognized names.

Demand for name brands. American consumers have developed a strong predilection for nationally recognized brands and designer-name merchandise because to them these goods denote higher quality and (often) status. Name brands once exclusive to stores such as Saks Fifth Avenue, Neiman-Marcus, and Bloomingdale's now appear in thousands of off-price stores around the country.

Not long ago a consumer, after finding and paying for a bargain, might conceal it in a shopping bag bearing the logo of a prestigious store. Now that shopper buys at a designer discount store, uses *its* bag, and boasts about having discovered a great bargain. It's a mark of status to be able to say "I got it on sale," thereby demonstrating that the shopper is discriminating and has avoided paying the usual retail price.

Disenchantment with traditional retailers. Department store policies also have contributed importantly to the success of off-price retailers because of their diminishing customer service, too-tight inventory controls, and, to many, unacceptably large markups.

Many department stores and specialty retailers have quietly adopted a new pricing strategy. To determine the regular price of an item, they normally double the wholesale price. This is called keystoning. Now some stores are introducing merchandise at keystone plus 15%, which means that when items go on sale they are marked down only to the keystone price. Many price-wise consumers, discouraged by the sales tickets they see, have switched their patronage to off-price retailers.

Consumers have been antagonized by other policies too. Poor service, too-frequent sales, and a lack of distinctive merchandise have eroded shoppers' loyalty. For example, post-recession sales promotions, designed to generate store traffic, often have backfired. They taught consumers to wait for "sales."

3 Joseph H. Ellis, "The Warehouse Club Industry: An Update," Goldman, Sachs & Co. (New York: January 17, 1985).

4 Malcolm P. McNair, "Significant Trends and Developments in the Postwar Period," in *Competitive Distribution in a Free, High-Level Economy and Its Implications for the University,* ed. A.B. Smith (Pittsburgh, Penn.: University of Pittsburgh Press, 1958), p. 1.

Evolution of the trend

The development of off-price retailing adheres very well to the "wheel of retailing" hypothesis originated by Malcolm P. McNair in a 1958 article that became a classic in the marketing literature.[4] The theory states that institutional change in the industry takes the shape of a "more or less definite cycle." Each cycle has three phases, entry, trading up, and vulnerability. The *Exhibit* illustrates how the small, specialty retailer was displaced by the department store, which subsequently became vulnerable to the discount retailer, then to OP retailers.

Entry phase

"The cycle frequently begins with a bold new concept, the innovation," McNair wrote. "Somebody got a bright new idea." The innovator "attracts the public on the basis of the price appeal made possible by the low operating costs inherent in his innovation." The innovators of off-price retailing were Edward Filene and Frieda Loehmann, who started their businesses early in this century.

In 1909 Edward Filene, son of the founder of Filene's, got the idea of using the basement of his Boston establishment as an outlet for leftover goods from manufacturers and other retailers. He sold this merchandise at low prices, reduced at regular intervals. In 1920 Frieda Loehmann opened a clothing store under her Brooklyn apartment. She paid cash to top makers for garment overruns and sold them at deep discounts for cash. By the time she died at age 88 in 1962, "Momma" Loehmann was a force in retailing women's wear; now the chain has 61 stores in 25 states.

Filene's Basement and Loehmann's stores feature a bare-bones shopping environment distinguished by pipe-rack displays and communal dressing rooms. Salesclerks are more interested in ringing up sales on a cash-and-carry basis than offering advice. To please their suppliers, in the early days conventional off-pricers scissored manufacturer's labels from their merchandise so that customers could not be sure what brands they were buying. But astute shoppers deciphered the thinly disguised codes on price tags.

Trading-up phase

"As he [the innovator] goes along, he trades up, improves the quality of his merchandise, improves the appearance and standing of his store, attains greater respectability," McNair wrote. As their operations have matured, even the off-price veterans have changed their marketing policies – somewhat. While Loehmann's still specializes in closeouts, excess apparel, and samples from manufacturers, it is also filling its racks with private-label merchandise, thus ensuring continuity of merchandise. The largest off-price chain retailer, Marshalls, is also trading up. Its new stores in Denver, Colorado feature a more opulent look. They have no pipe-racks and their product mix has been expanded to include jewelry.

Off-price apparel stores have also changed the way they merchandise and advertise their goods. While once they seldom advertised by brand and put their wares on the floor without the labels, now some off-price outlets are touting brand names through the media. The Dress Barn piques consumers' interest by asking: "Why shop at Macy's or Bloomingdale's when you can get the same thing for less?" Most OP soft goods sellers still refrain from advertising by brand, although most do leave the labels in clothes destined for the selling floor.

Factory units such as Warnaco Outlet Store and Manhattan's Brand Name Fashion Outlet have altered their identity as they matured. Factory outlets historically were located adjacent to the mills, thus providing a means for producers to sell their irregulars and overruns. Warnaco's and Manhattan's have expanded their product mix by carrying brands in addition to their own.

Off-price establishments are also moving. Just as freestanding retail operations first located in downtown districts, off-price and factory outlet stores began as separate operations. It was only a matter of time before off-price and factory outlet operators grouped together in much the same way as the earliest shopping centers developed. In the OP field there are now two types of shopping centers: mall outlets dominated by manufacturers and off-price centers dominated by retailers. The tenant mix in a typical mall stresses soft goods. A fairly typical proportion is 20% men's apparel, 35% women's apparel, 20% children's apparel, 10% shoes, 10% housewares, and 5% gifts and miscellaneous.

The phenomenon of grouped off-price stores is proliferating; an estimated 75 to 90 are now operating in the United States, and at least 100 are in development. To date, most have been conversions either of existing shopping centers or of real estate once designated for other purposes.

Some of the titans in the shopping center industry are becoming involved in the off-price phenomenon. Their approach is to build from scratch, investing in prime real estate and adopting the typical mall architecture and construction. Factory Outlet Mall in Orlando, Florida, with 67 shops and 13 kiosks in 350,000 square feet, is claimed to be the nation's largest – at least for now. Willow Chase Center, under construction in Houston, will be a 360,000-square-foot installation. With its Williamsburg-style architecture, colorful awnings, and landscaped walkways, it looks on paper as plush as any of the best suburban or regional malls.

Vulnerability phase

According to McNair, as the innovative institution matures it enters a stage characterized by "topheaviness, too great conservatism, a decline in the rate of return on investment and eventual vulnerability. Vulnerability to what? Vulnerability to the next revolution of the wheel, to the next fellow who has a bright idea and who starts his business on a low-cost basis, slipping in under the umbrella that old-line institutions have hoisted."

The phenomenal growth of off-pricers has inspired imitators – including some started by retailing giants. In 1983 Dayton Hudson opened four stores in California called Plums – The Elegant Discounter. In the scramble for a foothold in off-price retailing, Plums tried to create its own niche in the upscale market with a store design aimed at making the department and specialty store shopper feel comfortable. After operating Plums for slightly less than a year, Dayton Hudson sold the four-store chain to Ross Stores, Inc. because Plums failed to meet performance goals. Even while Dayton Hudson licked its wounds, headquarters in Minneapolis maintained that the merchandising concept has considerable potential. Sure enough, in late 1984 the chain announced it would test in the Miami market an OP home accessories store dubbed R.G. Branden's. Dayton Hudson said the outlet "will emphasize dominant assortments of value-priced, high-quality merchandise."

Ross Stores in California is considered a competitor in the moderate-to-better merchandise portion of the business, selling high-quality merchandise and catering to the affluent customer. Three retail magnates have joined forces to turn Ross Stores into one of the nation's most aggressive off-price operations. Stuart Moldaw, founder of the Pic-A-Dilly retail chain; Mervyn Morris, a founder of Mervyn's Department Store (now a unit of Dayton Hudson), and Donald Rowlett, formerly president of J. Brannam, an off-price retailer owned by Woolworth, bought the chain in mid-1982 from owner William Isackson. At the time of writing, Ross had a chain of 66 stores in California and planned to open 20 new units in the West.

As a representative of the emerging off-price store, Ross foreshadows problems to come. Off-pricers have heretofore bought for less and sold for less, and stocked closeouts and overruns. What distinguishes Ross from other off-pricers is its policy of buying 90% of its merchandise directly from manufacturers, which enables its stores to sell more current fashions. Ross also has abandoned the no-frills look. The carpeted, contemporary interiors feature extensive graphic displays to help shoppers locate merchandise (a substitute for sales help). The trading-up process pursued by Ross may eventually be reflected in higher prices – which, in another turn of McNair's wheel of retailing, will open the field to a new innovator.

The establishment fights back

Lawrence Phillips, president of Phillips-Van Heusen Corporation, began a speech to the Menswear Retailers of America in 1983 with, "I know of no subject commanding as much attention of top management as the question of off-price retailers and how one should compete against them." Traditional department stores and discount chains are challenging the success of off-pricers with several strategems. A few have chosen to *compete* tooth-and-nail; some have opted to *avoid* conflict and have withdrawn from competition; and others have decided to *diversify* by starting their own similar outlets.

Competitive strategies. Some department stores and mass merchandisers have joined in the off-price game by trying to match their competitors' low prices, which is a switch from the 1970s when the economy was generally robust and competition less intense. Such big chains as Carter Hawley Hale, The Broadway, Federated Department Stores, Bullock's, and May Company of California have at one time or another recently featured drastic price reductions on brand-name merchandise. Coupled with this policy is seemingly endless promotion. Traditional retailers do not like to admit that off-pricers are affecting their business; nevertheless, an upsurge in newspaper advertising indicates that they are putting on more sales.

The proliferation of designer brands at the off-price level, the search for uniqueness of merchandise, and the strain for better profit margins have led many specialty stores, department stores, and mass merchandisers to put new stress on private labels. Private labels not only guarantee exclusivity for whoever sells them but they also give retail stores more flexibility in setting prices. In this trend the retailers are following some organizations that have long relied on private branding. One of them is J.C. Penney Company, which has fashion labels like Fox, Hunt Club, Stafford, a young men's line called Gentry, and an infant's grouping called Nana's Pet. In 1983 Penney's introduced a women's wear collection created by Halston, a designer. Called Halston III, the line is an all-encompassing, related assortment of sportswear, career clothes, evening wear, active apparel, and accessories.

Among the traditional department stores, Lord & Taylor is a leading user of private labels, with such goods accounting for some 30% of sales. In menswear, in-house merchandise represents more than 50% of sales. Carter Hawley Hale and Macy's each derive about 15% of sales from private-label goods, which is double the level of a few years ago.

In addition to more active promotion and a move toward the private label, department stores and some manufacturers have pursued combative strategies to halt the off-pricers. To keep their high-fashion image, some department stores have threatened to cease ordering from designers who sell to outlets they consider to be less desirable. Bergdorf Goodman in New York City stopped carrying Halston clothes after the designer had created the line of clothing for J.C. Penney. The line included $100 dresses, compared with $1,000-$2,000 for a typical Halston dress at Bergdorf.

Full-price department stores have also applied pressure to manufacturers that sell their goods to both conventional and off-price outlets. In June 1983 several executives of Federated Department Stores announced at a New York retail seminar that their chain would not do business with manufacturers that sell "fresh merchandise" to both department and OP retailers in the same trading area. Likewise, some manufacturers have publicly vowed to cease doing business with cut-rate retailers. General Mill's Izod Lacoste unit has done so, and Phillips-Van Heusen placed an ad in *Women's Wear Daily* stating, "If you cheapen our brand, we won't sell to you." In a variant on this attack, the Jack and Jill Shop in Memphis dropped the Health-Tex line of children's clothing after 23 years because the supplier opened a mall outlet store and was selling the same merchandise at sizable discounts.

Fearful of losing their merchandise sources, some off-price stores have resorted to the courts. Burlington Coat Factory Warehouse filed suits against Interco, R.H. Macy, and Charlotte, North Carolina-based Belk Stores and several of its suppliers, charging collusion in price setting. Burlington also filed suits against Federated Department Stores and Esprit. These lawsuits accuse the Ohio-based retailer and California-based sportswear marketer of conspiring to prevent Burlington from doing business with Esprit. Later, Toys "R" Us, Inc. charged Federated and General Mills' Izod Lacoste with price fixing. The lawsuit alleged that the companies conspired to prevent Izod apparel from being sold by the Toys "R" Us children's clothing division. The suit was eventually dropped.

Avoidance strategy. Retailers who have low stakes in the market segment invaded by off-pricers may take the approach of conceding the market. Then the particular retailer concentrates on more lucrative segments while trying to keep costs low. Likewise, Allied Stores has expressed determination to retain the high-quality and high-fashion segments of the retail business. Its top executives believe that despite the increasing number of people shopping at off-price establishments, there will always be shoppers who want the service, status, and security they find in a traditional department store.

Diversification strategy. Several of the most successful retail companies have diversified and entered the off-price merchandising field themselves. As I mentioned, Associated Dry Goods, owner of Lord & Taylor, acquired Loehmann's in 1983. Federated, which Filene's joined in 1929, has started a new off-price chain called Filene's Basement after the original. It now has 15 stores. I have already recounted the fate of Plums, Dayton Hudson's venture.

K mart is another retailer trying to protect its integrity while enthusiastically entering the off-price market. It has opened 29 off-price outlets called Designer Depot, which carry prestigious labels such as Gloria Vanderbilt and Calvin Klein at large discounts. It plans to be operating 100 stores by 1986. K mart also is experimenting with an off-price gift and housewares store called Accents.

One of the most aggressive entrants is Zayre, a Massachusetts-based discount chain. Off-price sales are the fastest growing part of its business. In 1984 it added 49 outlets to its chain of women's Hit or Miss stores, which now number 401, and expanded its T.J. Maxx family clothiers from 118 to 156 stores. In early 1984 Zayre started distributing the Chadwick's of Boston, Ltd. off-price catalog, offering women's fashions at discounts up to 50% below retail. Zayre stressed that the brand-name merchandise featured in this catalog was entirely the current season's as well as its own exclusive labels.

Ten of the 23 apparel merchants ranked by *Fortune* among the 50 largest U.S. retailing companies control off-price chains. This is the first time that retail titans have diversified into stores that sell name-brand and designer-label apparel at large reductions from the "retail" price on a daily basis.

Turn of the wheel

Although off-price retailing has been heralded in some quarters as the greatest retailing phenomenon of this decade, the blossom of the early 1980s may already have begun to shed some petals. Industry analysts indicate that the rapid growth of off-pricers in the first part of this decade has slowed. The appearance of a few casualties among the newcomers, such as Plums and Gap Stores' Taggs, indicates that the field may be getting crowded and the concept more difficult to adopt. Apart from the upswing in the economy, a large part of the deceleration in growth rate of off-pricers can be attributed to better attacking and counterpunching by conventional retailers.

Even so, the retailing arena has been radically changed by the influx of off-pricers. While no form of retailing has ever put another form out of business, the rest of this decade is likely to witness stiffer competition among off-pricers and more effective retaliation from conventional retailers.

Stiffer competition will bring a shakeout in the off-price arena. The main casualties are likely to be small, undercapitalized, independent companies. To survive the shakeout, off-pricers will have to pay close attention to market positioning. One of the small companies that is trying to carve out a market niche is Titus MacDuff, a subsidiary of Minneapolis-based Juster Bros. that carries men's and women's dress and business apparel. Titus MacDuff stores' tactic is to offer more services and stay open at times that best suit the clientele. The hours are from 5 p.m. to 9 p.m. weekdays, 9 a.m. to 5 p.m. Saturdays, and noon to 5 p.m. Sundays. To meet their pledge to offer more customer service than most off-pricers, Titus MacDuff stores have a tailor on hand for alterations and sales help to wait on shoppers.

As the wheel of retailing continues to turn, it is likely that the sturdiest, most innovative, and financially healthiest off-pricers will survive and continue to keep the traditional retailers on their toes. On their part, the established retailers will take advantage of intrinsic weaknesses of many OP organizations – such as weak service and noncontinuity of assortment – to keep competitive as the battle for market niches goes on. ⊽

Reprint 85309

Automation alters retailing

Retail institutional change shows a mixture of direct and indirect responses to trends in the environment. Such trends are interwoven with economic, technological, demographic, attitudinal, and other shifts, with the threads of accelerated rates of change running through the whole fabric. One significant combination of these influences produced the "automobile age," characterized by marked expansion of suburban living and the domination of suburban shopping centers. Since that time the emphasis has swung from transportation to information processing and communications, and the computer is replacing the automobile as the dominant factor that is affecting retailing.

At the same time, on a parallel track, a dichotomy of even earlier origin has been developing in consumer motives, attitudes, and habits. The world of routinely purchased, staple, everyday merchandise is splitting off from the world of more specialized goods and services which involve an element of ego-enhancement. This dichotomy in consumer purchasing is closely related to the greater premium placed on time. Increasingly consumers seek to accomplish routine buying as expeditiously as possible, leaving themselves more time for interests and activities and for the specialized purchasing which these activities require. An important part of the evidence for this dichotomy is the increase in recent years in nonstore retailing, mail order and in-home buying, and the concomitant growth of specialty store retailing....

With an automated telecommunication system of shopping for routine household supplies, not only could goods be selected from wider assortments than any one store currently offers, but the time and energy required would be enormously reduced. As consumers gain more time and greater freedom to pursue interests and activities, many trends that are not only apparent today, but will also gain fresh momentum, hasten the development of new ones. There will be a chain reaction of secondary effects, from shifts in family living styles to alterations in the demand for services.

The transition will be difficult. Though the details of the end results are almost impossible to anticipate, it seems clear that it will be consumers who benefit. The challenge to retailing is to think and plan for this result.

From
Malcolm P. McNair and
Eleanor G. May,
"The Next Revolution of the
Retailing Wheel,"
HBR September-October
1978, p. 91.

IDEAS FOR ACTION

The "branding" effect of a good corporate name is a potent marketing tool.

In Services, What's in a Name?

by Leonard L. Berry, Edwin F. Lefkowith, and Terry Clark

A name cannot make or break a product or company. It was not the name Edsel that doomed Ford's ill-fated car brand; the letters IBM, and the words they stand for, were not the critical ingredient in IBM's success. What matters is how well a company's goods or services meet its customers' needs.

Having said that, however, we contend that a well-chosen name can give a company a decided marketing edge over comparable competitors, and that the branding effect of a strong corporate name can be especially important for service companies. Why? Because in services the company name *is* the brand name.

Services do not lend themselves to individual branding the way tangible products do. Goods can be positioned and marketed with specific, appropriate brand names: Pampers, Alka Seltzer, Black Flag. Consumers may be loyal to such brands without ever knowing that the goods came from Procter & Gamble, Miles Laboratories, and American Home Products.

NYNEX

Although a service vendor may have a variety of offerings – first class, business class, and coach; or checking accounts and loan services – consumers tend to perceive all of them as components of a single brand. Think of such businesses as Avis, Federal Express, and Holiday Inns. Each conjures up an overall brand image.

For this reason, selecting a name for a service organization can be critical to a total marketing strategy, especially for new companies in very competitive markets and for companies expanding their range of services or their geographic reach.

Anyone can cite examples of successful companies with lackluster names; performance, after all, is primary. So how important, really, is a service brand name? The answer is that strong branding can accelerate market awareness and acceptance of a high-quality service, while weak branding can accelerate failure for a poorly conceived or delivered service.

Consider the difficulties of Allegis. Like Edsel, the name Allegis has probably come in for more than its fair share of criticism – a phenomenon that happens to support our thesis. The name itself was merely an extension of a flawed business strategy, a plan to create a systems concept in business travel by putting the well-known brands, United Airlines, Hertz, Hilton, and Westin Hotels, under the Allegis umbrella.

It was widespread skepticism about the *strategy* that turned the name into a lightning rod for criticism. To be sure, one can find flaws with the name. When introduced, it was defined as a combination of "allegiance" and "aegis," and the very fact that it needed to be explained – and its pronunciation made clear – signaled a problem. But this is hindsight. Had the strategy been sound and well executed, we obviously would not be citing Allegis as a flawed brand name.

Federal Express furnishes a contrasting example. We can now say that this is a strong and appropriate brand identity: Express delineates the nature and speed of the service, and Federal suggests a far-flung, perhaps governmentally sanctioned enterprise. But without its superlative ability to track and deliver parcels, and without its courteous employees and its professional-looking uniforms, trucks, envelopes, and advertising, the Federal Express brand would not be an example of excellence. The name was part of an overall operating strategy backed up by a sophisticated, cohesive branding program.

Four useful tests

Given the difficulty of judging brand names isolated from performance, are there any hard-and-fast rules for naming a service company? Beyond avoiding obvious negative connotations, there are no absolutes. But we have found four tests useful for assessing the branding potential of an existing or proposed name. A strong service brand should possess some, if not all, of these characteristics:

Leonard L. Berry is Foley's/Federated Professor of Retailing and Marketing Studies and director, Center for Retailing Studies at Texas A&M University. Mr. Berry's latest book is Service Quality – a Profit Strategy for Financial Institutions *(Dow Jones-Irwin, 1988). Edwin F. Lefkowith is president of a marketing and communications consultancy, Lefkowith Inc., in New York City. Terry Clark is assistant professor of marketing at the University of Notre Dame.*

1. Distinctiveness. It immediately identifies the service supplier and distinguishes it from competitors.

2. Relevance. It conveys the nature of the service or the service benefit.

3. Memorability. It can be understood, used, and recalled with ease.

4. Flexibility. It is broad enough to cover not just the organization's current business but also foreseeable expansions.

Let's take a closer look at the four tests and then examine how a cohesive branding and communications program allows a service company to exploit a brand image.

Distinctiveness. A company that wishes to establish a proprietary position in the marketplace clearly should avoid a generic-sounding name. Words like "Allied," "United," and "National" tell us little about what the enterprise delivers. They are empty baggage, and overused to boot. Allied who? Which United? National what? More words are needed (Van Lines, Stores, Airlines, Parcel Service) merely to identify the company's line of business. The day is past when a company added "National" to distinguish itself from local or regional competitors.

Years ago many financial institutions took names like "Commerce," "Merchants," "First National," and "First Federal." (In Texas alone, there are more than 60 S&Ls using "First Federal" in their name.) Now that financial services have become more competitive—financial institutions are expanding both geographically and in the services they offer—such names are inadequate to set a company apart from its rivals.

One way to set yourself apart is to use a word (or words) uncommon to the service category. Meridian is an example from financial services. Another approach is to use a proper name: Chase, Barnett, J.P. Morgan, McDonald's, Marriott. Names like these stand out in a competitive environment if well supported with distinctive marketing communication. They have the arbitrary (not literal or descriptive) quality that lawyers recognize as one ingredient of an effective trademark.

AmericanAirlines

IBM

A third option is to use fabricated words, which are becoming increasingly prevalent, in part because real words are getting harder to trademark. Some have drawn fire for being too gimmicky, too obviously the product of a computer, but others serve their purpose well—names like Primerica, Exxon, Crestar.

Relevance. A name that conveys the essence of a service helps identify and position the company clearly in customers' minds—an important factor for companies selling intangibles. Ticketron suggests both the nature of the service and the electronic means by which it is delivered. Humana suggests the human touch, personalization, sensitivity—positive connotations for a healthcare organization. Visa is relevant for a worldwide financial service because it implies international access.

By relevance we do not mean that a name should give a simple, literal description of the service, because description leads to greater length and less distinctiveness. Overnight Delivery Services, for example, would be a relevant name but is weaker than Federal Express, Personal Touch Health Care, weaker than Humana. Names that resonate with indirect connotations, rather than literal descriptions, are also more likely to meet the third test, memorability.

Memorability. Several factors affect how memorable a service brand is. Distinctiveness is one. Pathmark is more memorable than Grand Union, NYNEX more memorable than U.S. West. But a name that is distinctive because it is complex or based on difficult or foreign words many consumers do not recognize, may flunk the memorability test.

Brevity and simplicity are generally assets. A name that is easy to understand when heard or read, and easy to pronounce, will encourage memorability; a short word also lends itself more easily than a long word to effective graphic treatment in a logo. Moreover, consumers tend to derive shorthand equivalents for long words. In some cases—like Pan Am—this does not pose a problem; but in other cases the nickname is unflattering, like "Monkey Ward" for Montgomery Ward.

While the name Aetna is brief and distinctive, one could argue that it is difficult to pronounce when first encountered. The company has addressed this problem through its "Aetna, I'm glad I met ya" advertising line, but companies contemplating new names should probably consider whether they want to expend their marketing resources on pronunciation (or on explanation, as with Allegis).

When it can be done with restraint, an unusual spelling immeasurably aids the memory. "Citibank," not much of a fabrication—but surely more distinctive than its former appellation, First National City Bank—stands out because of the unusual "i." Given the particular target audience, Toys "R" Us, with the "R" reversed, is inspired. Parents and grandparents who buy from this chain's stores evidently find the cute name and graphic appropriate. But for nearly all businesses, overdoing cuteness produces a brand name memorable only for its gimmickry.

Marriott

Flexibility. Most companies change and expand over time, sometimes with the result that they outgrow their original names. In evaluating a name, a company would do well to consider any changes in direction it is likely to pursue, so that the name it selects is broad enough to grow with the lines of business.

Geographical references can be a limiting factor, and many companies have lived to regret their regional names. When "First National Bank of Hometown" expands into several states, it has a problem. Western Hotels became Western International (a confusing identity) and ultimately adopted Westin, a fabricated name with a less regional connotation. Allegheny Airlines changed to USAir as it expanded its system. (And while the carrier shed its derisive nickname "Agony Airlines," the newer name does not accommodate route expansion beyond the national border.)

Delta, on the other hand, need not change its name to reflect its reach. For one thing, it has earned a strong brand position. For another, while "delta" has a regional association, the word has other meanings and is therefore not as limiting as "Air South" would have been, and as the more specific Allegheny was.

Any purely descriptive term can become a straitjacket. A venture that has evolved into a total transportation enterprise will naturally have more trouble communicating the larger scope of its offerings to customers if its name still includes "trucking" or "rail." A name can also keep management from recognizing the company's opportunities; it can inadvertently become a kind of mission statement that limits managerial perceptions.

A word that draws its descriptive power from connotations is usually more flexible than one based on literal definitions. "Sentry" can cover more territory–literally and figuratively–than Insurance Company of North America or Government Employees Insurance Company.

As important as the power of the name is the support and reinforcement the company gives its chosen name with an integrated, coordinated communications program, encompassing everything from forms to advertising. Indeed, some names that seem less than optimal on the basis of the four tests have nonetheless gained strong brand recognition because of a coordinated marketing effort. American Airlines is no better than an average name, yet it is a powerful brand. The most important element, of course, is the airline's service quality, but the carrier also has a disciplined branding program: well-designed uniforms, a consistent use of graphics in all tangibles–from planes to ticket jackets–and persuasive advertising.

Humana and Visa

The name Humana wins high scores on all four of our tests. Created in 1972 when Extendicare chose to sell its nursing homes and concentrate on hospitals, it is distinctive, unlike the names of many competitors. As noted earlier, it is relevant to the company's business of health care and carries positive connotations. It is short and easy to understand and remember. And it is flexible enough to apply to all the various services the company offers: hospitals, insurance plans, health-care membership programs. The power of the name is evident in Humana's high ratings in market awareness surveys, and which is underscored by the company's performance record.

Another name with all four of the desirable characteristics is Visa. The credit card, originally called BankAmericard by the Bank of America back in 1958, was rechristened in 1977. The name is distinctive compared with competitors MasterCard and American Express. It is relevant; the name suggests that the card will open doors internationally. It is easily understood and pronounced not just in the United States but all over the world. The limiting reference to banks, cards, and America are all gone, so it is flexible; the numerous services provided under the Visa banner include traveler's checks and an automated teller network. The brevity of the tag lends itself to effective graphic treatment.

The case of Visa also illustrates the importance of a service brand name in the context of a marketing communications strategy. Consumer research in the early 1980s showed that Visa's brand image was slipping against the competition. The company responded with an advertising program carrying the line "Visa–it's everywhere you want to be," which underlined the fact that more merchants worldwide accept the card than competitors' cards. The campaign worked in concert with the suggestions of access in the brand name. Recent research indicates that Visa's brand image is now much stronger.

A brand image is a total concept based on far more than a name alone. It includes the integration of words, colors, symbols, and slogans, and the consistent application of these elements to send a clear and cohesive message to consumers. An employee's uniform, the design of a sign, graphics on all materials, and an effective advertising campaign should work together to brand the intangible service.

Graphic symbols can help make a fair name better and a good name great. The red umbrella used by The Travelers–symbolizing protection and shelter–strengthens the brand image of a company that has outgrown the literal derivation of its name. Merrill Lynch's bull is another strong brand reinforcer. And who thinks of Prudential without picturing the rock?

> A well-chosen name can't save a company whose service is poor.

Slogans can serve a similar purpose. "You're in good hands with Allstate" conveys with words and a visual image what consumers can expect from the company. Similarly, the concept of the "friendly skies of United" helps bring relevance to a dull name.

Brand image, of course, extends beyond name, logo, and advertising appeal. McDonald's supports its branding with everything from its M-like golden arches to menu items like Egg McMuffins and Chicken McNuggets. In short, a cohesive branding program requires effective blending of *all* communications elements and use of them consistently and imaginatively across services and media.

Still, at bottom, the quality of the service determines the success of the image. If you don't satisfy customers, the name won't help. But of course, if you combine good performance with a good name, you will generate the most powerful branding effect for your services.

Reprint 88502

Brandstanding: long-lived product promotion

Art Stevens

Although the public is generally not aware of it, a great deal of what it knows and believes about a wide variety of products comes through press coverage. Articles in the "living" section of the newspaper that describe the attributes of a brand of Burgundy or the advantages of down coats or enriched dog foods often arise from product publicity information distributed by the manufacturer.

While use of such techniques is widespread, many marketing strategists confine their promotion to advertising to keep the public aware of their products. They see it as the only way to obtain long-term attention, because the usual kinds of publicity run out of gas before a product loses its potential consumer appeal.

Yet product publicity—used either separately or in conjunction with advertising—can achieve the same long-term benefits and continued exposure as advertising. The effectiveness of this type of promotion is gradually earning recognition among competitive and aggressive brand managers, product managers, and promotion people.

Since a long-term approach to product publicity is especially well suited to promoting brand lines, which usually have longer commercial lives than individual products, let's call it *brandstanding.*

Links that gain attention

Brandstanding promotes products by linking them to events, issues, or ideas of inherent interest to consumers.

Traditional product publicity—whether it introduces a new product or promotes a long-standing one—focuses on some feature of a product and describes it as mellow, nontoxic, low in calories, durable, or any of thousands of other possible characteristics that appeal to the public.

By contrast, brandstanding seldom features product characteristics. By selecting or engineering links that connect the product or brand to an event of public interest or an area of public concern, brandstanding establishes a rapport between consumers and a product.

Competitive events

A promotion for Blue Ribbon rice is an excellent example of brandstanding. American Rice, Inc. organized a competition among high school bands in the Houston area. Billed as the "Battle of the Bands," it was aimed at black households with incomes of less than $12,000. Blue Ribbon rice presented a "Blue Ribbon Award" to the winning band. A sales tie-in consisted of advance-sale, reduced-price tickets with proof of purchase of the rice. The teenagers involved sold some 1,400 advance tickets.

Six Houston papers, eight radio stations, and four television stations, including all three network affiliates, covered the Battle of the Bands. Moreover, a major black radio station broadcast the competition. The promotion not only increased sales of Blue Ribbon rice substantially but also apparently generated a lasting link of goodwill toward the product: sales continued to reflect brand loyalty many months later.

Examples of brandstanding through sports events abound. Cholesterol-conscious consumers, in particular, linked physical fitness and health to Mazola corn oil after makers of the product sponsored events like the 10-kilometer (6.2-mile) "minithon" in New York's Central Park. In fact, sports-events brandstanding has proliferated to such an extent that many sports events are known by the sponsors' names, such as the Bonne Bell Road Race in Boston.

Consumer issues

Linkage to events represents but one approach to brandstanding; advertisers can use issues effectively also. For example, the Ames Division of Miles Laboratories employs experts on diabetes to link a diagnostic product called Dextrometer to home care of the disease. These authorities are available for panel discussions, interviews on radio and TV programs, and other appearances. These experts discuss various problems of diabetics, including how they can live well, despite precarious health, through home management of the disease.

The Dextrometer, an electronic device that measures blood glucose levels, is a more accurate indicator of a diabetic's condition than traditional urine tests and thus fits in with the theme of diabetes control. Newspapers often contain features about and notices of the programs on which Ames-sponsored experts appear.

Such issue-oriented brandstanding promotions can have benefits that go beyond reaching the consumer. General Wine and Spirits Co., marketers of Eagle Rare bourbon, has joined forces with numerous organizations and persons in an effort to save the American bald eagle from extinction by preserving and rehabilitating the eagle's habitat.

General Wine and Spirits developed a brochure on the American bald eagle, in cooperation with the U.S. Fish and Wildlife Service, and has become an information clearinghouse on these birds. The company has worked with wildlife specialists to alter the conditions that threaten eagles—polluted rivers, hot wires on utility poles, hunters, overenthusiastic nature lovers who disturb the birds and thus inhibit their reproduction, and destruction of the tall trees that eagles require for their heavy nests.

The company also helps operate emergency centers that restore injured birds to health and then return them to the wild. All these activities are, of course, conducted in close cooperation with ornithologists, the Audubon Society, and other bird-loving groups.

The tie-in, obviously, is in the names—the American bald eagle and

Eagle Rare bourbon. Publicity about the company's efforts and programs aimed at saving eagles is, of course, far more likely to get feature coverage in the media than information about bourbon is. In addition, the idea of preserving an important element of our natural heritage appealed to the company's employees. Being part of a company that sponsors such conservation activities has apparently raised the employees' self-esteem. Productivity has increased.

Special conferences

Manufacturers can make effective use of conferences to persuade consumers to accept a wide spectrum of products. Norwich-Eaton Pharmaceuticals sponsored a national conference for teenagers at Emory University in Atlanta to acquaint young people with its contraceptive tablet, Encare Oval. The conference, titled "What's Happening?", was organized by Emory University to help teenagers understand sex, birth control, and pregnancy. Some 4,000 teenagers from across the country attended.

A feature of the meeting was a film on the history of contraception, which was produced by Norwich-Eaton. Dr. Robert A. Hatcher, an authority on contraception, was a consultant on the film and was available for discussion after the showing.

The company chose this means of promoting Encare Oval because of the importance of word-of-mouth communication in this consumer group. Reaching thousands of teenagers at the conference offered the possibility of reaching hundreds of thousands of teenagers. At the same time, the conference provided participants with important and reliable information.

Beyond television

Many products lack the appeal to gain television or radio coverage, and one of the most attractive aspects of brandstanding is its effectiveness in other avenues of communication.

Recently at Clark Lima, a crane manufacturer, plant construction had ebbed and orders for new machines had dropped precipitously. Management decided that, in order to grow, it had to reach the largest companies in the construction industry. The sales force was small, however, and could neither mount nor maintain a vigorous effort to contact the construction industry's giants.

Clark Lima overcame this problem through brandstanding. The company sponsored a symposium on construction issues. Representatives of more than 70 key prospects attended the symposium because of its appealing list of speakers and its timely subjects, which included government energy policies, the economy, labor, the environment, and insurance. The symposium received advance publicity as well as coverage in several national construction industry publications.

The program helped Clark Lima obtain a healthy segment of the crane market it considered crucial to its growth and established it as a company seriously concerned with the important issues facing the construction industry.

Basics of brandstanding

An effective brandstanding program must have the following characteristics:

1. The event or issue linked to a product must invite publicity. There must be sufficient newsworthiness or feature story interest to ensure media coverage.

2. The people attracted must be users or potential users of the product. Either the participants themselves or close associates of the participants, such as the mothers of the high school musicians in the Battle of the Bands, must be part of the market for which the product is intended.

3. There must be a meaningful or necessary link between the product and the events. The event can be linked to the effect of using the product, as with no-cholesterol Mazola corn oil. It can be associated with a

range of concerns or interests, as was the Clark Lima symposium. Finally, it can require proof of purchase, as Blue Ribbon rice's band contest did.

4. The link should be evident but not intrusive. The product must be treated as subservient to the event or issue.

5. A concurrent program of promotion must support the effort. Many companies take a marketing team approach, combining advertising, dealer promotions, point-of-purchase displays, and other methods of publicity with brandstanding. These techniques work together to produce interest, awareness of the link to the product, and product acceptance.

6. Follow-up evaluation of results is important. Brand managers who have extensive experience with brandstanding may be able to judge results while the promotion is taking place. Those who are not veterans, however, may want to use more objective means of evaluating results, such as analyzing sales figures or surveying participant and spectator attitudes.

There are good reasons for the growing use of brandstanding by product promoters. The technique overcomes the limitations of traditional approaches to product publicity. Usually products get media coverage only when they are new and are occasionally mentioned later in feature stories or roundup articles. By contrast, brandstanding is usable year after year, while it continues to maintain public awareness of the product and to foster goodwill.

Reprint 81339

Tactics for Retailers

Careful consideration of promotions reveals their disastrous short-term and long-term costs.

The Double Jeopardy of Sales Promotions

by John Philip Jones

For more than a decade, sales promotions have grown in importance, becoming the most popular tool in the marketer's kit. A brief look back helps to explain how tougher market conditions and shrinking profits pushed marketers to use promotions to fight for share. But a hard look at the numbers and a careful consideration of the logic of promotions reveals their disastrous short- and long-term costs – the double jeopardy of sales promotions.

During the 1970s, the number of stagnating markets overtook the number of growing ones.

Since World War II, consumer goods markets in the United States have been inexorably maturing – and gradually stagnating. They have been slowing in aggregate growth and eventually, in one market after another, stabilizing in total volume, except for annual increases of 1% or 2% caused mainly by population growth.

During the 1970s, an important change took place: the number of stabilized markets overtook the number of still growing markets (see the chart, "When Consumer Markets Flattened"). Now, more than a decade later, stable markets are much the rule and growing ones the exception. An examination of consumer usage data collected by Mediamark Research shows that only 13 out of 150 large consumer goods markets grew by more that 10% in 1989.

This lack of market vitality appears irreversible since it represents a seemingly permanent ceiling on consumers' purchase levels in all except a few areas – mainly financial and other services and high-tech, not the traditional categories of packaged goods and consumer durables. A number of important markets, including cigarettes, coffee, dairy products, and hard liquor, are actually declining.

This stagnation of markets has affected manufacturers in two ways. First, manufacturers find it harder

A practitioner with J. Walter Thompson for 27 years, John Philip Jones is now chairman of the advertising department at the Newhouse School of Public Communications, Syracuse University. He has written What's in a Name? Advertising and the Concept of Brands *(Lexington Books, 1986),* Does It Pay to Advertise? *(Lexington Books, 1989), and "Ad Spending: Maintaining Market Share,"* HBR *January-February 1990.*

to grow, in particular to improve their profits. With effortless earnings growth gone, manufacturers have been forced to adopt tougher (albeit reasonably successful) policies. All of the following strategies were plentifully evident during the 1980s:

□ Fighting with fury for market share, using promotions (generally a high-cost activity) as the main tactical weapon.

□ Seeking and exploiting small but growing segments of static markets, often through range extensions of existing brand names. This has led to a fragmentation of markets and a splintering of consumer franchises. There were 31 major brands of toothpaste in 1989, for example, versus 7 in 1979; 52 big brands of coffee, against 33 a decade earlier; and 28 models of Ford cars, compared with 7 in 1960.

□ Exploring untraditional product categories. Sometimes, however, this strategy backfired, as manufacturers applied their expertise less successfully than in their original fields of endeavor. For example, Procter & Gamble burned its fingers with ventures in orange juice (Citrus Hill) and potato chips (Pringle's).

□ Searching for more business overseas, such as McDonald's extensive overseas ventures.

□ Pruning costs, for instance, through reduced "theme" advertising and R&D expenditures. The danger with cutting R&D investments is, of course, the risk of eating the seed corn.

□ Finally and most significant, embarking on mergers and acquisitions, despite their steeply rising cost, in a search for scale economies and diversification.

The second effect on manufacturers stems partly from the growing market stagnation and partly from

When Consumer Markets Flattened

50 Major Consumer Goods Market Categories

	1967	1972	1977	1982
Still Growing	45	41	25	8
Reaching Plateau	5	9	25	42

Source: U.S. Department of Commerce, Bureau of the Census, Census of Manufactures, 1986.

the inflationary conditions of the 1970s. Business became accustomed to declining income (measured in real terms). During the nine years of high inflation, 1974 to 1982, aggregate corporate profits were static in real terms in 1979 and declined in 1974, 1975, 1980, 1981, and 1982.

Even profit itself came to be regarded, at least for awhile, as a less than adequate measure of corporate performance. "'Profit,' it cannot be said often enough, is an accounting illusion," wrote Peter Drucker at the time. "The announcement of 'record profits' is being greeted with skepticism by the Stock Exchange and with hostility by the public at large."[1]

During the 1970s, managers got into the habit of simultaneously boosting the list prices of their goods and making deep promotional price cuts. Producers therefore sliced profit away before they could benefit from it. The habit of mind associated with this procedure has not totally disappeared. Indeed, it offers the most plausible explanation for a tacit and possibly unconscious shift of goals on the part of many businesspeople. Despite a good deal of talk about the importance of profit, the actual pursuit of profit appears to have given way de facto to a search for growth in naked sales volume.

> Managers' heavy use of promotional price cuts sliced away producers' profit.

These two factors have led to much puzzlement and frustration. But they have certainly not led to any slackening of the competitive impulse. Competition–in particular competitive response–has become increasingly aggressive as manufacturers react in frustration to what they see as the inertia of markets. Their yardstick of success is market share. The initial competitive drive and the reaction it generates can cancel one another out, but the drive continues unabated because manufacturers have an atavistic fear of relaxation.

Manufacturers regard sales volume and market share as the keys to the future. This view is not entirely fallacious insofar as volume can represent a source of repeat business and of manufacturing and marketing scale economies. But producers' concentration on sales volume has caused them to neglect the price they pay and the earnings they are obliged to sacrifice as a result of the marketing plans they embark on so optimistically.

But there is an even more worrisome set of problems for manufacturers than massive, and often concealed, costs created by these attempts to boost short-term volume at their competitors' expense–ill effects that come to life in the long term. These short- and long-term outcomes represent a double jeopardy that managers of consumer goods companies unthinkingly and unwittingly encounter as a routine part of their marketing operations.

Promotions in the Short Term

The saturation of markets and the urge to drive up market shares have been major underlying causes of a significant change of emphasis between theme advertising (in advertising accounting parlance, "above the line," because it represents actual outlays) and promotions ("below the line," because they sacrifice income). During the past decade and more, manufacturers have increased promotional expenditures more than their advertising budgets until promotions accounted for an estimated 66% of total expenditures above and below the line in 1986, compared with 58% in 1976.[2]

Manufacturers have pumped increasing quantities of money into promotions, believing that promotions have a greater and more immediate proportionate effect on sales than theme advertising has. Historically, the responsiveness of sales to promotional activity is not very much in dispute, but there are enormous concealed problems in the proper measurement of such effects.

A promotion enables a manufacturer to buy tonnage sales on a once-and-for-all basis. It rarely stimulates repeat purchases. And although a promotion normally has a measurable short-term effect on sales, the downside is that in most cases manufacturers pay an exorbitant price. The only explanation for this is their failure to calculate rigorously enough what they are really paying for the tonnage.

In most circumstances, promotions mean price reductions. Even manufacturers' own terminology disguises this fact, calling them "investments." They are in reality income sacrificed; they should appear on the income side of the ledger (as a reduction, a negative item), not on the expenditure side (as money paid out). Trade promotions, accounting for 37 percentage points of the 66% of the total advertising dollars spent on promotions,[3] are virtually always rebates, even when described as "slotting allowances" and "display incentives." Of consumer promotions, which account for the remaining 29 percentage points, the most important are coupons and various types of temporary price reductions (TPRs)–price rebates printed on the labels, banded packs, free samples, and so on. These devices, both those directed at the trade and those at the consumer, are mostly variations of price cutting.

Given enough historical data to calculate a coefficient of price elasticity, the sales effect of price cutting can be quantified, though with a good deal of trouble. This number is simply the percentage by which sales of a brand will increase immediately as a result of a 1% reduction in price. It is preceded by a minus sign, demonstrating that lower prices cause sales to go up and vice versa.

The elasticity can of course be calculated for sales into the retail trade as well as for sales to the consumer, and there are some interesting differences between the two. The focus here, however, is on the consumer. But trade and consumer promotions can be connected. In particular, the retailer does not always retain the profit from a trade promotion but sometimes passes it to the customer, for example, by doubling the value of manufacturers' coupons.

Price elasticity is essentially a measure of how easily the consumer will accept a competitive brand as a substitute for the brand being examined. Low elasticity means that substitution is difficult and a change in price will not affect demand for the brand very greatly. The opposite also holds: high elasticity means that a price change greatly affects demand. As the number of competitors grows–which tends to happen despite slow growth in markets–we would logically expect price elasticities in general to rise. A survey by Gerard Tellis, a professor at the University of Southern California, provides some evidence to support this hypothesis.[4]

Calculations of price elasticity are not simple, but they have often been made. They are almost always based on a narrow range of price variations, which means that they should not be extrapolated too far outside this range. They are nevertheless useful for sales optimization and profit maximization, a process in which I participated in the early 1960s.

A number of estimates of the average price elasticity of groups of brands have been published. The most recent major study, reported in Tellis's article, reviews data on 367 brands that appeared in the academic literature from 1961 to 1985. Certainly, the most striking feature of Tellis's survey is the high level of the average price elasticity, −1.76. This means that for an average brand, a 1% price reduction would boost sales by 1.76%. Of course, manufacturers do not vary their prices in 1% increments; a more realistic 10% price reduction would lift sales by 17.6%, an impressive figure. But this increase alone provides an extremely incomplete picture of the effect of the price reduction, as I will demonstrate later.

Sales and Profit Outcomes of a 10% Price Reduction

Variable Cost (as a percent of NSV)	*Price Elasticity Level*	*Effect on Sales*	*Effect on Net Profit (if 5% of NSV)*	*Effect on Net Profit (if 10% of NSV)*
40%	-2.2	+22%	+20%	+10%
50	-2.2	+22	-24	-12
60	-2.2	+22	-67	-34
40	-2.0	+20	No change	No change
50	-2.0	+20	-40%	-20%
60	-2.0	+20	-80	-40
40	-1.8	+18	-20	-10
50	-1.8	+18	-56	-28
60	-1.8	+18	-92	-46
40	-1.6	+16	-40	-20
50	-1.6	+16	-72	-36
60	-1.6	+16	-104	-52

The table "Sales and Profit Outcomes of a 10% Price Reduction" displays the effect of a 10% price reduction based on price elasticities of −1.6, −1.8, −2.0, and −2.2. Tellis argues that typical marketplace elasticities may be much higher than the −1.76 average he worked out from the 367 cases. The empirical support for this claim is more tenuous, however, than that for his −1.76 average. Estimates based on European experience suggest that even this figure may be too high.[5] I have therefore limited the calculations to the range of four coefficients, which covers not only Tellis's average but also elasticities on both sides of it.

The sales projections in the table give ample support to the view that promotions can shift merchandise. The attraction they hold for brand managers is therefore understandable, particularly if managers find themselves in the uncomfortable situation of running brands whose shipments during the year have been unexpectedly slow and whose sales targets have to be met by December 31. The pressure is especially great if a brand manager's career is on the line.

But the attractive volume figures are not the whole story; the brand managers must look at the effect on costs. To do this, they have to make assumptions about cost structures. In the table, I have worked out alternatives on the basis of ratios that are reasonably typical for real brands: a variable cost representing 40%, 50%, and 60% of net sales value (NSV),[6] and net profit representing 5% and 10% of NSV.

The obvious feature of the profit calculations is that most of the sales increases provided by the price reductions yield a lower profit than before the sales rise. Indeed, some of the resulting profit reductions are disastrously large. The reasons for this unappealing outcome are an increase in variable costs (including raw materials, packaging, and labor) required by the extra sales volume, in conjunction with a reduction in NSV that applies to all sales resulting from the lower price.

Manufacturers undertake a certain amount of promotion for defensive reasons—for instance, to maintain high distribution and display for brands in an increasingly concentrated retail trade, especially the supermarket trade. This is understandable, although manufacturers should not neglect the countervailing force to retailers' strength, which is using consumer advertising to pull the merchandise through the retail pipeline and, perhaps equally important, making sure that retail buyers are aware of this activity.

Although it is difficult to distinguish offensive from defensive motives in promotional activity, I believe that the former are generally more important. Indeed, it seems clear that in most circumstances, manufacturers that promote heavily are deliberately exchanging profit for volume; in other words, making less profit on more sales or, to make the point more crudely, slicing into their own margins in dumping their merchandise.

Promotions in the Long Term

Looking beyond the distressing short-term effects, the manufacturer may be able to spot the even more worrying long-term legacy of promotions. There are three related points to consider about the long range:

1. There is overwhelming marketplace evidence that "the consumer sales effect is limited to the time period of the promotion itself."[7] A price-off promotion causes sales to rise, but once the promotion stops, they return to their original level. The "blip" on the A.C. Nielsen consumer purchases graph looks like the silhouette of a top hat. The reason is simply that the strategy for such a promotion aims to move merchandise by bribing the retailer and the consumer. When the bribe stops, the extra sales also stop. (In an exceptional circumstance, when a brand is on

a strongly rising sales trend, a promotion admittedly can put sales more or less permanently a notch higher than at the beginning.)

Some commentators have argued that a portion of promotional money has a long-term, franchise-building effect.[8] There is a little truth in this argument when it relates to promotions that encourage repeat purchase. But TPRs and coupons—which together account for the lion's share of promotion budgets—have just about the weakest long-term effect of any below-the-line activity. TPRs in particular lack the customary stress on building a consumer franchise that features the brand's competitive benefits or builds warm, nonrational associations with it. These are factors that might encourage the public to buy the goods on a more continual basis. As a consequence, promotions bring volatile demand while franchise building leads to stable demand.

> Managers at Unilever describe a vicious circle: promotion, commotion, demotion.

A promotion often also produces what Nielsen calls a "mortgaging" effect by bringing forward sales from a later period. Thus full-price sales following the promotion period may be even slower than they would otherwise have been. This prolongs the period when the manufacturer is paying a heavy promotional subsidy to the consumer.

All this leads to a significant weakening of the brand. A parallel point, for which there is patchy evidence, is that brands supported more by advertising than by promotions often carry a higher-than-average list price without much trouble and tend therefore to be more profitable. The consumer will pay the premium price because the advertised brands have offered more psychological added values than heavily promoted brands.

2. Promotions fuel the flames of competitive retaliation far more than other marketing activities. As a result, they bring diminishing returns with frightening rapidity. When the competition gets drawn into the promotion war, the effect can be a significant muting of the sharp sales increases predicted by the original price elasticity coefficients—with an even more disastrous effect on the profit outturn of the promotions.

The long-term result of such retaliation is sometimes the elimination of all profit from total market categories. There is no shortage of examples of this self-destructive effect. Two dramatic instances I remember are the market for laundry detergents in Denmark during the 1960s and the once-large market in Britain for fruit concentrates, which were mixed with water to make soft drinks. In both markets, heavy promotions eventually caused strong brands to degenerate into virtually unbranded and unprofitable commodities.

3. Promotions are said to devalue the image of the promoted brand in the consumer's eyes. This agrees with common sense, although there is little evidence to support it. Indeed, the argument may not be quite as powerful as it appears because an established consumer franchise takes a long time to decay as people's familiarity with and usage of the brand do more to maintain the image than external marketing stimuli do. On occasion, promotions undoubtedly have had an unfavorable influence on consumers' brand perceptions. This evidently happened to Burger King in the late 1970s and early 1980s, when the chain became locked in a promotion war with McDonald's.

As a rule, promotions can never improve a brand image or help the stability of the consumer franchise. At Unilever, a saying describes the vicious circle as promotion, commotion, demotion.

Consumer advertising, on the other hand, can strengthen the image. This represents a long-term effect in addition to short-term sales generation, and it leads to a growing perceived differentiation of the advertised brand from rival brands. Differentiation reduces a rival's ability to substitute for the advertised brand, thus leading to greater stability (that is, less elasticity) of consumer demand. (I should note that certain informed observers doubt whether the low creative quality of present-day campaigns actually leads to as much image building as past advertising was capable of doing.)

The Return on Advertising

But if promotions exact massive short-term costs and bring about worrisome long-term problems, can advertising investments promise anything better in either the short or long term?

The strictly short-term effect of advertising can, on occasion, be quantified through a calculation of the advertising elasticity of a brand. This number measures the percentage increase in sales to be expected from a 1% increase in advertising weight. Preceding the coefficient is a plus sign, since (it is hoped!) an increase in advertising will produce growth in sales.

Calculating an advertising elasticity involves complex regression calculations, but (as for price elasticity) the computation has been carried out in

Sales and Profit Outcomes of a 50% Advertising Increase

Variable Cost (as a percent of NSV)	*Advertising to Sales Ratio*	*Advertising Elasticity Level*	*Effect on Sales*	*Effect on Net Profit (if 5% of NSV)*	*Effect on Net Profit (if 10% of NSV)*
40%	4%	+0.1	+5%	+20%	+10%
50	4	+0.1	+5	+10	+5
60	4	+0.1	+5	No change	No change
40	4	+0.2	+10	+80%	+40%
50	4	+0.2	+10	+60	+30
60	4	+0.2	+10	+40	+20
40	4	+0.3	+15	+140	+70
50	4	+0.3	+15	+110	+55
60	4	+0.3	+15	+80	+40
40	6	+0.1	+5	No change	No change
50	6	+0.1	+5	−10%	−5%
60	6	+0.1	+5	−20	−10
40	6	+0.2	+10	+60	+30
50	6	+0.2	+10	+40	+20
60	6	+0.2	+10	+20	+10
40	6	+0.3	+15	+120	+60
50	6	+0.3	+15	+90	+45
60	6	+0.3	+15	+60	+30
40	8	+0.1	+5	−20	−10
50	8	+0.1	+5	−30	−15
60	8	+0.1	+5	−40	−20
40	8	+0.2	+10	+40	+20
50	8	+0.2	+10	+20	+10
60	8	+0.2	+10	No change	No change
40	8	+0.3	+15	+100%	+50%
50	8	+0.3	+15	+70	+35
60	8	+0.3	+15	+40	+20

hundreds of cases. The spread of research based on single-source scanner data will make it easier to make such calculations in the future.[9]

The most recently published examination of advertising elasticity, based on 128 cases, yielded an average short-term advertising elasticity of +0.22.[10] This figure jibes well with earlier studies. The difference between this coefficient of +0.22 and the average price elasticity of −1.76 is certainly large. But it would be extremely dangerous and costly to conclude that promotions are therefore more effective. The major difference between promotions and advertising is that promotional price reductions cost the manufacturer much more money than advertising increases do, so that it is misleading to evaluate their relative effectiveness by their sales effects alone.[11]

In the table "Sales and Profit Outcomes of a 50% Advertising Increase," I am concerned solely with the operational changes that a manufacturer is accustomed to making in the marketing variables. Business does not operate with 1% advertising variations any more than it does with 1% price changes. From my experience of advertising pressure testing and the difficulties of measuring its effects, 50% is the minimum uplift in the advertising appropriation that will get the needle to swing.

It is strikingly obvious from the table that, despite the small sales effects of the extra advertising, this volume produced good profit increases in most cases. This is quite different from the effect of the price reductions analyzed in "Sales and Profit Outcomes of a 10% Price Reduction" when serious earnings erosion undercut the substantial sales growth.

But before we rush headlong out of promotions and into advertising, thereby making the advertising agencies our friends for life, let me remind readers that the world is a confusing place and that there are some additional complications to be examined.

From Theory to Practice

By helping project the sales volume and profit that are likely to follow marketing actions, mathematical techniques are meant to sharpen the efficiency of corporate practice. This discipline is rarely applied in the United States and in other sophisticated marketing environments, however, because few manufacturers will take the considerable trouble to develop the tools – that is, to estimate the price elasticity and advertising elasticity of their brands. This is more than a once-and-for-all process because the actual outturn of promotional and advertising activities may differ slightly from predictions, so producers must monitor price and advertising elasticities continuously and adjust them as necessary.

Obviously, the first task is to do a good deal of homework to produce the elasticity coefficients. In addition, I make three operational recommendations:

Price Elasticity and List Price. The first possibility a manufacturer should consider is a permanent price increase for the particular brand. At the lower levels of price elasticity, the loss of sales from a 5% or 10% price increase would be so small, and the added revenue from the higher price so significant, that the price reduction would probably lead to a net increase in the income earned by the brand. This is a realistic possibility for brands with price elasticities of −1.0 and less. If the elasticity is less than −0.5, the chance of a major profit increase is very good indeed.

Price Elasticity and Promotion Planning. Promotions must be carried out in a planned and well-disciplined fashion. To test the soundness of the planning for each brand's promotional program, manufacturers should estimate how much promotion is necessary for defensive purposes – that is, to maintain competitive levels of display in supermarkets (or whatever the arena is) and to counter aggressive promotional action of the largest and most direct competition.

This is of course a judgment call. But the projections of sales and profit from particular price reductions provide the best available data on which evaluation of the probable results of the manufacturer's own moves can be based. Moreover, the producer, with a good deal of trouble but little additional expense, can provide itself with something extra by way of background data. This will come from close analysis of the marketplace effectiveness of every promotion staged, which should include an objective evaluation of performance against initial targets.

This recommendation may appear rather trite and unnecessary, but I am aware of only a handful of manufacturers that make any effort to do this. An old adage, too easily forgotten, says that manufacturers should always strive to achieve a double benefit from their marketing programs: first, additional profit, and second, increased knowledge and expertise.

Advertising Elasticity and Advertising Planning. A common problem in computing the advertising elasticity of a brand is that the mathematics, no matter how skillfully executed, may show a complete absence of sales effect attributable to the advertising. There can be two reasons for this, mathematical insensitivity and inadequacy or (against the manufacturer's own judgment) an absence of any sales effect to be discovered.

There is no fundamental reason to be disheartened by the discovery that a well-loved campaign has no effect on sales. The fact may be disappointing, but the accurate intelligence itself should be welcomed.

It does, however, put the manufacturer in a difficult position. If management is obliged to conclude that the emperor in fact has few clothes, the most pressing task is to find out how to achieve a measurable effect that can be evaluated for its financial implications. This means embarking on an energetic program of experimentation, covering alternative advertising campaigns, budgets, media, and phasing, and this should go on until the manufacturer and the advertising agency manage to throw up some perceptible results (or are forced to give up in despair). The research costs will be heavy because the manufacturer must evaluate extensive market testing not only for short-term sales-generating effects but also for any long-term job it may be doing.

This work may involve something that can be monitored reasonably directly (for example, the advertising may be slowly modifying consumers' perceptions of brand attributes). But its effects could very possibly be well below the surface. For instance, the advertising may be doing a protective job for the brand in a competitive environment, and this may be measurable only when a cutback causes an erosion in market share – a very serious outcome that could take a long time to surface. This possibility means that experimentation, particularly if it involves downweighting, must be carefully evaluated over a long period of time.

But what should be done if, after giving advertising every chance, there is no perceptible short- or long-term effect? Quite frankly, the manufacturer should cut its losses. A brand can be maintained in effective distribution by a minimal level of promotional support and with only enough theme advertising to keep the brand name intermittently in front of the salesforce and the retail trade. And sometimes there is no theme advertising at all. Growth from brands that are modestly supported in this way is too much to expect, but they can maintain a low level of profitable sales, in some cases for decades. I was associated with such a brand, Lux toilet soap. Lux is sold extremely widely and is the market leader in a number of countries around the world. While it has received no theme advertising support in the United States since 1967, to this day it maintains a measurable and profitable market share.

A brand can be maintained with little promotion and advertising–just don't expect it to grow.

In regard to advertising that does have a demonstrable marketplace effect, it probably influences the consumer by strengthening the image attributes of the brand and hence its perceived difference from the competition. The process, which is stimulated by image-building advertising and nourished by repeat purchases, gives competitors difficulty in substituting for the brand (thus reducing the price elasticity of demand for it). With this protection, demand for the brand will be less responsive to promotional price cutting. This is the reason why larger and stronger brands have the balance of their marketing efforts tipped more toward theme advertising than smaller and weaker brands have.

Whatever a manufacturer decides to emphasize in a campaign, the goal is marketing efficiency. The mathematical technique I have described has demonstrated uses in furthering such efficiency. It can lift the veil that the frantic search for sales volume and market share throws over actual results. It can show manufacturers the nature of the double jeopardy they face when embarking on promotion programs without analyzing the short- and long-term consequences in costs and foregone profits.

Author's note: For their counsel and suggestions, I thank Simon Broadbent of Leo Burnett, William Weilbacher of the Bismark Corporation, and Boris Wilenkin of Unilever.

References

1. Peter F. Drucker, *Managing in Turbulent Times* (New York: Harper & Row, 1980), pp. 29, 11.

2. Estimates by Donnelly Marketing. More recent, unpublished figures from Batten, Barton, Durstine & Osborn, New York, jibe with these estimates. The most recent estimate of below-the-line expenditure is 69%.

3. Simon Broadbent, *The Advertiser's Handbook for Budget Determination* (Lexington, Mass.: Lexington Books, 1988), p. 28.

4. Gerard J. Tellis, "The Price Elasticity of Selective Demand: A Meta-Analysis of Econometric Models of Sales," *Journal of Marketing Research*, November 1988, p. 331.

5. One analysis produced an average price elasticity of −1.32, according to Simon Broadbent in "Price and Advertising: Volume and Profit," *Admap*, November 1980, p. 536. Andrew Roberts calculated −1.67 in "The Decision Between Above- and Below-the-Line," *Admap*, December 1980, p. 590.

6. Taking published estimates of advertising-to-sales ratios for the main U.S. industries, *Advertising Age* has analyzed them according to advertising's percentage of sales and its percentage of margin (indirect cost). From these data, it is possible to extrapolate the average ratios of variable cost by industry. "Advertising-to-Sales Ratios, 1989," *Advertising Age*, November 13, 1989, p. 32.

7. James O. Peckham, Sr., *The Wheel of Marketing* (privately published but available through A.C. Nielsen, second edition, 1981), p. 69.

8. See, for example, Robert M. Prentice, "How to Split Your Marketing Funds Between Advertising and Promotion," *Advertising Age*, January 10, 1977, p. 41.

9. For an examination of this innovation, see Magid M. Abraham and Leonard M. Lodish, "Getting the Most Out of Advertising and Promotion," HBR May-June 1990, p. 50.

10. Gert Assmus, John U. Farlet, and Donald R. Lehmann, "How Advertising Affects Sales: Meta-Analysis of Econometric Results," *Journal of Marketing Research*, February 1984, p. 65.

11. This point is trenchantly argued in Simon Broadbent, "Point of View: What Is a 'Small' Advertising Elasticity?" *Journal of Advertising Research*, August-September 1989, p. 37.

Reprint 90505

Ideas for Action

Edited by
Douglas N. Dickson

A breeze in the face

Thomas F. Schuster

A man once worked on the 89th floor of the Empire State Building. One muggy August day, he began to imagine how nice a breeze in his face would feel. When he opened the window, he suddenly realized he could probably get the world's best breeze in the face – simply by jumping out and falling face downward. By the time he reached the sidewalk, however, he understood what a high price he was paying for that breeze in the face.

There is such a thing as too much price promotion.

Through my marketing experience I have watched too many of America's major manufacturers and retailers of brand-name consumer products opt for a metaphorical breeze in the face – by relying too much on price promotion to stimulate short-term volume. These companies suffer the historically high price exacted for the thrill of this breeze – the death of their full-price, full-margin business over the long haul.

Because they have overused price promotions, for example, department stores now do less than half their normal sales volume at full price (and full margin), versus 80% just a few years ago. Leading up to this situation is the fact that there are too many department stores; each can generate only so much volume per square foot. Squeezed between discounters below and specialty stores above, their managers believe they *need* to promote to survive. Moreover, retailers have an age-old tendency to overdo a good thing – and they all "know" price promotion works.

They've been wrong. Department stores have overpromoted to the extent that most of their shoppers do not routinely buy at full price. They wait for a sale.

Promotion becomes overpromotion when it is so frequent that it depresses regular, full-price business by loading up consumers at a discount. It pays them to wait for the next sale rather than buying at full price. Of course, a certain amount of price promotion is necessary to generate traffic and consumer trial, especially of new items, but the most successful lines do such promoting only once or at most twice a year.

The way you've structured distribution directly affects your ability to control promotion. If you have a wide distribution network, with little control over your distributors, you cannot control price promotion. If you have selective distribution, you can do a lot to make certain that your distributors aren't overpromoting. Finally, if you have exclusive distribution, like Steuben Glass with just one outlet in each city – then you can control both price and promotion. The message is that if you don't watch distribution, you will lose control over price.

If you begin to hear the following warning bells, you're overpromoting. The first bell sounds when certain customers ask checkout clerks when a line will go on sale – before they buy. The next bell sounds when post-promotion analysis shows no increase in volume or profits. The final bell tolls just before Chapter 11, when you do business only during a sale.

Failure & near failure

Overpromotion needlessly gives away profits while simultaneously eroding the base of full-price business. Three examples will help explain its devastating impact.

The silver business illustrates the peril and irony of overpromotion. After 15 years of overpromotion, the silver market is still shrinking, most of the domestic silver companies have disappeared, the industry has lost consumer credibility, and full-price business doesn't exist.

It all began with a shift in demand. By the early 1970s, a change in consumer life-styles caused a decline in big weddings. Silver flatware and hollowware lost much of their importance and desirability; sales dropped dramatically. Most of the old-line silver companies failed (or refused) to recognize the decline as a fundamental shift in consumer demand. They reasoned instead that a good old-fashioned sale would get their silver business back on track. The price of silver had nothing to do with the rampant sale activity that ensued – it was the result of marketing

Thomas F. Schuster is president, U.S. operations, Coats Viyella Knitwear, Inc., with responsibility for several branded and private-label apparel divisions. He has more than 15 years of senior-level marketing experience, including terms as senior vice president and principal of Hartmann Luggage Company and president of Great American Knitting Mills (Gold Toe and Arrow socks).

misjudgment. To make matters worse, companies kept retail prices artificially inflated to make the planned "sales" affordable; consumer savings were largely imaginary.

The sale activity began at 20% off retail prices. Then one particularly aggressive company discovered that 30% off worked even better. The sheep syndrome took over as competitors quickly followed with their own bigger markdowns and destroyed the first company's competitive edge. By the late 1970s, silver products sold only when they were marked 50% off the inflated retail price.

One large company finally ended up with two separate wholesale price lists: a department store list with year-round "sale" wholesale prices and a specialty store list with much higher wholesale prices. Both lists suggested "normal" retail prices that were openly regarded as a joke. The manufacturer explained that department stores could sell their products only when they were on "sale" and needed lower wholesale prices to pay for the promotions. Specialty stores could still do some "normal" business and therefore could pay higher prices for the merchandise which, in turn, provided the manufacturer with its only chance of making a profit. The whole approach was illegal, unethical, and illogical–the result of a desperate company trying to remain profitable in a terminally overpromoted industry.

At one point, Gorham tried to shake off the overpromotion fever. The company realized that the market for sterling flatware was still shrinking, no matter what discount it offered. Gorham went to year-round, true-value prices. But the new approach was too late to change the rules. The industry had taught customers to wait for a sale. Soon Gorham was back to running sales of 50% off inflated retail prices.

Retailers of bras have watched their margins shrink over the last five years because of too many sales. Manufacturers have been hit even harder. What business does exist is more expensive since it comes in lumps only during sale periods.

The bra industry did not recognize consumers' slow but steady change to softer, more fashionable bras from functional support ones. Concurrently, retail prices began to break the $20 mark for the first time. Many bra companies saw their volume fall off.

Manufacturers and retailers went for a quick breeze in the face by turning to price promotions until today, all agree they can generate retail volume only at 20% or more off regular retail prices. They have successfully trained customers to wait for a sale–but these same customers still buy an average of only six bras a year. The result is constant unit volume at lower prices, which means lower profits.

The men's sock industry is standing on the windowsill, trying to decide whether to jump off and feel that breeze. Department stores have pushed them onto the ledge by declaring a need for more price promotions to build market share. But will it work?

Probably not, because it's virtually impossible to expand the market for dress socks. The average male consumer goes through 12 pairs of basic socks in a year. All the price promoting in the world can't change this.

Customers never buy at full price–they know to wait for a sale.

Department stores are pushing for the promotions not to sell more to individuals but to take business away from competitors.

At Gold Toe, we fought these trends. As a matter of policy, we sold only to department stores. Gold Toe's special heel and toe reinforcement has earned it an intensely loyal consumer base and two-thirds of the average retailer's sock business. It has long reminded its accounts that when 80% of sales are at full price, the business continues to grow each year. Further price promoting is unnecessary, won't pay out, and may hurt sales at full price and full margin.

Nonetheless, several Gold Toe retailers argued that they could increase market share with more frequent promotions. Recently, retailers stepped out of line in two major cities to price-promote Gold Toe on their own. Other Gold Toe retailers in those cities immediately responded. Consumers got their Gold Toe socks for 20% less, and total consumption and each store's market share remained constant over the course of the year. But, boy, did those stores give away profit dollars!

Pretty poor economics

A look at the economics of a store promoting a staple product on its own to "build market share" tells the story. The graph in *Exhibit I* clearly illustrates that the break-even point on unit volume goes up very sharply as stores discount–it is highly unlikely that such promotion will break even on gross profit dollars. The graph reflects simple arithmetic. At a common discount of 25% off, a store must double unit volume just to break even on gross profit dollars.

At the normal retail price of $1, the company makes 50 cents when it sells one sock. At 25% off, selling one sock will generate only a 25-cent profit. *Exhibit II* shows that, to make the same amount of profit (50%), the company will have to double its unit volume.

More important, even this theoretical relationship does not hold. Other stores in the same market will always, eventually, meet the lower price. It's highly unlikely therefore that unit volume can ever actually double. In fact, consumption of and demand for staples remain constant over time. Even if promotion volume doubles, the number of units sold each year stays the same.

In this example, the result of the promotion is a 10% decline in the store's gross profits. As *Exhibit III* shows, the store normally sells 100 units a year of a $3.50 retail item at a 50% gross profit. It promotes at 25% off during a month that normally accounts for 10% of annual unit volume. When the promotion doubles volume for the month, the store feels lucky. But in the end, the store does not increase long-term consumption and sells the same 100 units for the full year.

Unit volume is unchanged, but gross profit dollars are down 10%; at full price the profit would have been

Exhibit I **Where you can break even**

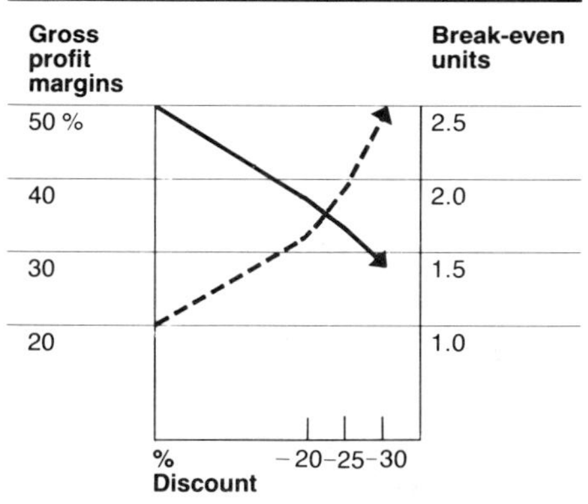

Exhibit II **Breaking even at 25 % off**

	Normal price	25 % off	25 % off break-even point
Units sold	1	1	2
Retail sales	$1.00	$ .75	$1.50
Whole-sale cost	–.50	–.50	–1.00
Gross profit	$ .50	$ .25	$ .50

Exhibit III **The cost of a promotion**

	Units sold at 25 % off	Units sold at full price	Total for the promo-tion	Total without promo-tion
Units	20	80	100	100
Retail price	$ 2.63	$ 3.50		
Margin	.333	.50		
Gross profit	$17.52	$140.00	$157.52	$175.00

$175. In addition, expenses were up because the promotion meant the store had to handle double the usual units during the month of the promotion.

In the long run, giving away profit dollars is a minor expense in overpromoting. The real cost shows up later when consumers learn the multibillion-dollar lesson all too well – don't pay full price for anything.

Packaged-goods manufacturers have discovered how good a breeze in the face from discounts can feel – and how much it can cost. Manufacturers have offered discounts without any trade-buying restrictions – "forward buying." Campbell sells up to 40% of its annual soup volume during a six-week discount period. This increases the company's manufacturing and distribution costs without increasing long-term consumption.

Campbell's managers defend their actions by pointing out that they have also introduced premium-priced line extensions whose profits offset the discounted sales of the basic line. But that strategy doesn't justify the original overpromotion. There is no basic relationship between the two strategies. It just doesn't make sense to offer unlimited discounted merchandise.

Avoiding the breeze

The best way not to fall on your face is not to jump in the first place. Try to offer the best product instead of the cheapest, or offer some difference to generate trade support and consumer pull-through without cutting prices. Gold Toe ships its retailers 98.5% of an order within 48 hours and gives consumers readily identifiable product quality. As a result, Gold Toe does 80% of its volume at full price and full profit.

Next, zealously police your distribution to make sure retailers don't need to promote to remain competitive. A manufacturer can't legally set retail prices, but it can legally refuse to open new accounts. Gold Toe religiously clung to selective distribution and only opened department store accounts. As a result, its accounts didn't have to compete with discount stores.

Hartmann Luggage suffered the overpromotion fate when it took a different tack several years ago. To increase its volume quickly, the company began to sell to highly visible discount luggage stores in addition to the prestigious full-price department stores it already had. Although Hartmann claimed to be antipromotion, these discounters cut the price at their own expense, which forced department stores to put the line on sale often. Tiring of dwindling profits, department stores eventually began to replace Hartmann with more profitable lines. Hartmann sales shrank more than 50% in its largest New York department store accounts. As Hartmann became less visible – and less prestigious – in department stores, it lost its attractiveness to the discounters and they began to de-emphasize the luggage as well.

Department store accounts will pay a lot more attention to full-price business if the same line isn't sitting with the discounter up the block. Manufacturers should avoid the breeze in the face of bumping sales by expanding distribution to anyone whose check won't bounce.

Remember to work with retailers to rediscover the rest of the marketing mix, to boost sales and profits over the long haul. Train your salespeople to advise and guide their accounts on the total department category and not just on their particular line. Remember that retailers properly place their self-interest first. Manufacturers must learn to analyze retailers' businesses from their point of view.

At Gold Toe, sales representatives were positioned as "sock consultants" who worked with department store managers to build volume and profits for the entire department. They understood main-floor sales per square foot by each product category and could recommend the appropriate sock department size, layout, lighting, and display, as well as explain regional consumer preferences. Since most socks are sold from pegs, consultants even analyzed sales and profits per peg for the retailer.

When Hartmann Luggage worked with a major department store account to analyze its store-by-store stock position, it discovered serious out-of-stocks on key SKUs, revised basic stocks, and nearly doubled the account's retail sales – all at full price.

Manufacturers and retailers have also discovered the value of in-store display. Gold Toe's sock consultants use display kits to work with its accounts and lay out featured items of the month. As in food stores, display alone can pump up sales; the sizzle sells the steak.

Coming back up

But what if your retailers heavily price-promote already? How do you get out of this situation without killing your volume? Use a break-even analysis to show graphically that you're in business to generate profits, not sales volume. Work with key account managers toward a common overall goal: to limit promotional activity to the bare minimum. In that way, you ensure that promotional events retain their effectiveness, generate incremental sales and profits, and are infrequent enough to protect and maintain day-to-day full-price business.

The best way to avoid a long fall is not to jump in the first place.

Help your accounts understand that getting away from unnecessary price promoting is not impossible, but it is a slow and usually painful process. Jack Schultz, president of B. Altman's, is doing it. In 1986, he refused to repeat several major price promotions run by Altman's during the 1985 Christmas selling season. Having earlier trained its customers to wait for a sale, he's now starting to get out of the fix.

If you've gotten trapped into overpromotion, you can do several things to escape:

1 Eliminate your least important fringe promotions, both to cut down on the frequency and visibility of promoting and to retrain customers to forget about sales.

2 As a manufacturer, strictly allocate the quantity of off-price units you'll allow retailers to purchase and hold them to quantities they can sell during the event for which they're intended. At Gold Toe, we allowed each account to purchase only 20% of the prior year's net shipments at promotional discount–and no more. This helped us ensure our control over our profit mix, prevented the shipping department from going crazy, and discouraged overpromoting. Every account was treated in the same way.

3 Cut back or contain the amount of trade discounts. Don't make promotions too profitable. If you sell sale units to the trade at 20% off, they may think they can retail those units alone at 20% off. If you increase your promotional discount to 30% off, you may encourage accounts to run the sale at 20% off and use their pocketed 10% to fund another promotion later on.

4 Help retailers test the way they want to lower consumer discounts. Along with several other manufacturers of branded apparel basics, Gold Toe found net store profits to be greater with a 20% off sale than with a 25% or 33 1/3% off sale. Higher discounts didn't generate enough additional unit volume to pay out.

5 Encourage new promotion approaches. Rather than promoting Gold Toe at a flat 25% off, Bamberger's successfully ties the consumer discount to the number of pairs purchased: consumers save 20% if they buy one to eight pairs and 25% if they buy nine or more. Average unit sales–and profits–have skyrocketed.

6 Don't be swayed by the argument that promotion doesn't hurt you but brings customers into the store. This line of thinking hinges on the promotion's ability to create incremental traffic. But the more promotions, the less effective each becomes, and the less incremental traffic it creates. Too much of a good thing quickly becomes too much of a bad thing in retailing.

Every breeze in the face has a price that must be paid, sooner or later. If retailers and manufacturers work together, they can control their promotional destiny–and profits–and preserve their long-term health.

Reprint 87613

Pulling away from push marketing

Alvin A. Achenbaum and F. Kent Mitchel

Restoring the power of pull marketing can help manufacturing productivity.

There was a time, about 40 years ago, when manufacturers of packaged goods themselves determined the marketing strategies behind their products. Making use of the power of their brands, these companies – producers of food, tobacco, beverages, toiletries, and health and beauty aids – sought to motivate consumers to buy their products through the then-passive trade distribution system.

This "pull" marketing through advertising, point-of-purchase materials, and packaging helped the manufacturers build and maintain market share by fashioning consumer franchises for their brands. The price premiums these franchises permitted yielded the funds necessary to maintain large advertising and promotion budgets as well as sizable product development budgets.

Epitomizing the dynamics of pull marketing were such giants as Procter & Gamble, General Mills, Gillette, General Foods, and Bristol-Myers. They were considered the most sophisticated of the bunch, largely because they seemingly controlled their own destinies.

Two other factors abetted the development of pull marketing. One was the rise of self-service in distribution, in which the consumer picks the item off the shelf without a salesperson's or order-taker's intervention. The other was network television, the golden medium for reaching a mass audience quickly, cheaply, and effectively. Now, however, this formula of brand differentiation, in-store communication, and mass advertising, predominant in American life since the end of World War II, is drastically losing ground. The distribution system is assuming a much bigger role.

Price-off promotions – consumer coupons or trade allowances – have come to dominate manufacturers' promotion and advertising budgets. It is not unusual when more than 80% of a retailer's packaged merchandise is acquired on a trade deal or when more than 50% is bought via some type of consumer coupon – dozens of which arrive weekly in the Sunday paper. The results are intensive price competition, a weakening of the franchise that brands have heretofore enjoyed, and reduced margins for the producers of packaged goods.

These manufacturers have drifted into this era of "push" marketing not through design but as a consequence of a number of reinforcing factors, some of them socioeconomic. Unless they reverse this trend, they will risk crippling their marketing productivity.

What pushes push marketing

What forces and developments have moved manufacturers away from pull marketing?

Society's well-known shift from homogeneousness to heterogeneity in values and life-styles. This shift opens the gates to market segmentation, with a consequent proliferation of brands and line extensions as a manufacturer's main strategy for finding possible growth opportunities in often very flat markets. Beer is a prime example.

Segmentation by life-style of most mass advertising media. Today, only network TV is a truly mass medium, but more viewing options (partly as a result of cable, syndication, and VCRs) are causing audience fragmentation here too. The smaller audiences have caused steep rises in media delivery costs, so advertisers no longer see TV advertising as the efficient primary

marketing tool it once was. In prime-time network TV, moreover, the cost of a major schedule is simply beyond the means of most national brands.

The spread of market information and R&D technology, which has made effective product differentiation difficult to achieve and harder to

Alvin A. Achenbaum is a principal of Canter, Achenbaum, Associates Inc., a New York consulting firm specializing in marketing management. Formerly he was with three advertising firms – among them J. Walter Thompson, where he was executive vice president and director of corporate planning and marketing services. F. Kent Mitchel is president of the Marketing Science Institute in Cambridge, Massachusetts. He recently retired after a 36-year career with General Foods, where he was vice president, marketing staffs.

maintain. Technology – computer-integrated manufacturing is a good example – has reduced the advantages of scale and made production innovation less proprietary. The net result: most brands lack distinctiveness, which leaves price as the chief indicator of consumer value.

And toward push marketing?

Consolidation through merger and acquisition (like much of business generally) in the retail packaged-goods trade. No longer content to be the conduit for suppliers' individual brand strategies, these combinations boast the scale and managerial ability to enforce demands on the manufacturers. They expect the manufacturers to support *their* marketing strategies. In the grocery business, witness Super Valu stores in Minnesota, once strictly a wholesaler, now a big retailer. And Ralph's on the West Coast and Supermarkets General in New York: both wield a great deal of clout with packaged-goods manufacturers.

Retailers' hearty appetite for trade deals. Enjoying the cash flow they get from such allowances (estimated to be more than four times the trade's profit), they resist manufacturers' attempts to limit them. Since profit margins permit only a certain amount for marketing, large trade-deal expenditures reduce the funds available for franchise-building mass advertising.

The unfortunate focus of many businesses on short-term results. This stems partly from flat markets and partly from Wall Street pressure for fast earnings growth. Price promotion is far more reliable than advertising for producing quarterly volume – though advertising may be more efficient in the long run at building the business.

These forces and trends have shifted a great deal of market power to the retailers, who can now use allowances and coupons for their own purposes and, in the process, reduce their dependence on the manufacturers. The trade is not necessarily concerned with building the category and product volume vital to manufacturers' growth. For manufacturers, competition through price promotion reduces the wherewithal for research and development, for packaging, and for advertising to maintain brand distinctiveness.

What brand marketers can do

After 15 years, these trends are now institutionalized among national marketers and the national trade; change will be difficult to bring about. Makers of national brands have two options for dealing with this predicament.

The first is to accept the situation and recognize the retailer's power, but to try finding a way to raise gross margins and at the same time maintain market share. Obviously, that's not easy to do. It requires the manufacturer to become a low-cost producer while continuing to use trade allowances and price-off coupons as defensive marketing tools.

It forces the producer to cut manufacturing and distribution costs, minimize R&D expenses, dismantle the marketing structure built for pull-marketing purposes, and enhance the productivity of advertising (limited though it may be) and promotion through joint promotion of brands and umbrella advertising.

This option is likely to suit brands whose market shares rank number three or four. To be a low-cost producer and marketer is difficult, if not impossible, for a major manufacturer with a culture and organization built on success in mass marketing and with an overhead that can be pared only so much.

The other option, more appropriate for a number one or number two brand, is to return to a franchise-building strategy but in ways that recognize the retailer's power and the changed consumer environment. This would mean application of fundamental marketing verities to the altered marketplace, especially the verity that the role of marketing is not to undercut the competition but to create and keep customers.

The manufacturer following this strategy would acknowledge the importance of making the product fit the heterogeneous market. This means constant effort to make it somehow fit better – in packaging, preparation, use, storage, or purchase. The superiority can be as readily identified with the maker as the product, but different it must be or price will inevitably become decisive. It is usually far more effective to improve and differentiate established brands than to add new ones, if only because so few new entries are successful.

The manufacturer would continue catering to particular market segments. The country is so big and diverse, and product categories so thoroughly penetrated, that variety, not standardization, is what consumers want.

The manufacturer would strongly back these differentiated products with brand advertising. The role of advertising – outside of creating brand awareness – would be to reinforce the differences among brands to build a brand's distinctive reputation. To have leverage, the advertising must convey a message relevant to consumers: *what* the advertising says about the brand is far more important than *how* it is said. The key is in making the product fit consumers' life-styles.

Pull marketing works if it's properly focused.

The manufacturer would try to improve both its message and its media coverage in market segments and local markets. As markets become more segmented, media prices escalate out of proportion to audience growth. The old methods of valuing the media may no longer apply. Media cost per thousand packages sold, say, may be more useful than audience CPM.

The manufacturer would work with retailers to enhance the brand's in-store appeal. Through better point-of-purchase material, decor, or events, for example, the manufacturer may be able to help the merchandiser build the kind of traffic receptive to the purchase of the brand. The manufacturer obviously must understand the retailer's strategy so the product can be presented in a way that fits it.

Taking steps like these will be difficult if the manufacturer's people don't pull together. A slew of executives normally participate in decisions about resource allocation, including advertising and promotion. They do not all reach for the same goals, nor do they have the same values or even similar experience with which to gauge the expected results.

Salespeople like trade money; it makes their jobs easier, and their reward system is tied to volume. Brand managers like coupons because they help bring in the quarterly volume. Most brand managers are heading for general management, and their tenure in brand marketing is short-lived; they have less interest in an extended franchise of the brand. Senior managers, responsible to stockholders for earnings performance, may choose action that appears to shift the priority away from franchise development.

The leadership task is to unite all elements of a top brand's marketing organization and focus them to build the consumer franchise. In this way they can offset the damage push marketing inflicts. ⛉

Reprint 87301

Better marketing at the point of purchase

Consumer goods manufacturers can use such tools as displays and promotions to gain a competitive edge in retail outlets

John A. Quelch and Kristina Cannon-Bonventre

Retail stores have become the newest battleground in the war of consumer goods manufacturers to win customers. As advertising costs soar, retail sales efforts deteriorate, and consumers become more discriminating, manufacturers are discovering the need to reach potential buyers directly at the time and place at which the buying decision is made – the point of purchase. Manufacturers are finding that such tools as well-designed displays, distinctive packaging, price and sample promotions, and in-store advertising can provide them with a competitive edge. To make point-of-purchase programs work, manufacturers must be able not only to devise attractive displays but also to tailor them to various kinds of retail outlets. Finally, manufacturers must effectively execute their programs by clearly delineating their responsibilities vis-à-vis those of their retailers and by choosing the best means of servicing them.

Mr. Quelch is assistant professor of marketing at the Harvard Business School, where he specializes in consumer marketing. Among his recent articles is "It's Time to Make Trade Promotion More Productive" (HBR May-June 1983). He also wrote, with Hirotaka Takeuchi, "Quality Is More Than Making a Good Product" (HBR July-August 1983). He is coauthor with Paul Farris of the book Advertising and Promotion Management *(Chilton, 1983).*

Ms. Cannon-Bonventre is an assistant professor of marketing at Northeastern University in Boston. Formerly she was a research associate at the Harvard Business School, where she specialized in consumer marketing and retailing.

The retail point of purchase represents the time and place at which all the elements of the sale – the consumer, the money, and the product – come together. By using various communications vehicles, including displays, packaging, sales promotions, in-store advertising, and salespeople, at the point of purchase (POP), the marketer hopes to influence the consumer's buying decision.

Partly because of the diversity of communications vehicles available and partly because effective POP programs can aid in competing for retailers' support, marketers need to manage their POP programs carefully so as to ensure that both retailers and consumers will see consistency and coordination in the programs rather than confusion and contradiction. Recent examples of innovative, well-managed POP programs include:

☐ Atari's Electronic Retail Information Center (ERIC), a computerized display installed in more than 500 stores that is designed to help sell computers. An Atari 800 home computer linked to a video-disk player asks a series of questions to help the retailer determine a customer's level of computer ability and product needs. ERIC then switches on a video disk that plays the most appropriate of 13 messages based on the customer's inputs.[1]

☐ Kodak's Disc Camera, launched in May 1982. A rotating display unit presented the disc story to the consumer without the need for salesperson assistance. In addition to the display unit, the POP program included merchandising aids, sales training and meetings for retail store personnel, film display and dispenser units, giant film cartoons, window streamers, lapel buttons, and cash register display cards.[2]

Illustrations by Katherine Mahoney.

☐ Ford Motor Company's showroom wine-and-cheese parties, started in Dallas and San Diego in 1982 to provide a "more comfortable [car] buying process for women" and to respond to the fact that 40% of new car purchases (valued at $35 billion) are now made by women. The auto showroom has traditionally been an uncomfortable environment for women, whom salesmen have often patronized or overpowered with technical details. The showroom events represent an effort to manage the point of purchase to attract an increasingly important customer segment.[3]

Innovative management of the point of purchase has been applied to a broad range of consumer product categories, including:

Candy, gum, and magazines, which depend on impulse purchases for a large percentage of their sales.

Personal computers and other new technical products that require in-store demonstration.

Pantyhose and vitamins, which because they include multiple items in each brand line must be presented especially clearly to the consumer and efficiently stocked.

Lawn and garden appliances, which are sold through several types of retailers, each of whom requires a different POP program.

Liquor and tobacco, which are prohibited from advertising in some media.

Automobiles and other mature, large-ticket items usually associated with intensive personal selling.

We believe that the expenditures of consumer goods manufacturers on POP communications will increase and that marketers who can manage events at the point of purchase well can gain competitive advantage. In this article we consider why managing the point of purchase is becoming more important, the roles of each element of the POP communications mix, and how consumer goods marketers can improve their management of the point of purchase.

Editor's note: All references are listed at the end of the article.

POP's new importance

POP expenditures are of increasing significance to marketers for three reasons. First, they often prove more productive than advertising and promotion expenditures. Second, the decline in sales support at the store level is stimulating interest among retailers in manufacturers' POP programs. Third, changes in consumers' shopping patterns and expectations, along with an upsurge in impulse buying, mean that the point of purchase is playing a more important role in consumers' decision making than ever before.

For the same reasons, retailers are becoming increasingly receptive to manufacturers' offers of POP merchandising programs. Even K mart stores, long off limits to manufacturers' sales representatives, now allow them to set up displays and offer planograms. The delicate power balance between the manufacturer and the trade is such, however, that retailers will not give up control of the POP readily, particularly at a time when its importance is growing. Moreover, the pressure on retailers to carve out distinctive positionings to survive heightens their determination to control store layouts, space allocations, and POP merchandising.

Hence, at the same time that their interest in manufacturers' POP programs is rising, retailers are becoming more selective than they once were and beginning to impose constraints, such as restricting the height of displays to preserve the vistas in each department and on each floor. To maintain consistency in store formats and to take advantage of volume discounts, Sears, Roebuck and Company recently centralized all fixture ordering at headquarters.

Improving communications productivity

Marketers are carefully examining alternatives and supplements to media advertising, which has roughly tripled in cost since 1968. POP programs cannot substitute for media advertising, nor are they as easily controlled in the store since they are implemented on someone else's turf. They can, however, reinforce and remind consumers about the advertising messages they have seen before entering the store. POP programs help improve productivity in the following ways:

Low cost. While reaching 1,000 adults through a 30-second network television commercial costs $4.05 to $7.75, the cost per thousand for a store merchandiser or a sign with a one-year life is only 3 cents to 37 cents.[4] These figures reflect the low production and installation costs of POP materials and the fact that the same POP materials are seen repeatedly by consumers and salespeople.

Consumer focus. POP programs focus on the consumer but also provide a service to the trade. Because they help move products off the shelves into consumers' hands, POP expenditures are often more productive than off-invoice price reductions to the trade, which risk being pocketed and therefore withheld from the consumer.

Precise target marketing. POP programs can be easily tailored to the needs of local markets or classes of trade in response to marketers' increasing emphasis on region-by-region marketing programs and on account management of key retail customers. In addition, particular consumer segments can be precisely targeted. Revlon's Polished Ambers Dermanesse Skin programmer, a nonelectronic teaching aid used at the point of purchase to suggest appropriate cosmetic combinations to black women, exemplifies a targeted approach that could not be undertaken efficiently via media advertising alone.

Easy evaluation. Alternative POP programs can be inexpensively presented in split samples of stores. Stores equipped with check-out scanner systems can quickly provide the sales data needed to evaluate the impact of POP programs for the benefit of both manufacturer and retailer.

Declining retail sales push

Manufacturers are increasingly questioning whether they can rely on retail sales clerks to push their products at the point of purchase. The quality of retail salespeople appears to have declined as their status has diminished. Their high turnover rate (often more than 100% per year) reflects their relatively low educational level and remuneration.

Sales positions are increasingly being viewed as dead-end jobs since more retailers now prefer to hire university-trained managers.

To reduce labor costs and remain price competitive, retailers such as Sears have cut the number of clerks covering the floor in favor of centralized checkouts. Consumers have developed the impression that salespeople are less attentive and knowledgeable when, in fact, they have to cover more shoppers and product lines than before.

To cut costs while extending opening hours, retailers have also shifted to inexperienced and uncommitted part-time salespersons, who often know little about a product's features and cannot demonstrate its use.

Thus, retail salespeople increasingly lack both ability and credibility. Effective POP programs can compensate for such sales weaknesses by enabling the manufacturer to maintain control of the message delivered to the consumer at the place and time of the final purchase decision. Marketers who provide the most attractive, educational, entertaining, and easy-to-use POP programs are likely to win the favor of store management. Their products are also likely to receive more push from overextended retail salespeople because an effective POP program can increase their credibility and facilitate the selling task.

Changing consumer expectations

These days consumers are inclined to seek special deals and wait for sales before they buy large ticket items or stock up on small items. As a result, consumer demand for such products as cosmetics and home furnishings fluctuates more widely than ever before. Retailers are interested in POP merchandising techniques and displays that can productively occupy consumers while they are waiting for sales help. For this reason and because of union restrictions on part-time personnel, Bell Phone Centers, for example, offer consumers many POP aids, including demonstration units.

The increasing use of automatic teller machines and vending machines, the expanded use of self-service store formats, and the advent of computerized shopping mall guides all indicate that consumers who value speed and convenience are becoming amenable to helping themselves at the point of purchase. This trend is evident, for example, in hardware stores, where manufacturers such as McCulloch and retail chains such as ServiStar are providing more and more display centers to present their product lines.

Many consumers wish to do their shopping quickly and efficiently; yet, at the same time, the longer they are in a retail store, the more likely they are to buy. Purchases planned least often were, according to one survey, auto supplies (94%), magazines and newspapers (91%), and candy and gum (85%).[5] Drugstore purchases, too, were largely unplanned – 60% of them, including 78% of snack food and 69% of cosmetics purchases.[6] An average of 39% of department store purchases were unplanned, ranging from 27% of women's lingerie purchases to 62% of costume jewelry purchases.[7] Effective POP programs not only present useful information efficiently; they can also make shopping entertaining and remove some of its frustration.

The point-of-purchase communications mix

How can consumer goods marketers address the different – and sometimes conflicting – interests of the manufacturer, the retailer, and the consumer at the point of purchase?

Using displays effectively

For one thing, they can use well-designed displays. They attract consumer attention, facilitate product inspection and selection, allow the access of several shoppers at once, inform and entertain, and stimulate unplanned expenditures. Because additional display space can expand sales without any change in retail price, consumer goods marketers increased their spending on POP displays 12% annually between 1980 and 1982. Well-designed displays respond to the needs of both the retailer and the consumer.

They reduce store labor costs by facilitating shelf stocking and inventory control, minimizing out-of-stock items, and lowering the required level of back-room inventory. For example, automatic feed displays such as 7-Up's single-can dispensers eliminate the need for store clerks to realign shelf stock.

Good displays are designed for a particular type of store and often for a specific store department. For example, the Entenmann Division of General Foods realized that its display designs in the bakery sections of supermarkets were not transferable to the cash register areas, where the company wished to sell its new line of snacks, so it developed an additional range of displays.

Good displays reflect the likely level of trade support. There is no point in designing a large display that will not generate the retailer's required level of inventory turnover. Likewise, there is no point in offering the trade a permanent display for a seasonal product. Richardson-Vicks, for example, redesigns its display each year rather than provide a permanent fixture because retailers give floor space to Vicks Cold Centers during the winter months only.

Well-designed displays are versatile and can accommodate new products. Max Factor, for example, provides retailers with a floor-stand display consisting of a series of interchangeable trays and cartridges. New product lines, packed in similar trays, can be easily inserted, while the cartridges can, when removed from the floor stand, double as counter display units.

Manufacturers must, of course, also keep their own interests in mind when they are designing displays. For example, Johnson & Johnson's First Aid Center provides supermarkets and drugstores with a permanent display for more than 30 of its first aid items.[8] By creating a strong visual impact at the point of purchase, the display presents Johnson & Johnson as a large, well-established company that offers consumers the convenience of easy product selection and "one-shelf shopping" for all their first aid needs. It also discourages retailers from stocking only the fastest-moving items. In addition, the display carries the company name and thus prevents the retailers from using the display to stock other products. At the same time, it helps Johnson & Johnson preempt competition in slow-moving product categories in which the retailer can justify stocking only one brand.

While displays such as these are becoming prevalent in self-service environments, other innovative displays are being developed to supplement the efforts of salespeople. For example, Mannington Mills' Compu-Flor, a small computerized display placed in floor covering retail outlets, is programmed to use a potential consumer's answers to eight questions about room decor. The terminal then displays three to ten appropriate Mannington styles for the customer to choose from. When idle, the machine beeps periodically to attract consumers. Mannington had placed the units in 700 stores by the end of 1982 at a cost of $8 million, an amount equal to the company's advertising budget.

Mannington found that Compu-Flor selected styles for customers more efficiently than salespeople (who had trouble remembering all the styles in the product line), encouraged salespeople to push Mannington products rather than those of its two larger competitors (Armstrong and Congoleum), and boosted the number of sales closed on a customer's first store visit.[9]

Compu-Flor is just one of a number of computerized video displays at the point of purchase that provide a standard controllable message from manufacturer to consumer, a way of engaging customers' attention while they are waiting for sales assistance, and entertainment.

A package is more than a container

Packaging has many functions beyond acting as a container for a product.

Appropriate packaging, of course, attracts attention at the point of purchase. Manufacturers such as Nabisco and Kellogg use the same package design for many items in their product lines to present a highly visible billboard of packages to consumers at the point of purchase. In 1979, Nabisco standardized the package design of its chocolate-covered cookies; the market share for this product rose from 24% to 34% by 1981.[10]

Standardized packaging also permits easy identification of brands, types, and sizes. Private-label suppliers have imitated the color codes used to identify various sizes of disposable diapers made by the brand name manufacturers. Similarly, packaging communicates product benefits and identifies target groups. Contrast the packaging of Marlboro cigarettes, aimed at men, Virginia Slims, targeted at women, and Benson & Hedges Deluxe Ultra Lights, with a silver package designed to appeal to elitists among both men and women.

And the right packaging limits the potential for pilferage of small items. The manufacturer of Fevertest, a plastic strip that, when placed on the forehead, indicates the presence of fever, added size and value to the product by enclosing the strip in a wallet, packaging the wallet in a blister pack, and displaying the item on pegboards at supermarket and drugstore checkout counters.

Consumer and trade expectations of product packaging should not discourage marketers from innovation, though frequent changes in package size and design breed trade resistance, especially when existing shelf configurations cannot easily accommodate the new packages. Reflecting the shift to self-service car maintenance, Kendall and Arco recently began to sell oil in plastic containers with built-in pouring spouts.

Making shopping fun

Manufacturers are increasingly using consumer promotions to make shopping exciting. These include premiums, coupons, samples, and refund offers in or on product packages to help them stand out and break through the visual clutter at the point of purchase. Package-delivered promotions have the further advantage of being inexpensive in comparison with consumer promotions offered in magazine advertisements or direct mail campaigns.

Manufacturers are also becoming aware that retailers favor manufacturers whose promotions bring consumers into the store. For example, some sweepstakes promotions, such as Brown Shoe Company's Footworks contest, encourage the consumer to match symbols in an advertisement with those on a store display or package in order to enter the contest. Retailers also like promotions that tie into store merchandising themes and cross-sell other products (promotions built around recipes or complete home

decorating services, for instance) and promotions that avoid the use of special price packs that require retailers to replace existing shelf stock and set up new Universal Product Code entries in store computer systems.

In-store advertising media

Manufacturers can extend to retailers a number of innovative approaches for reinforcing brand awareness and delivering advertising messages at the point of purchase. These include:

Commercials broadcast over in-store sound systems.

Moving message display units with changeable electronic messages.

Customer-activated videotapes and video disks that show merchandise such as furniture that is too bulky to be displayed on the department floor; the videotapes can also be played in window displays to present, for example, designer fashion shows.

Television sets installed over cash registers to show waiting customers commercials for products that are usually available nearby.

Advertisements on carts used in supermarkets and other self-service outlets.

Danglers and mobile displays that use available air space rather than limited floor space.

Implementation steps

Recognizing the significance of the point of purchase is not enough. Consumer goods marketers must pay more attention to developing effective POP programs and, even more important, to ensuring that they are properly implemented at the store level.

Before developing a POP program, managers must have a clear understanding of their marketing strategy – which products are being delivered to which markets through which channels of distribution. Given the marketing strategy, marketers should go on to answer such questions as:

What must happen at the point of purchase to satisfy consumer needs?

Which channel members – manufacturers, retailers, consumers – are willing to perform which functions?

Which members can perform them most cost-effectively?

How should the functions be allocated?

How should the pricing structure for the product (and for the POP program) reflect this allocation of functions?

Program development

Once they answer these questions, marketers can work out the specifics of the POP program – objectives, vehicles, and budgets. Here are five principles that should guide this process:

1 Integrate all elements of the POP communications mix. The package, for example, cannot be designed independently of the display. All POP vehicles should communicate consistent and mutually reinforcing messages to both the trade and the consumer.

2 Offer the trade a coordinated POP program for an entire product line rather than a collection of POP materials for particular items. To further impress the trade, make sure that the POP program is easy to understand and financially realistic.

3 Link POP assistance to trade performance. High-quality displays, for example, should not be given away to the trade unless linked to a quantity purchase or paid for with cooperative advertising dollars earned on previous purchases.

4 Assume that various POP programs will be necessary for distribution channels. The traditional hardware store and the self-service mass merchandiser, for example, differ both in store environment and in type of customer; the ideal POP program for each will not be the same.

5 Integrate POP communications with non-POP communications. Television advertising should tell consumers in which stores and departments they can find the advertised product and should include shots of product packages and displays to facilitate consumer recall and brand identification at the point of purchase. Sometimes a POP display becomes the basis for a television advertising campaign, as in the case of the Uniroyal POP unit, which invited the consumer to drill a hole in a Royal Seal tire to demonstrate that no air was lost if it was punctured.

Program execution

Any POP program is only as effective as the quality of its implementation at the store level. Effective implementation requires that managers, first, recognize the execution challenge. Many innovative approaches to managing the point of purchase fail because responsibilities for such tasks as stocking and maintaining displays are not clearly allocated or, once allocated, are not properly performed. Under these circumstances, cooperation between manufacturers and retailers can quickly turn into recrimination.

Consumer goods marketers are often too eager to assume POP responsibilities themselves. To increase their control over the execution of their marketing programs, they might enhance effectiveness and reduce expense to make the programs work by appropriately compensating the retailers.

Two recent examples highlight the risks of ineffective execution at the point of purchase:

- ☐ General Entertainment Corporation failed in its 1982 attempt to market popular music cassette tapes from floor-stand displays in supermarkets partly because its field sales force could not maintain display inventories of 168 stockkeeping units, many of which changed every few months.
- ☐ Binney & Smith, manufacturer of Crayola crayons and other arts materials, quickly placed 1,500 special merchandising units called Crayola Fun Centers in a variety of distribution outlets following their introduction in 1980. But efficiently servicing the displays proved difficult, and Binney terminated the contract of the servicing firm handling this task.

In general, the greater the number of stockkeeping units in a display and the greater the diversity of channel environments in which the displays are placed, the more complex and challenging effective execution becomes.

Next, managers must evaluate the execution alternatives. Consumer goods marketers usually have three options for carrying out POP programs – to use their own salespeople, to contract with brokers or service merchandisers, and to rely on the retailer. The evaluation should center on comparative costs, degree of marketers' control over the execution, and the relative importance of effective POP merchandising in leveraging a product's overall marketing program. The more important it is, the more justification the marketer has for using a direct sales force.

One important reason for the success of L'eggs was the company's decision to have its own salespeople deliver the product on consignment to stores and to assume total responsibility for managing the point of purchase. Yet the ability of the L'eggs salespeople to stock product displays efficiently had a negative twist; although it enabled L'eggs to introduce numerous line extensions, their addition complicated the product selection process at the point of purchase and made it seem inconvenient in the minds of many consumers.

To ensure the freshness and integrity of its snacks, Frito-Lay's 9,000 van salespeople visit 300,000 outlets each week. Beyond taking orders, they are trained to advise retailers about how to allocate shelf space in the snack food section according to a six-point space management program. Yet, despite the clout of its sales force, Frito-Lay could not persuade supermarkets to stock its new line of Grandma's cookies at supermarket check-out counters; they are now being displayed in the cookie sections.

These two examples deliver an important message. Even when a company has the sales force to ensure the execution of a POP program, it must never lose sight of the needs of consumers and the trade.

Many consumer goods marketers cannot afford their own sales forces and must rely on brokers or service merchandisers. Both are often unfairly demeaned. A good broker is sometimes more effective than a direct sales force in managing the point of purchase, as many big companies, including H.J. Heinz and Pillsbury, know well. Because they carry a number of noncompeting product lines, brokers enjoy economies of scale that enable them to visit retail stores more often than a manufacturer's sales force to check stocks, reset displays, and offer planograms. Brokers can establish close relationships with retailers in their local areas and organize blockbuster promotional events for their principals. For frozen food manufacturers, brokers are especially important to managing the point of purchase. Frequent store visits are essential because freezer space is limited on account of equipment and energy costs, and stores carry little, if any, back-room inventory.

If your company uses brokers or service merchandisers, here are four approaches to ensure that they effectively execute your POP program:

1 Check the size of the broker's sales force against the company's product line commitments. Is the brokerage firm overextended? How important is your business to the firm?

2 Develop a POP program that is creative yet easy to implement. As a result, your company may gain more attention from the broker's salespeople (and, therefore, the trade) than the broker's other principals.

3 Compensate the broker appropriately for the POP tasks you expect him or her to perform. Do you provide bonus incentives to broker salespeople for additional display placements?

4 Evaluate POP performance. Do you buy display audits to compare your share of display space with your market share? Do you occasionally play the customer, visit stores, check displays, and ask sales clerks for information?

These same principles are relevant whether the retailer, a broker, or a direct sales force is responsible for executing the POP program. The most important point for the consumer goods marketer to recognize is that an effective POP program never runs like clockwork. It needs constant attention and reevaluation.

Many consumer goods marketers are increasing their expenditures on POP programs. In 1982, for example, Elizabeth Arden, Inc. raised its POP budget by 40%.[11] What these marketers recognize is the old adage that the difference between success and failure often depends on the last 5% of effort rather than on the 95% that preceded it. In consumer marketing, that last 5% manifests itself at the point of purchase just before consumers choose what to buy.

References

1 "Firms Start Using Computers to Take the Place of Salesmen," *Wall Street Journal*, July 15, 1982.

2 "Kodak's Dazzling Disc Introduction," *Marketing Communications*, July 1982, p. 21.

3 "Wine, Baubles, and Glamor Are Used to Help Lure Female Consumers to Ford's Showrooms," *Marketing News*, August 6, 1982, p. 1.

4 "Consumer Product Marketing: The Role of Permanent Point-of-Purchase," *POPAI News*, vol. 6, no. 2, 1982, p. 5.

5 "POPAI/Dupont Consumer Buying Habits Survey," *Chain Store Age/Supermarkets*, December 1978, p. 41.

6 "Drug Store Buying Decisions: 60 Percent In-Store," *POPAI News*, vol. 6, no. 2, 1982, p. 1.

7 D.N. Bellenger, D.H. Robertson, and E.C. Hirschman, "Impulse Buying Varies by Product," *Journal of Advertising Research*, vol. 18, 1978, p. 15.

8 "Marketing Textbook: Case History J&J First Aid Shelf Management System," *POPAI News*, vol. 6, no. 2, 1982, p. 8.

9 Lawrence Stevens, "A Computer to Help Salesmen Sell," *Personal Computing*, November 1982, p. 62.

10 Don Veraska, "More Than One Tough Cookie Wrapped This One Up," *Advertising Age*, August 9, 1982, p. M-14.

11 "A Facelift for Elizabeth Arden," *Business Week*, August 23, 1982, p. 101.

Reprint 83614